The
Closed Captioning
Handbook

D0139000

54455189

The
Closed Captioning
Handbook

Gary D. Robson

2800-9922

778.523
R667c

ELSEVIER

AMSTERDAM • BOSTON • LONDON • NEW YORK
OXFORD • PARIS • SAN DIEGO • SAN FRANCISCO
SINGAPORE • SYDNEY • TOKYO

Focal Press is an Imprint of Elsevier

Focal Press

East Baton Rouge Parish Library
Baton Rouge, Louisiana

Focal Press is an imprint of Elsevier
200 Wheeler Road, Burlington, MA 01803, USA
Linacre House, Jordan Hill, Oxford OX2 8DP, UK

Copyright © 2004, Elsevier Inc. All rights reserved.

No part of this publication may be reproduced, stored in a retrieval system, or transmitted in any form or by any means, electronic, mechanical, photocopying, recording, or otherwise, without the prior written permission of the publisher.

Permissions may be sought directly from Elsevier's Science & Technology Rights Department in Oxford, UK: phone: (+44) 1865 843830, fax: (+44) 1865 853333, e-mail: permissions@elsevier.com.uk. You may also complete your request on-line via the Elsevier homepage (http://elsevier.com), by selecting "Customer Support" and then "Obtaining Permissions."

Recognizing the importance of preserving what has been written, Elsevier prints its books on acid-free paper whenever possible.

Library of Congress Cataloging-in-Publication Data
Robson, Gary D.
  The closed captioning handbook / Gary D. Robson.
    p. cm.
  ISBN 0-240-80561-5
    1.   Motion pictures- -Titling. 2. Television programs- -Titling. I. Title.
  TR886.9.R63 2004
  778.5'235- -dc22

                                                          2004002310

British Library Cataloguing-in-Publication Data
A catalogue record for this book is available from the British Library.

ISBN: 0-240-80561-5

For information on all Focal Press publications
visit our website at www.focalpress.com

04 05 06 07 08 09   10 9 8 7 6 5 4 3 2 1

Printed in the United States of America

In loving memory of my parents.
I miss you both.

TABLE OF CONTENTS

12 Realtime Voice Writing 149

13 Offline and Nonlinear Captioning 161

TABLES OF ILLUSTRATIONS

List of Figures

List of Tables

FOREWORD

As a longtime captioning advocate and former president of a captioning organization, the efforts of Gary Robson have not escaped my notice over the years. While there have been advances in television captioning since its inception in 1980, there has been very little effort by anyone in the captioning industry to document these for posterity except for my dear friend and colleague Gary.

I come from a big deaf family. At last count, I have counted over 200 relatives and countless friends who are deaf themselves. My parents, being deaf, loved the movies, and later television, when it came into being for us in the late 1940s. I remember watching Kate Smith singing on my grandparents' old Dumont black-and-white set without even understanding her. Thankfully, Sid Caesar had enough humor that did not require sound amid his antics with his sidekick, Carl Reiner. There was also Red Skelton, who gave us deaf people enjoyment in viewing television in those days—yet something was missing. The sound track, while it existed for millions of people out there, did not prove useful for the remaining millions who were deaf and profoundly hard-of-hearing (those who could not hear enough to appreciate what was said on television). Funny as it may seem, the lack of captioning, or rather, the lack of "access" to the sound track, made most of us "imagineers." We often "imagined" what was said, whether it was right or way off the point, yet we did enjoy television under these parameters.

As a young child, I had a burning desire to make a difference in the world, and I took to captioning as one of my causes on behalf of the community. My first effort was to attend a panel discussion in 1976 at St. Ann's Church in New York City. Being 31 years old at that time, I was relieved to see executives of ABC and NBC in attendance explaining the new development called "closed captioning." I will let Gary explain what closed captioning is elsewhere in this book. That gave me the inner fire to eventually have everything captioned on television.

It has been a long journey since then, but we are getting there, with the help of pioneers like Mac Norwood, John Ball, Julius Barnathan, Larry Goldberg, Jeff Hutchins and, of course, Gary Robson.

In 1982, I was appointed chairman of the National Association of the Deaf (NAD) TV Access Committee. This committee was an extremely active one then, battling various technologies that were in play then, along with the reluctance of some television networks to further captioning. It was always the "chicken and egg" thing. The television industry looked to the number of decoders as a benchmark whether to caption more. The deaf and hard-of-hearing looked to the number of hours being captioned as a benchmark to buy decoders. With the advent of the Television Decoder Circuitry Act of 1990, as Gary details in this book, the "chicken and egg" dilemma went away, and the number of hours has steadily increased since then.

When I became President and Chief Executive of the National Captioning Institute (NCI) in 1993, I made it my mission to make captions available "24 hours a day, 7 days a week, 365 days a year on 500 channels." In addition, I worked very diligently with the home video companies to increase captioning on home videos. During the drafting of the captioning provisions of the Telecommunications Act of 1996, I walked the halls of Congress to ensure that nothing was compromised. Sure enough, it never has been, and it has taken the foresight and will of Congress—and subsequently the Federal Communications Commission (FCC)—to ensure this access.

After my resignation from NCI, I was a consultant to the National Association of the Deaf, working with the FCC to draft regulations that currently stand today, with the goal of having close to 100% of new television programs captioned by 2006. Yes, the journey is almost complete, but we must remain vigilant to be sure captioning is not an afterthought, but part of the process of creating entertainment for television and movie theaters. Ironic as it may seem, captioning unfortunately is the very last step in the production process. We cannot produce captions in the middle of an editing session of a television program. The captions must wait until the sound is created, edited and mixed. Oftentimes the time between a producer finishing a television program and its being aired is a matter of hours. Thanks to our friends in the captioning industry, this has never been an issue—it's the old adage "the show must go on" that keeps us going.

Gary and his wife, Kathy, have been pioneers in their own right, bringing realtime captions to television stations in the San Francisco Bay area before they went national. In addition, they owned a captioning hardware/software company that produced equipment for realtime captioning for newscasts, live programming such as the Oscars, and sporting events. One only needs to watch a football game to appreciate the efforts of such realtime captioners who work with specialized hardware and software that Gary and others have created to spell 128 names on both sides of a football team accurately in realtime throughout a game. This is one of the nuances of captioning that people take for granted.

But there is another side to Gary that we all remain thankful for. He is the self-appointed captioning industry "chronicler." No one else has taken the time and effort to chronicle and document all that has happened with such an infant, but extremely important cottage industry, that is no longer a "cottage." Gary's Captioning FAQ on his website is a classic all by itself. If anyone in the world scratches their heads and says, "where do I find this and that regarding captioning?" 95% of the time it would be found in Gary's FAQ.

His first caption-related book, *Inside Captioning*, was a first step in chronicling the development of the captioning industry. Now, *The Closed Captioning Handbook* and the following pages will be a testament to what has happened and evolved in captioning. It's safe to say it will be a "biblical" tome for captioning—this book will always be referenced by those in the captioning industry in the years to come. The industry owes it to Gary Robson. Honestly, without Gary, there is very little out there documenting the development of captioning, from both a historical and technical point of view.

After going through the book, one will find that there's a lot more to captioning than just putting words on a screen. It is not a simple process. We have thrown all of our technological weight at making the process more effective and efficient, but it remains a labor-intensive effort to put such words on the screen for deaf and hard-of-hearing people to enjoy, understand, and appreciate television. If Gutenberg brought the printed word to everyone, captioning has brought "visible sound" to those of us who are deaf and hard-of-hearing.

As I write this foreword, I am babysitting my three deaf grandchildren, Joshua (7 years old), Brittany (5), and Courtney (3). I looked out of my home office and saw them watching the Cartoon Network with captions. I asked Joshua if he was watching the cartoon animation or reading the captions. He said, "Oh...both." If that doesn't hit home for you, it did for me, and on behalf of everyone in the deaf and hard-of-hearing community, we have Gary Robson to thank for making this subject documented, true, and important for those of us who need and live by it.

Philip W. Bravin
Sioux Falls, South Dakota
November 16, 2003

PREFACE AND ACKNOWLEDGMENTS

I have a lot of people to thank for what appears between these covers.

Joanne Tracy, my editor at Focal Press, guided the development of the book, handled all of the administrative burdens, took the proposal through peer review, and helped me at many stages. She also kept out of the way and let me do my work. That's a wonderful combination of traits in an editor.

Kathy Robson, my wife and a world-class stenocaptioner, provided material for me, proofread my work, and kept my personal world from shutting down as I worked on this book.

David Blanchette of VITAC, **Marty Block** of Voice to Text, **Gerry Field** of the National Center for Accessible Media (NCAM), **Phil McLaughlin** of EEG Enterprises, and **Dwight Wagner** of VITAC helped with technical proofreading and fact-checking. If any errors managed to find their way past this group, they are probably due to misunderstandings on my part.

Many others from government agencies, trade associations, consumer groups, research organizations, standards committees, and private companies were kind enough to talk with me and share information for the book, and I hesitate to name any for fear of leaving anyone out.

The product vendors listed herein provided me with reams of product literature, programming manuals, photographs, and more. Obviously, I couldn't use it all, and I hope I did an appropriate job of selecting a representative sampling of what's available in the market today. There are a few vendors whose products are not illustrated or well-described here, and in most cases it's because they did not respond to my inquiries, but this was generally rare.

Like any serious author, I have attempted to keep the material in this book as factual and unbiased as possible. Readers should be aware, however, that I have had business dealings and relationships with many of the companies listed in *The Closed Captioning Handbook*. In the interests of full disclosure, therefore, let me briefly explain some of these relationships:

- I was co-founder, Chief Technology Officer, and Chairman of the Board of **Cheetah Systems, Inc.** for almost 11 years before selling it to ErgoBilt in 1997. This culminated in a long and painful lawsuit against ErgoBilt. I have no interest, financial or otherwise, in Cheetah's current incarnation as **Cheetah International**, which has a completely separate set of owners and is no longer affiliated with ErgoBilt.

- I was co-founder and Chief Technology Officer of **Cheetah Broadcasting**, which ceased operations in 1998.

- I worked for **VITAC** as Chief Technology Strategist starting in 1998, and for its parent company, **WordWave**, as Director of Internet Technologies until 2000.

- I performed consulting work for **Softel** on the design of their realtime closed captioning system in 2003.

- I performed consulting work for **CaptionTV** and **IPCO** on the design and development of their CC+ caption filtering system from 2001 through 2003. I have a patent currently pending on part of this process, but I have no financial stake in the company or its products.

- I chaired the **Consumer Electronics Association** (CEA) working group that developed the EIA-708 standard for about a year, taking over after most of the work was already complete. I was also a member of the subcommittee that developed EIA-608.

There have already been two books published about closed captioning technology and law: *Inside Captioning* (CyberDawg Publishing, 1997), and *Alternative Realtime Careers* (NCRA Press, 2000). I wrote them both.

I decided to create this book instead of putting out a new edition of one of the others for several reasons. First, *Alternative Realtime Careers* is a book focused upon a specific audience: court reporters and stenocaptioners. This book is aimed at a very different group: broadcasters, engineers, and people interested in the nitty-gritty details of closed captioning.

Since I first wrote *Inside Captioning* and created the Closed Caption FAQ on the Internet, I've received hundreds—or maybe thousands, I haven't counted—of emailed questions about captioning. The world of captioning has expanded far beyond where it was in 1996, and it was clearly time for a brand-new and differently structured book.

The Closed Captioning Handbook covers the technical details of analog line 21 captioning, and also covers captioning of DTV, computer media, DVDs, movie theaters, and more, with extra chapters on CART and audio description for the blind. I structured it to answer the questions I most often see in my email in-box, putting the focus on what people ask for the most.

Clearly, this book can't replace all of the standards documents that apply to captioning, but it does explain each subject well enough for the majority of people.

INTRODUCTION

In our fast-moving world, anything set down in print can become obsolete. In an attempt to prevent—or at least postpone—this problem, we have established a Web site for this book which will contain updates and news flashes. We make no guarantees concerning the frequency with which the site will be updated, but there will always be information there. The URL for the site is:

`www.captioncentral.com/handbook/`

It contains a lot of information related to the book, and will serve as a set of living appendices for those who need more up-to-date information.

Conventions Used in This Book

Sample captions in this book are set in the `Lucida Console` typeface, which is a commonly available monospaced font that works well in user interfaces for simulating captions as well.

Web addresses (URLs) are set in the `Courier New` typeface to set them apart from the surrounding text.

Numbers, when referring to data bytes or character codes, will always be written in hexadecimal (base 16) unless noted otherwise. Whether in hex or spelled out in binary, numbers are represented in UIMSBF (unsigned integer most significant bit first) format.

Throughout this book, all references to DTV apply to the digital TV broadcast standards from ATSC, including high-definition TV (HDTV), enhanced-definition TV (EDTV), and standard digital TV (SDTV). In the world of closed captioning, all advanced television (ATV) signals carry captioning in the same way, regardless of aspect ratio, interlacing, or resolution.

A Note on Sample Code

All of the sample code segments in this book, whether SAMI, SMIL, RealText, or Visual Basic, were tested and run on my computer, and then transferred into the book with copy & paste. Obviously, I can make no guarantees if you are running different versions of programs than I used, but these were all fully functional programs or code snippets at the time the book was written.

All of the sample files and code segments can be downloaded on the Web at:

www.captioncentral.com/handbook/samples/

The Visual Basic functions were written and tested in VB 6.0. Why did I use Visual Basic instead of C or C++ or C# or Java or Perl or Cobol or any of the other dozens of possible programming languages? Because just about every programmer can read VB, even if they don't use it. Basic was the first programming language learned by millions of programmers, so they have a basic (no pun intended) familiarity with the language. The syntax of languages like Java can be confusing to programmers familiar with other languages, but Basic is very straightforward and easy-to-read.

1 WHY CLOSED CAPTIONING?

From the beginning, closed captioning has been a way for people who can't *hear* the audio of a movie or TV show to *see* the audio. Words and sound effects are expressed as text that can be turned on and off at the viewers' discretion, as long as they have a caption decoder.

Since laws like the Television Decoder Circuitry Act have made decoding capabilities nearly ubiquitous, the benefits of closed captioning now extend far beyond the deaf and hard-of-hearing communities. Consumers use captioning in noisy environments. Sports bars have TVs tuned to several games at once, with captions turned on to let their patrons follow all of them. Broadcasters capture transcripts of live shows from the captioning. Internet video stores are keyword searchable using caption text. The caption data stream contains links for interactive television and filters for removing objectionable content. Extended data services in field 2 include station and program identification, time of day clock, and much more.

Closed captioning has been shown to be a tremendous help in learning environments for hearing as well as deaf and hard-of-hearing people. In "Adult Literacy: Captioned Videotapes and Word Recognition," a doctoral thesis by Benjamin Michael Rogner,[1] adult students that used captioned video presentations progressed significantly better than those using traditional literacy training techniques.

People retain about 20% of what they hear, 30% of what they see, and 50% of what they hear *and* see, according to "Dales Learning Cone of Experience."[2] Augmenting an auditory experience with captions more than doubles the retention and comprehension levels.

---

[1] The full text of this dissertation is available online at
     www.captioncentral.com/resources/papers/rogner.html
[2] Wiman and Mierhenry, *Educational Media*, Charles Merrill, 1969.

Television captioning began as a community service, offered on newscasts by a few networks and television stations. Now, laws mandate captioning on most programming in the United States and Canada, and the requirements are becoming ever stricter. The price of captioning has dropped dramatically since the '80s, to the point where the captioning costs are a small percentage of the overall cost of a broadcast.

Technology has advanced at the same time, making captioning possible not just on TV shows, but on videotapes, DVDs, streaming video, digital TV, and more.

The question that titles this chapter should really be "Why *Not* Closed Captioning?"

Defining Terminology

The first attempts at visual accessibility used **open captioning**, meaning that the captions could not be turned off. Today, the term "open captioned" usually refers to video with decoded captions burned in. Some TV stations use open captioning during emergency broadcasts. You can also produce videotapes with open captions for applications where the display device doesn't have an integral decoder, such as projection video systems or kiosks.

Closed captioning can only be seen with an appropriate decoding device, as it is "hidden" in Line 21 of the vertical blanking interval (VBI). This allows people who find the captioning distracting to turn it off.

Open captioning is permanently burned in to the video, and can't be removed or turned off.

Subtitling is perhaps the most confusing term in the captioning business. In the U.K. and Australia, "subtitling" refers to closed captioning using Teletext. In theaters and broadcasts in the U.S., it refers to something more akin to open captions, often in a different language from the sound track. On DVDs, it refers to something quite similar to closed captioning. Typically, however, captions contain not only dialog, but sound effects, onomatopoeias, and other visual cues as well, whereas subtitles contain only dialog.

Subtitlers assume that the viewer can hear the audio, but can't understand it, either because it's in a different language or it's blurred and indistinct. Captioners assume that the viewer cannot hear the audio at all. You will see captions like [FOOTSTEPS APPROACHING] or [TELEPHONE RINGS], which would never appear in a subtitle. Subtitles are usually centered at the bottom of the screen, but captions are typically placed to provide a visual cue as to who is speaking, and often have explicit speaker identification in the caption.

Just to confuse things further, however, DVDs can be both captioned and subtitled. The DVD format allows for multiple subtitle languages, and many video producers consider the subtitles to be a substitute for closed captioning. For the most part, they are, as they can be turned on and off like closed captions, and they contain the dialog of the video. Unfortunately, DVD subtitles often omit the placement cues, sound effects, and other information deaf and hard-of-hearing viewers rely on.

The process of placing closed captions on a video signal is called **encoding**, and the device that makes them visible is a **decoder**.

An Overview of Line 21 Closed Captioning

The North American standard for analog broadcast TV, which is called NTSC, delivers approximately 30 frames of video per second. In actuality, it is an interlaced 59.94 Hz signal, which produces 29.97 frames per second, but for the purposes of this introduction, 30 fps is close enough. In Chapter 15 (Caption Timing), we'll explore the ramifications of the odd frame rate and how it affects captioning.

Each frame is divided into lines, and each line is divided into individual dots called pels (short for "picture elements") or pixels. The first 21 lines of each frame, known as the vertical blanking interval, or VBI, are not visible on the television screen. Those lines contain data used by video equipment for a variety of purposes, the most important of which is synchronizing the frames so your TV can find the top of the frame.

In the U.S., line 21 of the VBI is reserved for closed captioning and related information.

Since the NTSC signal is interlaced, there are actually two line 21 "fields," each of which can hold two characters of data. The signal referred to as line 21 field 2 is actually contained in line 284. These fields form two independent streams of data in the TV signal, which control codes further divide up into the following data channels shown in table 1-1.

Table 1-1: Captioning Data Channels

Name	Location	Type of Data
CC1	Field 1, Channel 1	Primary closed captioning. CC1 data receives priority in all captioning equipment, and should be synchronized perfectly with the audio.
CC2	Field 1, Channel 2	Special use captioning that doesn't have to be closely synchronized with the video or audio.
CC3	Field 2, Channel 1	Secondary closed captioning. This can be used for applications like a second language or "easy-reader" simplified captions. Like CC1, captions in CC3 should be synchronized with the audio.
CC4	Field 2, Channel 2	Another special use non-synchronous caption channel.
TEXT1	Field 1, Channel 1	Primary text services.
TEXT2	Field 1, Channel 2	Secondary text services. Can also be used for interactive TV (ITV) links, which are broadcast-related Web addresses (URLs).
TEXT3	Field 2, Channel 1	A third text channel. The FCC discourages use of TEXT3, and it is rarely used.
TEXT4	Field 2, Channel 2	Discouraged and rarely used, like TEXT3.
XDS	Field 2	Extended data services. XDS is packetized data containing information about the program, channel, network, time of day, and content advisories.

Captioning Symbols and Logos

Captioned programs are often identified by one of the symbols shown in figure 1-1. The icon on the right is a generic CC icon, which can be used by anyone. The icon on the left is trademarked by the National Captioning Institute, and may only be used on programs that they caption.

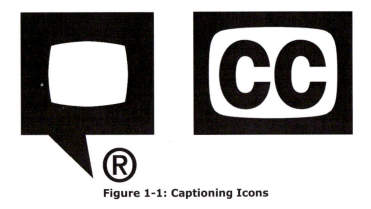

Figure 1-1: Captioning Icons

Artwork for the generic CC icon is available for downloading in a variety of formats and resolutions from the Caption Central Web site at:

`www.captioncentral.com/resources/artwork/`

You can also find artwork for the audio description icons and ratings (content advisories) icons for some of the rating systems in that same section of the Caption Central Web site.

2 A BRIEF HISTORY OF CAPTIONING

The proliferation of closed captioning we see today is the result of over half a century of development, experimentation, lobbying, and legislation. In this chapter, we'll hit the highlights of the long, rocky road captioning has taken, and look at the milestones we're expecting to hit in coming years as well.

1947 Emerson Romero develops the first "captioning" of movies. His process consisted of making text-only frames and splicing them into the film. The end result is similar to the dialog frames in silent movies.

1949 J. Arthur Rank shows a captioned movie in London, showing the captions on a smaller screen in the lower left-hand corner of the main screen. An operator had to manually insert each caption slide into a second projector.

Clarence O'Connor and Edmund Boatner organize Captioned Films for the Deaf (CFD), an organization whose goal is to provide free access to captioned movies for deaf people.

Deaf and hard-of-hearing people enjoy the first color open-captioned film, *America the Beautiful*.

1958 Malcolm (Mac) Norwood becomes the first Chief of Media Services for the CFD until his retirement in 1988.

1959 The Captioned Film Act (Public Law 85-905) provides federal funding for the CFD to open caption feature films.

1960s IBM and the United States Central Intelligence Agency (CIA) create the first computer-aided transcription (CAT) system, whose goal is fast translation and transcription of data in other languages, using a monstrous mainframe computer. This is the core technology that will later lead to realtime translation as today's captioning systems use it.

1962   The Captioned Film Act is amended to provide CFD with $1.5 million for training, production, acquisition, and distribution of educational media and to provide for research into educational media for the deaf.

1970   The National Bureau of Standards (NBS) begins researching the possibility of transmitting a standard time signal in the VBI. The project is eventually abandoned, but it brings about the idea of putting data in the VBI and eventually leads ABC to suggest putting captions there.

1971   First National Conference on Television for the Hearing Impaired held in Nashville, Tennessee.

1972   A demonstration of closed captioning is held at Gallaudet University, where ABC and the National Bureau of Standards (NBS) show captions embedded in a broadcast of the *Mod Squad*.

         The Caption Center at WGBH is established as the first TV captioning agency.

         The first nationally broadcast open-captioned program, *The French Chef*, with Julia Child, airs on PBS.

         The BBC announces Ceefax Teletext service, which will lead to captioning (the British call it "subtitling") in seven years.

1973   PBS begins broadcasting *The Captioned ABC News*, a late-night, open-captioned rebroadcast, with commercials replaced by stories of special interest to the nation's deaf and hard-of-hearing community. More than 190 PBS stations carry the program, which airs for nine years.

         StenoComp is founded by Herbert Avram, Patrick J. O'Neill, and William Eisner to commercialize the computer-aided transcription (CAT) system they developed for the IBM/CIA project. The first to purchase one of the systems was a court reporting firm owner in Los Angeles, California, by the name of Frank O. Nelson.

1975   PBS files a petition with the Federal Communications Commission (FCC) to reserve a segment of the television signal for transmitting captions.

1976   The FCC reserves Line 21 of the vertical blanking interval (VBI) for transmitting closed captions.

1978   StenoComp files Chapter 7 bankruptcy.

1979   EEG Enterprises builds first Line 21 caption encoders.

National Captioning Institute (NCI) formed.

First program captioned ("subtitled") on the BBC using Ceefax Teletext.

1980   The first home caption decoder (NCI's TeleCaption I) becomes available. It is manufactured and sold by Sears, Roebuck and Co.

First closed-captioned TV program airs. ABC does *The ABC Sunday Night Movie*, NBC does *The Wonderful World of Disney*, and PBS does *Masterpiece Theater*.

First captioned TV movie is *Force 10 From Navarone*.

IBM becomes the first company to caption a TV commercial.

1981   (The International Year of Disabled People)

Captioned home videos become available. Among the first: *Close Encounters of the Third Kind*, *The China Syndrome*, and *Chapter Two*.

1982   First realtime captioning system developed by TSI. The InstaText system ran on a Jacquard minicomputer.

First realtime captioning goes on the air during the *Academy Awards*, with Martin Block of NCI performing the captioning.

Australian Caption Centre (ACC) opens.

First captioned television program shown in Australia—*The Barchester Chronicles*.

NCI begins regular realtime closed captioning for ABC's *World News Tonight*.

First live sporting event captioned—the *Sugar Bowl* (college football).

Canadian Captioning Development Agency (CCDA) is formed.

1983   Line 21 realtime captioning hits Canada, with the World Conference on Captioning in Ottawa.

1984   PBS broadcasts *The Voyage of the Mimi* with English and Spanish captions, marking the first dual-language captioned series.

TSI, producer of the only realtime captioning system, files Chapter 7 bankruptcy.

1985   American Data Captioning (later to become VITAC) opens its doors.

The Kellogg Company becomes the first corporation to fund captioning of a television series (*Family Ties*).

1986   First tests of audio description of *Mystery!* take place in Boston at the WGBH Educational Foundation.

Computer Prompting and Captioning (CPC) develops a prompting system that outputs closed captions at the same time as the prompter text.

Xscribe Corporation introduces the microcomputer-based XCS-1 realtime captioning system, which swiftly replaces the Jacquard-minicomputer-based InstaText system throughout the industry. The XCS-1 used the CP/M operating system.

1987   Subtitled Videos Project established to provide access to video titles in Australia—over 800 videos captioned in the following ten years.

1988   PBS conducts a national test of Descriptive Video Service (DVS) during the entire season of *American Playhouse*.

1989   The rock group Living Color produces the first closed-captioned music videos. The group's producer, Ed Stasium, has a deaf daughter.

1990   Television Decoder Circuitry Act of 1990 is signed into law.

Americans with Disabilities Act passes.

The Electronic Industries Alliance (EIA) forms the Television Data Systems Subcommittee (TDSS) to create standards relating to closed captioning.

Cheetah Systems, founded by my wife, Kathy Robson, and me, releases the PC-based CAPtivator Online realtime captioning system, which runs under DOS. The company was renamed Cheetah International after we sold it in 1998.

1991   The Australian Caption Centre (ACC) creates the National Working Party on Captioning (NWPC).

C-SPAN begins captioning floor proceedings of the United States House of Representatives (in February) and the U.S. Senate (in November).

First official standard for line 21 closed captioning is adopted by Television Data Systems Subcommittee (TDSS) of the Electronics Industries Alliance (EIA). The current (2003) revision of this standard is CEA-608-B.

1992   Canada Caption, Inc. (CCI) is formed to raise money to fund captioning in Canada.

Hillsborough County, Florida, becomes the first county in the U.S. to provide realtime captioning of all county supervisor meetings.

Fremont, California, becomes the first city in the U.S. to provide realtime captioning of all city council and school board meetings.

1993   Television Decoder Circuitry Act takes effect.

The Clinton Inaugural: A PBS Special is closed-captioned and described. The program is the first live broadcast accessible to blind and visually impaired people through Descriptive Video Service.

TRIPOD Captioned Films established to open-caption first-run movies on 35 mm film, and make them available to show in movie theaters.

The Corporation for Public Broadcasting and WGBH establish the CPB/WGBH National Center for Accessible Media (NCAM).

Jerry Lefler transmits realtime text into a CompuServe chat room.

1994   Information Superhighway speech by Vice President Al Gore becomes first captioned public event in cyberspace. I set up and engineered the cybercast, and Jack Boenau did the realtime captioning. The captions are broadcast on CompuServe.

The first ergonomic stenotype keyboard (the Gemini writer) is designed by my brother, Bill Robson, and me, and introduced by Robson Technologies, Inc.

Support for the TeleCaption I decoder is no longer required.

Realtime broadcast to the Internet Multicast Backbone by RealTime Reporters, of Santa Cruz, California for Sun Microsystems.

1995 *Live! with Derek McGinty*, by Discovery Communications, becomes the first regular weekly show to be captioned in cyberspace. The captioning is delivered on America Online and the Internet by Cheetah Broadcasting and Caption Colorado.

My Closed Captioning FAQ (frequently asked questions) goes online. As of this writing, it now contains over 100 questions and answers, and resides on the Web at `www.captioncentral.com/caption_faq/`

1996 The Society of Motion Picture and Television Engineers (SMPTE) forms a working group for captioning standards on MPEG digital video, which is used on DVDs.

1997 Bill Clinton's second presidential inauguration becomes the first to be simultaneously captioned live on television and the Internet.

First official standard for DTV closed captioning is adopted by Television Data Systems Subcommittee (TDSS) of the Electronics Industries Alliance (EIA). This standard was then called EIA-708. The current (2003) revision is CEA-708-B.

Microsoft announces the Synchronized Accessible Multimedia Interchange (SAMI) format for closed captioning of multimedia presentations, on CD-ROM and the Web.

1998 The Telecommunications Act of 1996 officially takes effect, so the clock starts ticking on mandatory closed captioning.

Activision releases *Zork Grand Inquisitor*, the first computer game with full closed captioning.

RealNetworks introduces "RealText" for captioning Internet broadcasts that use streaming audio and/or video and their G2 player.

1999 "Voice writers" demonstrate viable realtime translation using speech recognition technology, opening up the possibility of speech-based realtime captioning. Jim Bouck becomes the first certified realtime verbatim reporter (RVR).

Microsoft releases the *Encarta* encyclopedia on CD-ROM with captioning on all of the video clips.

2000 First milestone in the Telecommunications Act of 1996, requiring 450 hours per quarter (roughly 5 hours per day) of captioning on new (first aired in 1998 or later) English-language programs by all broadcast networks.

FCC adopts Report and Order mandating captioning on DTV.

The National Center for Accessible Media (NCAM) releases MAGpie, a free program for captioning multimedia.

2001   First Telecomm Act milestone for Spanish-language captioning, requiring 450 hours per quarter of captioning on "new" Spanish-language programs.

2002   Support for the TeleCaption II decoder is no longer required.

First Caption Quality Initiative (CQI) conference is held.

AudioScribe releases a speech-based realtime captioning system called SpeechCAP, and demonstrates it using a CNN broadcast.

The Telecomm Act requires 900 hours per quarter (roughly 10 hours per day) of captioning on "new" English-language programs by all broadcast networks. The definition of "new" is expanded to include all digital (DTV) programming first shown after July 1, 2002.

2003   The Telecomm Act requires at least 30% of all "old" (first aired 1997 or earlier) English-language programs to be captioned.

Closed-caption service providers form the Accessible Media Industry Coalition (AMIC) to address quality issues in captioning (among other issues). This is largely driven by the Caption Quality Initiative (CQI).

2004   The Telecomm Act requires 1,350 hours per quarter (roughly 15 hours per day) of captioning on "new" English-language programs and 900 hours per quarter (roughly 10 hours per day) on "new" Spanish-language programs.

2005   The Telecomm Act requires at least 30% of all "old" (first aired 1997 or earlier) Spanish-language programs to be captioned.

2006   The Telecomm Act requires virtually 100% of all "new" English-language programs to be captioned.

2007   The Telecomm Act requires 1,350 hours per quarter (roughly 15 hours per day) of captioning on "new" Spanish-language programs.

2008   The Telecomm Act requires at least 75% of all "old" English-language programs to be captioned.

2010   The Telecomm Act requires virtually 100% of all "new" Spanish-language programs to be captioned.

2012   The Telecomm Act requires at least 75% of all "old" Spanish-language programs to be captioned.

3 CAPTIONING STYLES AND CONVENTIONS

Many aspects of closed captioning have been standardized and codified. Despite efforts by several groups over the years, there are few accepted standards for quality and style of captions.

Measuring Quality

Though the FCC has been requested by deaf groups to mandate minimum quality levels, the FCC has declined to do so. Part of the reason is that quality needs to be quantifiable before it can be mandated. It's easy to say that all captioning must be 95% accurate. Defining what "accurate" means is another problem entirely.

In the early days of stenocaptioning, an important metric was the translation rate. As a stenocaptioner writes, the system is constantly looking up the incoming strokes in a translation dictionary—this process is described in detail in Chapter 11 (Realtime Stenocaptioning). The software tracks the number of "translates" (entries found in the dictionary) and the number of "untranslates."

Aspiring stenocaptioners were told then that if they could achieve translation rates of 98.5% or better, they were ready to apply for work at a captioning firm. Captioners going on the air were expected to be at 99% or better. With an average of five words on a row of captions, a 99% translation rate equates to one translation error in every 20 lines of captioning.

Realtime captioning software typically displays the translation rate on the screen, so that stenocaptioners can glance at their screen at any time to see how they're doing (see the upper-right corner of figure 10-4). Watching translation rates became something like a video game for stenocaptioners. Software vendors added decimal places so that the screen would show the difference between a 99.3% rate and a 99.33% rate.

A rite of passage for stenocaptioners was (and still is) the first "hundred percenter"–a broadcast with a perfect translation rate. Most stenocaptioners can tell you exactly when their first hundred percenter occurred and what they were captioning at the time.

The problem with using translation rates as a gauge of quality is that they don't take into account mistranslates or misfingerings. The majority of the bloopers in Chapter 11 are 100% translates. Every stroke was found in the translation dictionary. The problem is that they were wrong. If a captioner hears, "Steve's now coming," and writes "Steve's not coming," the meaning is completely changed, yet it's a valid perfect translation.

This led to the development of the TER, or Total Error Rate. A review would be done of a broadcast after the fact, finding and marking every error. The TER looked quite different from the translation rate. It wasn't uncommon for a stenocaptioner with a mature translation dictionary to consistently achieve 99.8% or better translation rates with TERs under 99%. In fact, a 98% TER was generally considered acceptable (roughly one error in every ten lines).

The TER concept, too, has its problems. One is the definition of an error. Is a missing comma an error if it doesn't change the meaning of a sentence? How about failing to put "New York Times" in quotes or italics? If a three-syllable word isn't in the dictionary, and translates as three shorter words or fragments, is that one error or three?

Trade associations have struggled with these questions on their certification exams for years. When the National Court Reporters Association (NCRA) developed their Certified Realtime Reporter (CRR) exam, this was the subject of some controversy. In a certification exam, just as in a legal quality standard, there cannot be subjective decisions. The grading process must be clear, objective, and consistent.

The CRR requires writing five minutes of professionally dictated material at reading rates of 180 to 200 wpm. It requires an accuracy of 96% to pass. That means a total of 38 errors is allowed. If you make 39, you fail the exam. There are other criteria that qualify as automatic fails, such as dropping ten or more consecutive words in two or more places.

With so few errors allowed, the definition of an error is obviously a critical issue for test-takers. NCRA provides lists of proper nouns and specialty terminology to the test-takers in advance, so that they won't be penalized for not having them in the translation dictionaries.

The National Verbatim Reporters Association (NVRA) is the trade association for voice writers and mask reporters. They, also, have a realtime certification exam, called the Realtime Verbatim Reporter (RVR), which is similar in construction and requirements to the CRR. It, also, involves five minutes of 180-200 wpm dictation with a required accuracy of 96%.

In both the CRR and the RVR, errors are defined as deviations from the original verbatim text. This would not necessarily be a good definition for captioning quality. A captioner can drop words without changing the meaning of a sentence. "Um, it happened–let's see–three times," could be turned into, "It happened three times" without affecting a deaf or hard-of-hearing viewer's comprehension of the material at all.

There are quantifiable issues, such as captions that are completely missing, but for the most part caption quality remains an elusive target.

Mixed-Case vs. All Uppercase

Captioning in the U.S. has traditionally been done in uppercase. This is often incorrectly interpreted as a technical issue, that line 21 doesn't support lowercase letters. Not true.

Several factors contributed to the uppercase standard. One of the primary factors was the original font for captioning, in which the lowercase letters were difficult to read. There were no true descenders (letters like lowercase y, j, and g were pushed up in the cell to make room for the descender to sit above the baseline), no anti-aliasing (smoothing of curves and diagonal lines), and the low resolution made it hard to distinguish some of the letters. Today's character generators in the decoders, on the other hand, produce lowercase letters that are quite clear.

Also, television captioning was developing at the same time as realtime translation technology for court reporters. Writing in all capital letters made the job of the stenocaptioner easier, as there was no need to worry about capitalization. A stenocaptioner working in mixed-case must differentiate between the color brown and the name Brown, for example. As online captioning systems became more sophisticated, they took over a lot of the issues, such as capitalizing the first word of a sentence, and capitalizing the word following an abbreviated title such as Mr., Mrs., or Dr.

Numerous studies have shown that mixed-case English is easier to read than English in all caps *in printed material*. Those studies have used typed or typeset text where print quality was not an issue. In the early decoders, where font quality was poor for lowercase, those studies were simply not applicable. As technology has advanced and the resolution of the character generators has improved, font quality has become less of an issue.

In other captioning venues, such as Internet streaming media, mixed-case is expected. People used to online chat environments consider uppercase to be the equivalent of shouting, and realtime streaming text online in all caps is very poorly received.

There are no technical barriers to mixed-case line 21 captioning any longer. Several captioning service providers have switched to mixed case, and more are experimenting with it.

Verbatim vs. Edited Captions

Perhaps the most-argued facet of captioning has been editing for reading speed, as opposed to presenting verbatim captions. Proponents of both schools of thought have valid arguments, and practices still vary widely.

It should be noted that the debate applies primarily to captioning for adults and students of secondary-school age. Few people claim that verbatim captioning of a show like *Sesame Street* would be readable by the majority of the intended audience. Generally, captions in children's programming are edited for comprehension and reading speed, with verbatim captioning only being used in poems and songs.

It also needs to be made clear before any discussion of caption reading speeds that reading static printed material is very different from reading captions. When reading a printed page for comprehension, the reading rate will vary, and the reader may go back to a previous paragraph for clarification. Obviously, this can't be done with captioning, where the reading rate is fixed. Also, a reader of printed material is focused only on the page being read, whereas a caption viewer has the video image on the screen at the same time, which may aid in understanding or may simply be a distraction.

As a final note, comprehension and reading rate may vary depending upon the viewer's level of deafness. A totally deaf viewer relies completely on the captions, and will tend to focus on the captioning to the exclusion of the picture. A 1999 study[1] found that deaf viewers of captioned video spend 82-86% of their time looking at the captions.

Although I have no hard research to back up my observations, I believe that hard-of-hearing people may tend to watch the captions less during familiar material, thus being affected less by changes in reading rate.

Why Verbatim?

Most proponents of verbatim captioning phrase the question as "why *not* verbatim?" They argue that there is no compelling reason for presenting the deaf and hard-of-hearing viewers with less information than the hearing viewers receive. When I worked at VITAC, our consumer advisory board was asked their opinion on the subject, and they responded unanimously that they wanted to get exactly the same information that hearing viewers received. The purpose of captioning, explained one, is to provide equal access, not partial access based upon someone else's interpretation of what I need.

---

[1]   Carl J. Jensema, Ramalinga Darma Danturthi, and Robert Burch, "Time spent viewing captions on television programs" - *American Annals of the Deaf*, 145(5):464–468 (2000).

Indeed, that sentiment runs strong through late-deafened adults, one of whom told me, "I'm *deaf*, not stupid. If I can't keep up, that's my problem."

Why Edit for Reading Speed?

This point of view is easily summarized. The purpose of television programming is to entertain or inform. If you can't understand what's going on, then you'll be neither entertained nor informed.

Many prelingually deaf people[2] have significantly slower reading rates than hearing people. Regardless of their intelligence, if English is their second language (after sign language), they cannot be expected to have the same comprehension levels as hearing people who grew up exposed to English. Believers in caption editing for reading speed say that as long as the meaning of the captioning isn't changed, editing increases accessibility without lessening the amount of information portrayed.

Drawing Conclusions

Dr. Carl Jensema has been involved in a number of studies that attempt to resolve the question of editing and comprehension. One oft-cited study, "Viewer Reaction to Different Captioned Television Speeds," performed for the Institute for Disabilities Research and Training, Inc. (IDRT) and funded by the U.S. Department of Education, measured viewers' comfort level at various reading rates.

In this study, 578 people were shown video segments with captions running at various speeds. The videos had no sound and the captions weren't tied to specific events on-screen. Viewers were asked to rate the caption speed on a five-point scale, as too fast, fast, OK, slow, or too slow. The middle rating, at which subjects felt the caption speed was comfortable, turned out to be 145 wpm. Interestingly, deaf people seemed to prefer slightly higher reading speeds than hearing people. Jensema attributes that to deaf people having more experience watching captioned television.

Before drawing the conclusion that all captioning should be rendered at 145 wpm, however, it is important to note several key points about this study.

First, this was not a comparison between verbatim and edited captions. There was no sound track to synchronize to, and viewers were not asked their opinion of verbatim captions.

Second, although 145 wpm was the mean comfortable level, the comfort level was still reasonable at speeds up to 170 words per minute. To quote from the study, "This suggests that most viewers are able to adjust to higher captioning rates and will not object to verbatim captions when the audio rate picks up."

---

[2]   The concept of prelingual and postlingual deafness is explained in Chapter 22 (CART and Live Event Captioning).

A very telling study, also for IDRT, was done by Jensema and Dr. Robb Burch in 1999. In this study, "Caption Speed and Viewer Comprehension of Television Programs," Burch and Jensema showed captioned video segments to 1,102 people and then tested their comprehension of the material presented in the captions. They had two sets of videos, one which presented straight facts to be regurgitated, and another which required the viewers to draw conclusions to answer test questions correctly.

Although there were differences based on a wide variety of demographics, the scores were generally consistent. In the analysis of the first set of videos (the "fact" set), the study stated:

> It had been expected that as the caption speed increased, the subtest scores would be lower because there were more words (and facts) being presented. This did not happen and it appears that subjects were generally able to absorb the material being presented, even when the speed reached 220 wpm.

> The fact tests in this study were based on 30-second video segments, a format that is very different from a typical viewing situation. However, the results suggest that the tests were measuring effectively and that, under these circumstances at least, caption speed has little influence on viewer's ability to absorb the facts presented in the captions.

Similarly, in the analysis of the other set of videos (the "conclusions" set), the study stated:

> The subjects did not display a trend toward a major drop in narrative test scores as caption speed increased. This was the same result that was obtained from the fact test scores. It is apparent that caption viewers are, in general, able to adjust to variations in caption speed and are able to draw correct conclusions from the captions they are viewing, regardless of speed.

Although age made little practical difference in the scores, education did. Those whose highest education completed was junior high school (representing both students and adults who had not completed school) scored significantly lower in the "conclusions" set of tests. To once again quote from the study,

> The results suggest that education had little influence on simple remembering of captioned facts, but that low educational achievement was a major factor in drawing conclusions from captions. This is especially true at the junior high school level, a finding that has important educational implications and deserves future study.

Of the 1,102 people who participated in the study, approximately 68% were deaf, and another 19% hard-of-hearing.

Jensema was a part of another study in 1996, along with Ralph McCann and Scott Ramsey, which measured the actual presentation speed of captioning on television.[3] They analyzed 205 television programs with a total of almost 850,000 words, and found that the average presentation rate for captioning was about 141 wpm. This varied depending upon the type of show, with sports shows averaging 106 wpm and talk shows averaging 177 wpm, although the highest burst speed was over 230 wpm.

From these studies, we can draw the conclusion that the majority of adult deaf and hard-of-hearing viewers can watch captioning at verbatim speeds without significant loss of comprehension. Although editing may be necessary for technical reasons, such as bursts of captioning that exceed the maximum line 21 bandwidth, editing for comprehension is not generally required.

Conventions in Caption Presentation

Few of the conventions listed here are universal, although the use of the double chevron (>>) for a change of speaker in roll-up captions is close. You'll see wide variations in style between captioning companies, and a few broadcasters require specific style guidelines to be followed.

The closest thing to an industry standard for captioning presentation at this point is a document from the Captioned Media Program (CMP) called "Caption Key: Guidelines and Preferred Techniques," which can be downloaded from the CMP's Web site at `www.cfv.org`.

The Caption Key document applies specifically to videos captioned for the CMP, a federally funded program that provides free loan of captioned materials to deaf and hard-of-hearing people. It does represent, however, many years of experience, research, and consumer feedback, and makes an excellent starting point for someone getting started in captioning.

Speaker Identification

Speaker identification is handled quite differently in roll-up and pop-on captions. In pop-on captioning, which is generally done in a studio with time for careful caption placement, the speaker is generally implied by the position of the captions, as shown in figure 3-1.

---

[3]   Carl Jensema, Ralph McCann, and Scott Ramsey, "Closed-captioned television presentation speed and vocabulary" - *American Annals of the Deaf*, 141(4):284–292 (1996).

Figure 3-1: Speaker Identification Shown by Caption Position

In the left frame, the caption is placed under the boy, and in the right, it is placed under the woman. Note that in both cases, since they're looking at the book, the caption is positioned so that it doesn't obscure the book. Such vertical movement is a good way to prevent covering important information, but should be kept to a minimum to prevent a "jumpy" look to the captions.

Narrators are usually captioned at the top center of the screen to differentiate them from on-screen speakers. Other off-screen speakers are shown by using italics.

In roll-up mode, a *change* of speaker is often indicated without explicitly showing who the speaker *is*. The universal symbol for a change of speaker is two right angle brackets–also called chevrons—at the beginning of a line, as shown in figure 3-2.

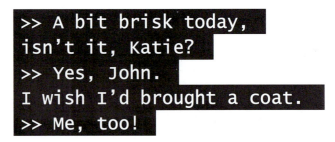

Figure 3-2: Speaker Identification Using Chevrons

When the speaker's name is indicated, it typically follows the chevrons and is followed by a colon.

With Teletext captioning (or "subtitling," as it's called there) in the U.K., color is frequently used for speaker identification. In a "talking head" program with two or three regular speakers, each is assigned a color. Throughout the program, for example, John's words might be in yellow, Katie's in cyan, and everyone else's in white. Although this capability is available in the U.S. with line 21 captioning, it is virtually never used.

Punctuation and Spacing

In roll-up captioning, a new line is generally started at the end of each sentence. Most online captioning software takes care of this automatically.

There should never be blank lines in roll-up captioning.

In pop-on captioning, an attempt should be made to keep sentences together in one caption, and not to have fragments of two different sentences in the same caption. There are times when more than one sentence will be in a single caption. With very short sentences (e.g., "Really? Is that so?"), it's better to combine them than to have two very short captions in a row.

When simultaneously displaying captions from two different speakers, as shown in figure 15-1, spread them apart and position them under the appropriate people.

In all captioning, avoid using two consecutive blank spaces. Just put one space after a period or question mark.

Acronyms and Abbreviations

In mixed-case captioning, acronyms and abbreviations are typically written as they would be on paper. In all-uppercase captioning, certain acronyms can look like words and make the sentence confusing. Even though the top sentence in figure 3-3 can be understood, it takes a moment to realize that "la" and "us" aren't words. The bottom sentence can be read and understood at a glance.

I LIVE IN LA, IN THE US.
I LIVE IN L.A., IN THE U.S.

Figure 3-3: Acronym Readability

As a general rule, if the acronym is pronounced as a word (e.g., NATO or FEMA[4]), then don't use periods. If it looks like a word, but each letter is pronounced (e.g., L.E.D. or I.T.[5]), use periods to avoid confusion.

---

[4]   North Atlantic Treaty Organization or Federal Emergency Management Agency.
[5]   Light Emitting Diode or Information Technology.

Sound Effects and Onomatopoeias

It is the captioner's responsibility to render any sounds that may be significant. If a shot is fired and everybody on the screen ducks, a caption like [gun fires] is required.

Typically, these are placed on a line by themselves in roll-up mode, or as their own caption in pop-on mode, although there are times when realtime captioners will pop up a caption like [applause] even when they're writing roll-up captions.

Captioning firms disagree on the use of descriptive sound effects versus onomatopoeia. As an example, if the video shows a bear with its teeth bared, should the caption read [bear growling] (a description) or grrrrr (an onomatopoeia)? The CMP Caption Key suggests using both, unless the source of the sound is on-screen and clear. In the bear example, "grrrrr" by itself would suffice, as would "boom" when an on-screen cannon fires.

Onomatopoeias are generally written as a part of the caption, just like any other word. Descriptions are typically set apart on a line by themselves and enclosed in square brackets. Where both are used together, the description is set on a line above the onomatopoeia, as in figure 3-4.

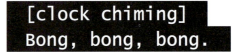

Figure 3-4: Using Descriptions and Onomatopoeias Together

It's important for the description of a sound effect to state what is making the noise, as long as it doesn't involve guesswork on the part of the captioner.

Even when captions are being presented in all capital letters, descriptive sound effects are generally written in lowercase.

Music

If music has lyrics, the words should be captioned, unless it's background music with people speaking over them. The caption should indicate what music is playing, by name if it's known (e.g., [Beethoven's Ninth playing]) or by description if it's not (e.g., [classical music playing]).

Lyrics use a music note (♪) at the beginning and end of each caption. Two consecutive music notes indicate the end of the song, as shown in figure 3-5, which is a pop-on captioning example.

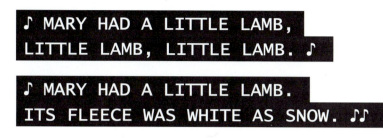

Figure 3-5: Captioning Song Lyrics

When there's background music that isn't instrumental to the plot, it is generally ignored in captions. If a father comes into his son's room and the stereo is blaring, that would be noted in the captions. If, a few moments into the scene, the father yells at the son to turn the music down, then the music is an important element, and everything up until that point should have some indication that the music is still playing. Typically, a single music note in the top-right corner of the screen shows this well.

Blanking the Captions

The goal of captioning is to provide deaf people with the same information that hearing people receive. There's no need, however, to provide the same information twice.

If a TV meteorologist puts up a graphic showing temperatures in various towns, and then proceeds to read the list, the captioner can simply blank the captions and allow deaf and hard-of-hearing viewers to read along. There's no need to duplicate the information (and cover part of the graphic) by captioning what the meteorologist says unless it's different than what the graphic shows.

You'll often see TV commercials that put a telephone number up at the end of the commercial, as the voiceover says "Call now at 555-1234." In these cases, the caption can read "Call now at," and be positioned directly above the telephone number. Similarly, if a Web site address (URL) is read aloud (e.g., "Visit us today at www.website.com") and displayed on the screen, the caption can just be positioned near the on-screen URL and say only, "Visit us now at."

4 CAPTIONING LAW

This chapter discusses laws relating to closed captioning. The material discussed here comes from text of laws, FCC reports, and other government publications, and contains personal opinions and interpretations of the author, who is *not* a lawyer. ***Nothing in this book should be construed as legal advice.*** If you have specific legal questions or issues, this chapter is intended only as a guide. Consult a qualified attorney before taking any legal action based on this information

The Americans with Disabilities Act

The Americans with Disabilities Act (Public Law 101-336), known as the ADA, is the best known of disabilities laws. When it passed, an estimated 44 million people were directly affected; over half of them because of hearing problems.

The ADA mandates wheelchair ramps, telephone relay services, and Braille labeling. It changed the designs of bathrooms, drinking fountains, telephone booths, and many other familiar structures. The changes brought about by the ADA are broad, sweeping, and ubiquitous. On the other hand, it barely mentions closed captioning.

The only direct mandate for captioning is in Section 402, which amends Section 711 of the Communications Act of 1934 to read:

> *Any television public service announcement that is produced or funded in whole or in part by any agency or instrumentality of Federal Government shall include*

closed captioning of the verbal content of such announcement. A television broadcast station licensee—

> *(1) shall not be required to supply closed captioning for any such announcement that fails to include it; and*

> *(2) shall not be liable for broadcasting any such announcement without transmitting a closed caption unless the licensee intentionally fails to transmit the closed caption that was included with the announcement.*

This requirement applies only to PSAs produced or funded by the Federal government, meaning that individual organizations—as well as state and local governments—are free to omit captioning if they desire, as long as there's no Federal money paying for the PSA.

Earlier in the ADA, however, in Title II, this loophole is dealt with in a rather roundabout way. In Section 201, a "public entity" is defined as:

> *(A) any State or local government;*

> *(B) any department, agency, special purpose district, or other instrumentality of a State or States or local government; and*

> *(C) the National Railroad Passenger Corporation, and any commuter authority (as defined in section 103(8) of the Rail Passenger Service Act).*

Section 202 then goes on to state that:

> *Subject to the provisions of this title, no qualified individual with a disability shall, by reason of such disability, be excluded from participation in or be denied the benefits of the services, programs, or activities of a **public entity**, or be subjected to discrimination by any such entity.*

This one paragraph is the foundation of virtually all captioning law springing from the ADA. Note first that the definitions exclude the Federal government itself. Although Title II does not require closed captioning of Federal proceedings, Congress did set an example in 1991 by instituting captioning of televised proceedings of both the Senate and the House on C-SPAN.

By not specifying directly that captioning is a method of accessibility, and that denying captioning constitutes discrimination, Section 202 falls far short of being a call for captioning. Title II was explained and discussed when local governments began instituting their own captioning.

Fremont, California, became the first city in the United States to provide captioning for all City Council and School Board meetings in 1992. Later, they added other meetings, such as planning commission. The ADA was not the primary driving factor in implementing captioning in Fremont, however. The city is home to the California School for the Deaf and a Gallaudet extension program. There was a strong grass-roots push for captioning, with one deaf community member summing everything up by stating, "All I'm asking for is what hearing people have had all along."

I approached several other cities in my research, asking what they would do if they were told that they would have to closed caption their televised city meetings because of ADA requirements. A representative of one city government explained that it was really quite simple in his mind. Captioning is expensive. They aren't required by law to televise their meetings. If they were told the televised meetings had to be captioned, they'd simply stop televising them. For obvious reasons, that official asked that I not use his name.

This attitude may be a part of the reason that the ADA hasn't been invoked in an attempt to force accessibility of local government broadcasts.

At least some schools, on the other hand, are taking Title II of the ADA seriously. In Legal Opinion M01-17 the General Counsel of the California Community Colleges Chancellor's Office compares ADA requirements imposed on colleges with section 508 requirements, and then states:

> As a result, if a college does not purchase available equipment or software which provides accessibility, OCR and the Chancellor's Office will not accept an argument based on undue financial hardship if a discrimination complaint is subsequently filed. This will typically mean that the college will be found in violation of the ADA and required to replace or modify the product, often at much higher cost.

Legal Opinion M02-22, from the same office, gets very specific:

> Applying these principles to the purchase or use of video materials, it is clear that the ADA and section 508 will generally require that colleges ensure that video material is captioned for students with hearing impairments.

And later on in the same document:

> Whenever possible, colleges should obtain a captioned version of the desired video from the publisher or copyright holder. If this option is not available, a college may choose to obtain written permission to caption the video from the publisher or copyright owner through a written agreement.

While this legal opinion applies only to California Community Colleges, other opinions concur. A September 28, 1993, letter from James P. Turner, Acting Assistant Attorney General in the Civil Rights Division of the U.S. Department of Justice, to Congressman John M. McHugh, states that:

> *Regulations implementing titles II and III [of the ADA] require the provision of auxiliary aids and services by public and private entities where necessary to ensure effective communication with an individual who is deaf or hard of hearing (section 35.160, p. 35721, of the title II rule; and section 36.303, p. 35597, of the title III rule, respectively). For individuals with hearing impairments, auxiliary aids and services include, but are not limited to, qualified interpreters, closed captioning, and transcription services such as computer aided real-time transcription (section 35.104, p. 35717, of the title II regulation; and section 36.303(b)(1), p. 35597, of the title III regulation).*

These exact words were also used in other letters from the Civil Rights Division, including a February 26, 1994, letter to an FCC Chief named Richard Engleman.

In the "ADA Guide for Small Towns," the Department of Justice explains to officials in local government that captioning must be provided where requested. To quote from the guide:

> *Achieving effective communication often requires that towns provide auxiliary aids and services. Examples of auxiliary aids and services include qualified sign language interpreters, assistive listening devices, open and closed captioning, notetakers, written materials, telephone handset devices, qualified readers, taped texts, audio recordings, Brailled materials, materials on computer disk, and large print materials.*

The City of Oakland, California, has been providing realtime closed captioning of its public meetings. In the background section of a resolution setting aside funds for further captioning, they stated:

> *Under Title II of the Americans with Disabilities Act (ADA) 42 U.S.C. 12101 et seq., state and local governments must ensure that communications with people with disabilities are as effective as communications with others. The U.S. Department of Justice regulations implementing Title II of the ADA require the provision of auxiliary aids and services where necessary to ensure effective communication with people with disabilities. For individuals with hearing*

impairments, auxiliary aids and services include qualified interpreters, closed captioning, and computer aided real-time captioning.[1]

The ADA effective communications requirement extends to city cable television programming. Page 35712 of the Title II regulation discusses this concept:

> *"A number of comments raised questions regarding the extent of a public entity's obligation to provide access to television programming for persons with hearing impairments. Television and videotape programs produced by public entities are covered by the ADA. Access to audio portions of such programming may be provided by closed captioning."*

The U.S. Department of Justice advises public entities to close (sic) caption audio portions of television programming unless doing so would result in a fundamental alteration in the nature of the television programming or in an undue financial and administrative burden. Closed captioning does not fundamentally alter the nature of television programming since it is only visible to those viewers who activate the captioning option on their television.

While there is no law on the books that comes right out and says, "State and local governments must provide closed captioning of everything they televise," that certainly seems to be the way a growing number of people are interpreting the ADA.

The Television Decoder Circuitry Act

Adoption of a new broadcast technology is almost always a chicken-and-egg situation, and captioning was no different. Broadcasters were loath to spend money on captions when only a tiny fraction of their audience could decode them, and consumers saw no reason to buy decoders when so few programs were captioned.

In the 1980s, deaf and hard-of-hearing people had to spend about $200 to purchase a TeleCaption decoder, and it cost broadcasters as much as $1,000 to caption a one-hour broadcast. Costs had to be driven down to spur acceptance.

The United States Government addressed this problem through the Television Decoder Circuitry Act of 1990 (Public Law 101-431). In a nutshell, the TDCA mandates that every television set manufactured or sold in the United States must have a built-in closed caption decoder chip, unless the picture is less than 13" in size.

---

[1] This is a reference to CART, which originally stood for computer-aided realtime translation. Now, most people in the industry call it communication assistance realtime translation.

Prior to the TDCA taking effect in July of 1993, the National Captioning Institute (NCI) estimates that there had been approximately 500,000 set-top caption decoders sold, representing well under 1% of the households in the U.S. With the advent of the TDCA, however, roughly 1½ million caption-enabled televisions were being sold in the U.S. each *month*! With no additional cost, captions could be provided in noisy environments like health clubs, bars, and airports. The audience for captioning expanded past the deaf and hard-of-hearing communities and into people learning English as a second language, children learning to read, quiet environments like hospital rooms, and many more.

Decoders, rather than being set-top boxes costing upwards of $100, were suddenly chips costing a few dollars. Awareness of captioning soared, as people experimented with the "CC" button on their remote controls, or found closed captioning on their on-screen menus. The higher level of awareness led more broadcasters to caption their programs. Captioning had definitely entered the mainstream.

The TDCA had far-reaching effects. Television manufacturers, rather than producing different models for each country, started shipping caption-enabled sets into Canada and Mexico. The proliferation of caption decoders encouraged more captioned programming, which in turn spurred design of related technologies, such as ITV links.

When the V-Chip was mandated, line 21 was the obvious place to embed the content advisory codes. With the decoder chips already decoding line 21, it was relatively simple to add V-Chip decoding in the same chip, so that it added little or no cost to the TV.

EIA-608

Section 6 of the TDCA states that, "The Federal Communications Commission shall promulgate rules to implement this Act within 180 days after the date of its enactment." This spurred the Electronic Industries Alliance (EIA) to form a subcommittee made up of industry representatives that had an interest in how the law would be enacted. The subcommittee included representatives from TV manufacturers, captioning companies, captioning software companies, captioning equipment manufacturers, and other related businesses.

The members of the subcommittee agreed almost unanimously that it was a good time to extend the original TeleCaption specification from the National Captioning Institute (NCI) and remove some of the limitations that it imposed. The resulting specification, EIA-608, allowed for greater flexibility in positioning captions, made minor modifications to the character set, and put into writing various assumptions that had been carried along since the beginning of closed captioning.

CEA-608-B, the current revision of the standard, is maintained by R4.3, the TV Data Systems Subcommittee of the Consumer Electronics Association (CEA). It may be purchased from Global Engineering Documents (`global.ihs.com`), and the current price as of this writing is $133.00.

Full Text of the TDCA

Part of the beauty of the TDCA is its brevity—less than 700 words for all that it accomplishes. The full text of the Act is:

Television Decoder Circuitry Act

An Act

To require new televisions to have built-in decoder circuitry.

Be it enacted by the Senate and House of Representatives of the United States of America in Congress assembled,

Short Title

Section. 1. This Act may be cited as the "Television Decoder Circuitry Act of 1990."

Findings

Sec. 2. The Congress finds that—

1. to the fullest extent made possible by technology, deaf and hearing-impaired people should have equal access to the television medium;

2. closed-captioned television transmissions have made it possible for thousands of deaf and hearing-impaired people to gain access to the television medium, thus significantly improving the quality of their lives;

3. closed-captioned television will provide access to information, entertainment, and a greater understanding of our Nation and the world to over 24,000,000 people in the United States who are deaf or hearing-impaired;

4. closed-captioned television will provide benefits for the nearly 38 percent of older Americans who have some loss of hearing;

5. closed-captioned television can assist both hearing and hearing-impaired children with reading and other learning skills, and improve literacy skills among adults;

6. closed-captioned television can assist those among our Nation's large immigrant population who are learning English as a second language with language comprehension;

7. currently, a consumer must buy a TeleCaption decoder and connect the decoder to a television set in order to display the closed-captioned television transmissions;

8. technology is now available to enable that closed-caption decoding capability to be built into new television sets during manufacture at a nominal cost by 1991; and

9. the availability of decoder-equipped television sets will significantly increase the audience that can be served by closed-captioned television, and such increased market will be an incentive to the television medium to provide more captioned programming.

Requirement For Closed-Captioning Equipment

Sec. 3. Section 303 of the Communications Act of 1934 (47 U.S.C. 303) is amended by adding at the end thereof the following:

"(u) Require that apparatus designed to receive television pictures broadcast simultaneously with sound be equipped with built-in decoder circuitry designed to display closed-captioned television transmissions when such apparatus is manufactured in the United States or imported for use in the United States, and its television picture screen is 13 inches or greater in size."

Performance And Display Standards

Sec. 4. (a) Section 330 of the Communications Act of 1934 (47 U.S.C. 330) is amended by redesignating subsection (b) as subsection (c), and by inserting immediately after subsection (a) the following new subsection:

"(b) No person shall ship in interstate commerce, manufacture, assemble, or import from any foreign country into the United States, any apparatus described in section 303(u) of this Act except in accordance with rules prescribed by the Commission pursuant to the authority granted by that section. Such rules shall

provide performance and display standards for such built-in decoder circuitry. Such rules shall further require that all such apparatus be able to receive and display closed captioning which have been transmitted by way of line 21 of the vertical blanking interval and which conform to the signal and display specifications set forth in the Public Broadcasting System engineering report numbered E-7709-C dated May 1980, as amended by the Telecaption II Decoder Module Performance Specification published by the National Captioning Institute, November 1985. As new video technology is developed, the Commission shall take such action as the Commission determines appropriate to ensure that closed-captioning service continues to be available to consumers. This subsection shall not apply to carriers transporting such apparatus without trading it."

(b) Section 330(c) of such Act, as redesignated by subsection (a) of this section, is amended by deleting "and section 303(s)" and inserting in lieu thereof ", section 303(s), and section 303(u)".

Effective Date

Sec. 5. Sections 3 and 4 of this Act shall take effect on July 1, 1993.

Rules

Sec. 6. The Federal Communications Commission shall promulgate rules to implement this Act within 180 days after the date of its enactment.

Plugging the DTV Loophole

The phrasing of Section 3 of the TDCA assures that traditional television sets have caption decoders. When the law was written, however, its authors didn't anticipate the separation of receiver circuitry from the display screen. At first, this was a fairly minor issue, affecting only equipment like TV receivers for computers. Since the receiver itself did not have a display bigger than 13" (or, indeed, any display at all), it was not subject to regulation by the TDCA.

The big hole, however, was DTV. It is common for DTV receivers and displays to be sold separately, and because of the wording of Section 3, captioning was not strictly mandated. The FCC stepped in to rectify this situation with Report and Order FCC-00-059, "Closed Captioning and Video Description of Video Programming, Implementation of Section 305 of the Telecommunications Act of 1996, Video Programming Accessibility."

This Report and Order, which took effect on July 1, 2002, specifically adds captioning mandates for DTV devices as follows (quoted directly from FCC-00-059):

- *All digital television receivers with picture screens in the 4:3 aspect ratio measuring at least 13 inches diagonally, digital television receivers with picture screens in the 16:9 aspect ratio measuring 7.8 inches or larger vertically (this size corresponds to the vertical height of an analog receiver with a 13 inch diagonal), and all DTV tuners, shipped in interstate commerce or manufactured in the United States must comply with the minimum decoder requirements we are adopting here.*

- *The rules apply to DTV tuners whether or not they are marketed with display screens.*

- *Converter boxes used to display digital programming on analog receivers must deliver the encoded "analog" caption information to the attached analog receiver.*

At the same time, the Report and Order added specific requirements for enhancements to closed captioning, based on Section 9 of the CEA-708 specification (known at that time as EIA-708). This spec not only covers the technical details of carrying caption data on a DTV broadcast, but adds significant enhancements, which are discussed in detail in Chapter 16 (DTV Captioning). The "Summary of Requirements" section of the Report and Order calls for a number of modifications to the spec, which were addressed by the CEA in the next revision (CEA-708-B).

The modifications are:

- *Decoders must support the standard, large, and small caption sizes and must allow the caption provider to choose a size and allow the viewer to choose an alternative size.*

- *Decoders must support the eight fonts listed in EIA-708. Caption providers may specify 1 of these 8 font styles to be used to write caption text. Decoders must include the ability for consumers to choose among the eight fonts. The decoder must display the font chosen by the caption provider unless the viewer chooses a different font.*

- *Decoders must implement the same 8 character background colors as those that Section 9 requires be implemented for character foreground (white, black, red, green, blue, yellow, magenta and cyan).*

- *Decoders must implement options for altering the appearance of caption character edges.*

- *Decoders must display the color chosen by the caption provider, and must allow viewers to override the foreground and/or background color chosen by the caption provider and select alternate colors.*

- *Decoders must be capable of decoding and processing data for the six standard services, but information from only one service need be displayed at a given time.*

- *Decoders must include an option that permits a viewer to choose a setting that will display captions as intended by the caption provider (a default). Decoders must also include an option that allows a viewer's chosen settings to remain until the viewer chooses to alter these settings, including during periods when the television is turned off.*

- *Cable providers and other multichannel video programming distributors must transmit captions in a format that will be understandable to this decoder circuitry in digital cable television sets when transmitting programming to digital television devices.*

For more information about DTV captioning and CEA-708, see Chapter 16 (DTV Captioning).

The Telecommunications Act of 1996

The Telecommunications Act of 1996 (hereafter the Telecomm Act) called upon the FCC to implement a broad mandate for captioning on American television. With the TDCA in force and tens of millions of caption-ready television sets already in the market, Congress felt it was time to force the broadcast industry to put captions on their programs.

The FCC was given some time to design and implement the mandate, and the clock officially started ticking on January 1, 1998. The requirements were imposed as a phase-in, originally only for English-language programming, but later adding Spanish as well.

A key facet of the Telecomm Act is that it applies to *broadcast* captioning. There is no mandate inherent in it for captioning of videotapes, DVDs, or streaming media on the Internet. It applies only to analog and DTV broadcast, cable, and satellite television.

One of the major objections broadcasters made is the massive cost of captioning their libraries of old video. Adding captions to newly produced programs is a tiny percentage of the overall cost of creating the program, but they said it would be a major burden to try and caption thousands of hours of archives in just a few short years.

To accommodate this, the FCC divided all television programming into two broad categories.

"Pre-Rule Programming" is anything that was first aired before January 1, 1998 (or, for DTV, before July 1, 2002). In essence, this covers everything that existed before the Telecomm Act officially took effect.

"New Programming" is anything aired after the Telecomm Act took effect, with the exception for DTV noted above.

The phase-in times are different for English and Spanish-language captioning, as captioning in Spanish-speaking environments is newer and not as widely used. Table 4-1 shows the schedule for new programming, and table 4-2 shows the schedule for pre-rule programming. For broadcasters that produce less than the total number of hours required, all of their new programming must be captioned.

For broadcast companies that produce more than one channel (e.g., multiple HBO and multiple MTV channels), the minimum hour requirements are *per channel*.

Table 4-1: Captioning Requirement Phase-In, New Programming

Hours per Quarter	English Language	Spanish Language
450	Jan 1, 2000	Jan 1, 2001
900	Jan 1, 2002	Jan 1, 2004
1,350	Jan 1, 2004	Jan 1, 2007
100% [2]	Jan 1, 2006	Jan 1, 2010

Table 4-2: Captioning Requirement Phase-In, Pre-Rule Programming

Captioning Required	English Language	Spanish Language
30%	Jan 1, 2003	Jan 1, 2005
75%	Jan 1, 2008	Jan 1, 2012

The method of captioning is taken into consideration as well. For example, the FCC recognizes that realtime captioning provides full access to a news broadcast, while using newsroom computer or prompter text does not.[3] Mandating realtime using stenocaptioners or voice writers could pose an undue economic burden upon smaller broadcasters, however. To strike a balance, the FCC ruled that news broadcasts captioned with newsroom computer/prompter methods would not count toward the requirement for the "big four" broadcast networks (ABC, CBS, Fox, and NBC) and their affiliates in the top 25 markets, nor would it count for cable or satellite networks reaching more than 50% of enabled households.

---

[2]   Exemptions still apply at the 100% level.
[3]   See ¶35 of FCC Order of Reconsideration MM Docket No. 95-176, from September 17, 1998.

Exemptions

Flipping through TV channels will show quickly, however, that we're nowhere near the mandated numbers in many cases. Why not? Because there are broadcasters that are exempt from the rules, and classes of programming that are exempt as well. Some of these include:

- "Small" video programming providers, meaning those with gross revenues of less than $3 million per year. In the case of broadcast companies owned by larger businesses, only the revenues of the broadcast company itself are counted, not those of the parent company. This means that a little $2 million public TV station remains exempt if it is purchased by a large broadcast conglomerate.

- Broadcasters for whom captioning would impose an "undue economic burden," words that we saw in the ADA as well. No broadcaster will be required to spend more than 2% of its annual gross revenues on captioning. This means that the smallest broadcasters affected by the law (those with $3 million in revenues) could be required to spend up to $60,000 per year, or about $165 per day, which doesn't buy much captioning.

- Brand new broadcast companies were given a four-year exemption to allow them to get fully up to speed. This expired at the beginning of 2002.

- Most "middle of the night" programming, which airs between 2 a.m. and 6 a.m. The entire ramp-up schedule is based on a target of 20 hours per day, which equates to roughly 1,800 hours per calendar quarter. The first milestone is ¼ of the target, the second is ½ of the target, and the third is ¾ of the target.

- Most commercials. Only commercials more than five minutes long have to be captioned.

- Locally produced non-news programming with "no repeat value," such as local commission meetings, grade school sports, and parades. These programs are *not* exempt if they are rebroadcast on another station. This exemption also does not exempt public meetings from ADA requirements.

- All programs in languages other than English or Spanish.

- "Non-vocal" music programming, such as symphonic music. Since there are no lyrics, there is nothing to caption. This exemption does *not* apply to music videos and music shows on networks like MTV.

- Instructional programming produced by local public television stations for individual schools that is not widely distributed.

- Public service announcements (PSAs) shorter than ten minutes in length.[4]

Broadcasters in the first two exempt categories are still required to maintain captioning on programs they broadcast that are already captioned. For example, a small (exempt) network affiliate is not required to caption the programming that they create, but they must make sure that nothing in their system removes captions from network programming that they show.

This does not apply, however, to programs that need to be edited. For example, if a station wishes to rebroadcast a movie that already has captions, but the movie will be edited for length or content, the captions must be edited or regenerated. The FCC considers this different from "pass-through" programming and does not require such programs to be recaptioned unless it is necessary to meet the minimum required number of broadcast hours.

Emergency Captioning

In 1970, fires ravaged California. Radio and television broadcasts warned residents about evacuations, but this was two years before the Caption Center at WGBH would be established as the first closed captioning service agency, and six years before the FCC would officially set aside line 21 for closed captioning. Officials drove around threatened areas announcing evacuations with loudspeakers, but this didn't help the deaf residents, either. Several deaf people burned to death in those fires because they didn't know what was going on.

This was only one of the tragedies that caused a flood of requests to the FCC to do something. They responded in 1977 by requiring that all Emergency Broadcast System (EBS) alerts must be presented "both aurally and visually." No longer could an emergency broadcast consist solely of a static slide saying "Emergency Bulletin" with a voice-over behind it. It was left up to the station how to present the EBS notice visually. It could be in the form of slides or crawls. In 1977, we were still five years away from the first broadcast captioned in realtime.

Also, the FCC requirement applied only to the EBS system, which was built for national emergencies. Local events often didn't use EBS. Also, EBS was used only on broadcast television stations, not on cable. In 1997, EBS was replaced with the Emergency Alert System (EAS), which requires alerts to be broadcast on *all* channels of a cable TV network. National emergencies, it would seem, were well covered.

When Hurricane Floyd hit the American coast in 1999, it hit hard. All of the local television stations were airing flood warnings to make sure that people got safely to high ground, but the EAS had not been activated. A deaf woman named Sharon McLawhorn was watching television

---

[4]   The ADA mandates that such PSAs *do* need to be captioned if they are produced by, or funded by, the Federal government.

that night, but she couldn't hear those storm warnings, and there were no captions. She went to bed not knowing what was coming, and woke up when the water was almost as high as her bed.

For over 24 hours she fought the elements, climbing and swimming to the roof of an adjacent trailer, and then to a different roof as the flood waters continued to rise. Eventually, she was rescued by helicopter.

Once again, it was time to update the laws to match available technology. The FCC's implementation of the Telecommunications Act of 1996 requires captioning, but with a long, slow phase-in period. At that time, broadcasters were required to caption approximately five hours per day, but the FCC didn't tell them which five hours, which allowed the stations mentioned earlier to broadcast flood warnings without captions.

On April 13, 2000, the FCC adopted a new Report and Order modifying their earlier rulings, and it requires all emergency broadcasts to be accessible to people with hearing disabilities. It does not specifically require closed captioning. The information may be presented using closed captions, open captions, subtitles, crawls, or any other method that puts a textual description of the emergency situation on the screen. In most cases, the easiest way to accomplish this will be realtime captioning, but stations that simply can't come up with the money or can't find a captioner are allowed to use whatever means necessary to get the information out in textual form.

No Fooling Around

This Report and Order differs from the earlier rulings on the Telecomm Act in several significant ways. The FCC recognized that requiring captions on sports, entertainment, and educational programming is a matter of equal access, but requiring captions or their equivalent on emergency broadcasts is a matter of life and death.

This ruling allows no exemptions. All broadcasters must comply, regardless of the size, age, profitability, or language of the station. There are no hardship exemptions of any kind. According to paragraph 18 of the Report and Order, there are 1,616 television stations in the United States, and all of them are required to comply.

There is also no ten-year phase-in period like the first Telecomm Act Captioning Report and Order. The ruling took effect 60 days from the publication date.

What's Actually Required

The FCC listed numerous examples of the kind of material this ruling covers, including "tornadoes, hurricanes, floods, tidal waves, earthquakes, icing conditions, heavy snows, widespread fires, discharge of toxic gases, widespread power failures, industrial explosions, civil disorders, school closings and changes in school bus schedules resulting from such conditions."

In a nutshell, deaf and hard-of-hearing people must have access to any broadcast that could directly affect their safety and that of their family and property.

Broadcasters that don't provide realtime captioning are allowed to summarize some of this information for deaf viewers, as long as all of the critical details are provided. It's okay to skip the reporter's musings about how this might affect next week's baseball game, but the captions must include evacuation routes, lists of affected areas, approved shelters, road closures, safety instructions, and other necessary information.

Rehabilitation Act of 1998, Section 508

Earlier in this chapter, it was noted that the Federal government conveniently exempted itself from the requirements of the Americans with Disabilities Act. In Section 508 of the Rehabilitation Act of 1998 (29 U.S.C. § 798), however, the government set a shining example of accessibility to electronic media for the private sector. The Act opens with a definition of what the Federal government must do to assure accessibility for its disabled employees:

> *(a)(1)(A) Development, procurement, maintenance, or use of electronic and information technology:*
>
> *When developing, procuring, maintaining, or using electronic and information technology, each Federal department or agency, including the United States Postal Service, shall ensure, unless an undue burden would be imposed on the department or agency, that the electronic and information technology allows, regardless of the type of medium of the technology–*
>
> > *(i) individuals with disabilities who are Federal employees to have access to and use of information and data that is comparable to the access to and use of the information and data by Federal employees who are not individuals with disabilities; and*
> >
> > *(ii) individuals with disabilities who are members of the public seeking information or services from a Federal department or agency to have access to and use of information and data that is comparable to the access to and use of the information and data by such members of the public who are not individuals with disabilities.*

(B) Alternative means efforts

When development, procurement, maintenance, or use of electronic and information technology that meets the standards published by the Access Board under paragraph (2) would impose an undue burden, the Federal department or agency shall provide individuals with disabilities covered by paragraph (1) with the information and data involved by an alternative means of access that allows the individual to use the information and data.

While Section 508 doesn't directly address captioning on broadcast television, it is clearly a mandate for captioning multimedia presentations (see Chapter 19 —Captions in Internet Streaming and Computer Media) and making Web sites fully accessible (see Chapter 20 — Accessible Web Site Design).

Section 508 requires that training and informational videos developed, maintained, procured, or used by a government agency be accessible, both with captioning and audio description. This also applies to distance learning programs used by or funded by the Federal government.

Captioning Complaints

Complaints related to Section 508 compliance should go directly to the agency that you believe isn't complying with the law. Telecomm Act complaints go to the FCC.

As a government agency, the FCC takes input directly from consumers. In fact, given the number of broadcasters in the U.S., it would be impossible for the FCC to police compliance with its rulings without consumer comments and complaints.

In its implementation of the Telecomm Act, the FCC decided to augment the consumer complaint process with random captioning audits.[5] Still, however, complaints are the primary means of dealing with noncompliance.

Any consumer can file a complaint up to the end of the calendar quarter *after* the one where the alleged violation occurred. In other words, if you have a captioning complaint about something that happened on July 4 (in the 3rd calendar quarter), you have until December 31 (the end of the 4th calendar quarter) to file the complaint. The complaint *must* be filed with the video programming provider in question first—*not* directly with the FCC.

The broadcaster has 45 days to respond to the complaint, unless it is filed during the same quarter when the violation occurred, in which case the broadcaster has until 45 days after the end of the quarter. In the example above, if the complaint was filed before the end of September (the last

---

[5]   See ¶118 of FCC Order of Reconsideration MM Docket No. 95-176, from September 17, 1998.

month in the 3rd calendar quarter), the broadcaster would have until November 14th (45 days into the 4th quarter) to respond. If the complaint was filed after the end of September, the broadcaster would have to respond within 45 days.

If the consumer and the broadcaster fail to work things out, or if the broadcaster fails to respond in the allotted time, then the consumer may file a complaint directly with the FCC. The broadcaster will have 15 days to file a response with the FCC. If the FCC agrees with the consumer that a violation has taken place, the broadcaster may face penalties, including fines.

All complaints, both to the broadcaster and to the FCC, must be filed in writing, which includes email as well as letters both mailed and faxed.

To file a complaint with the FCC, see the instructions on the FCC Web site at www.fcc.gov. Consumers and broadcasters should both keep copies of all correspondence related to complaints, including notes of telephone or TDD/TTY calls.

Jurisdiction of the FCC

The FCC has jurisdiction over broadcast television, including cable and satellite distribution, but not over private networks (such as in-house corporate news or school stations that aren't broadcast outside the school property) or non-broadcast video. Thus, the FCC does not have jurisdiction over videotapes and DVDs available for purchase or rental, video games, Internet streaming media, movie theaters, and videos shown on airplanes.

5 CONSUMER CAPTIONING EQUIPMENT

In 1980, the only way to watch closed-captioned television at home was by purchasing a set-top decoder from Sears and connecting it to your TV. As the prices of TVs dropped over the next ten years, we reached the point where an inexpensive TV cost less than the decoder did.

Decoders and their remote controls gained more functionality as the original TeleCaption I developed into the TeleCaption II, the TeleCaption 4000, and eventually the TeleCaption VR-100. Other companies introduced decoders with various special capabilities. Teknova, ViewCom, MYCAP USA, and SoftTouch all put their spins on the decoder market, ranging from multi-language decoders to computer connections for monitoring caption text.

When the Television Decoder Circuitry Act took effect in 1993, all TVs in the U.S.—except for small sets under 13"—had to have a decoder chip built in. As more broadcasters began including Extended Data Services (XDS) information in their signals, VCRs began to appear with decoder capability. The Time-of-Day packets in XDS allowed VCRs to set their own clocks, eliminating the blinking 12:00 that could be found in so many households around the country. If the VCR manufacturer had to include a decoder chip anyway to read the XDS, adding captions wasn't that much more effort.

The demand for set-top decoders began to evaporate, and even the venerable TeleCaptions disappeared from the market. Highly specialized units like SoftTouch's MagHubcap, shown in figure 5-1, still survive, but most of the others have gone out of production. The MagHubcap serves several purposes. It can act as a standard decoder with some extra options, like removing the black background behind the captions. It can also send caption text to your computer, and even act as a broadcast-quality character generator.

Figure 5-1: MagHubcap Caption/Data Recovery Decoder and Character Generator

Units like the MagHubcap don't find their way into too many homes. They are much better suited for engineers, caption industry insiders, and broadcasting applications. Most consumers looking to capture closed-caption data in their computers use a video capture card like the ATI All-in-Wonder, which is described later in this chapter.

Now, a new type of decoder has begun to appear that filters captions, and even mutes audio to eliminate obscenities based on reading the captions. The technical details of these devices are discussed in Chapter 18 (Other Line 21 Data). Decoders like the TVGuardian (pictured in figure 5-2) and the ProtecTV can still behave like an old TeleCaption, but they also offer caption censoring as an option.

Figure 5-2: TVGuardian Caption Decoder and Obscenity Filter

If you still have a pre-1993 TV, there's no reason to throw away that old decoder. Although the original TeleCaption I and TeleCaption II don't support all of the latest features in the CEA-608-B specification, most captioning will look fine on them. Almost all of the decoders manufactured after the TeleCaption II support a high percentage of the 608-B features, and should work fine on any TV system.

Connecting Equipment

There are two types of video connectors typically found on analog consumer equipment,[1] and a third that's used on the professional equipment. These are shown in figure 5-3.

---

[1]   There are other connectors as well, such as the DIN connector used for S-video, but these are different enough that they are rarely confused.

Figure 5-3: Video Connector Types

The antenna/cable connection carries many modulated video signals (channels) in a single cable. You need a TV tuner to extract any one specific signal. It uses a coaxial cable with an F connector on the end, which is usually threaded to screw onto the jack, and has a piece of bare copper wire sticking out in the middle.

RCA connectors are used for both audio and video, where the video cable carries a single picture without sound. You can *not* connect a decoder's video output to a television's antenna input just by purchasing an F→RCA cable adapter from Radio Shack. They are incompatible signal formats, and a modulator device is required to take the single video input and place it on Channel 3 or 4 for the television to extract.

BNC connectors are used on professional video equipment. The connectors are bayonet-style, and they slip on and twist to lock. You can connect professional video outputs to consumer equipment by using an RCA→BNC adapter.

Captions on Consumer Televisions

During the period between the passage of the Television Decoder Circuitry Act (TDCA) and the adoption of new technical standards for the decoders, there were some TVs manufactured that didn't comply fully with the standards. Companies that decided to build decoders into their sets before the law required it were largely guessing at what the requirements would be. Zenith, for example, made close to a million televisions in 1992 that had larger-than-normal caption text and some display oddities such as italic text being shown as black on a yellow background.

Setting these sets aside, virtually all other TVs in the U.S. follow the same standards. Nonetheless, they are not the same. There are several different caption chips available, as described in Chapter 9 (Decoding Equipment), and the implementation of the chips in the TV varies from manufacturer to manufacturer, or even from one model to the next.

Since TV manufacturers are constantly introducing new models, and specs change regularly, a listing of models and features would be obsolete before this book even hit print. Instead, let's examine some of the features you should look for when shopping for a TV with captions.

How Captions Are Turned On and Off

There are two common methods for turning captions on and off: A button on the remote control, or an on-screen menu.

Typically, the remote control button cycles between CC1, CC2, and none. If text modes are supported, they're included in the cycle. If you tend to turn captioning on and off relatively frequently, this is a feature you should look for.

When a menu is used, take a look at how deep into the menuing system you need to go to change the caption mode. With some TVs, captioning is one of the options that appears on the main list when you press the menu button. With others, you need to dig into sub-menus. There are TVs that take a lot of button-pushing to get the captions turned on.

Sometimes, the menus offer options other than just on and off. One example is the "caption on mute" feature. This feature is designed for hearing households that typically leave captions turned off. When the mute button is pressed to disable audio (when someone is on the phone, for example), the captions come on to replace the audio. When the audio is turned back on, the captions go away.

When checking out the caption features on a new TV, press a few buttons and watch what happens. On some sets, the same circuitry is used for the on-screen display (OSD) and for the captions. That means whenever you bring up a menu, the captions go away. If the OSD is used for displaying information like volume levels, even turning the sound up or down will disable the captions for a couple of seconds. If the set does support captions and OSD at the same time, the OSD will often cover the captions, at least partially, but this is better than having no captions at all while the OSD is on.

Language Support

TVs are not required to support captions in field 2. Most of the time, programs only have captioning on CC1, and all TVs support CC1. Shows that are captioned in two languages at once usually put the second language in field 2, like *60 Minutes*, which has English on CC1 and Spanish on CC3. If you have any interest in multilingual captioning, make sure to select a set that supports CC3 captioning.

Text Support

Early in the history of captioning, broadcasters experimented with placing different kinds of information in TEXT1. ABC, for example, put a program guide in TEXT1, showing viewers what programs were coming up and whether they were captioned. With the advanced program guides available in today's satellite and cable systems, this use for the text fields has all but died out.

The majority of the data you'll find in line 21 text fields nowadays is not intended to be viewed directly, such as ITV links and TV filter codes. These are described in detail in Chapter 18 (Other Line 21 Data).

For most people, then, having the ability to display line 21 text data on your TV screen doesn't make much difference.

Fonts

The FCC mandates the number of rows and columns of text on the screen, and where they will be located. Each character is located in a "cell" of a specified size and shape—described in Chapter 7 (Line 21 Technical Details).

Although the size and location of the cells are the same for all TVs, the text in those cells varies quite a bit. Decoder and television manufacturers are free to create their own text fonts, and vary the size of the letters within the cells. They may also change the speed and smoothness with which roll-up captions scroll. When selecting a TV, make sure to watch both pop-on and roll-up captions to see how readable they are for you.

Picture-in-Picture

When you use the picture-in-picture (PIP) feature on your TV, the sound you hear usually comes from the big picture—the small PIP is silent. Most sets display the captions from the big picture as well. If you're buying a TV with PIP, check on the captioning options.

Displaying captions on the small PIP doesn't work well. The text is so small that it's difficult to read. This feature is usually only found on very large high resolution sets.

If you're watching a program on the big screen, but you have the football game in PIP, you may want the audio from the program and the captions from the football game. Changing which picture is the "big" picture is typically easy. Changing which captions you see on it may require running through several menus.

Different TV manufacturers have very different ideas for handling captioning with PIP, some of which still haven't found their way into commercial TVs. Reviewing patents filed on these processes will show quite a few ideas that have never reached the market. Features like this make it even more important to try out the TV in the store before you buy it and take it home.

"Caption Volume Control"

This feature is strictly for digital television (DTV) sets. The CEA-708 standard for DTV allows for viewers to make the captions larger, so they're easier to read; or smaller, so they cover less of the picture. Look for this feature on DTV sets, and see how smoothly it works.

Caption Relocation

There are several devices available for broadcasters that allow them to shift captions around on the screen to avoid covering crawls and emergency broadcasts. As I write this, there are no television sets that allow home viewers to control where the captions appear, but the feature has been discussed by several manufacturers.

Making Captions Work with VCRs

When you have a caption decoder in your TV, there's nothing different or special involved in connecting a VCR. With an external caption decoder, there are two different setups, depending on your objective.

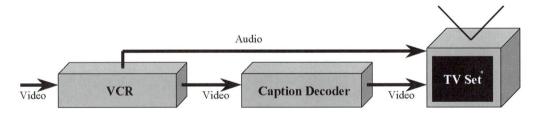

Figure 5-4: Connecting a VCR and Caption Decoder for Viewing

If you wish to watch TV with captions, use the setup shown in figure 5-4. The decoder displays any captions present in the video coming out of the VCR, whether it originates on a videotape, or it's being passed through from your antenna, satellite receiver, or cable box.

If you have separate connections for video and audio (stereo cables with RCA connectors), then the video goes through the decoder, and the audio goes directly from the VCR to the TV. If you use a single cable (a coaxial cable with F connectors), then it runs through the decoder.

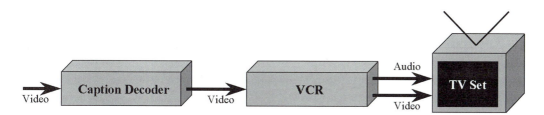

Figure 5-5: Connecting a VCR and Caption Decoder for Open-Caption Recording

On the other hand, if you want to record videotapes with open captions, you'll need to change to the setup shown in figure 5-5. The caption decoder puts the caption text on the picture *before* it gets to the VCR, which allows you to record tapes that can be shown on TVs or video systems that don't have caption decoders. When you play a closed-captioned videotape using the setup in figure 5-5, the video won't pass through the decoder, so you won't see the captions unless your TV also has a built-in caption decoder.

Making Captions Work with DVD Players

As Chapter 17 (Captioning and Subtitling on DVDs) explains in detail, there are two ways to store closed captioning information on a DVD. Each DVD that you rent or buy may use a different system, and many of them use both.

Closed Captions on a DVD are sent out to the TV set along with the video, and their display is controlled by the TV. Since they are created by line 21 code that's preserved (stored and regenerated, actually) on the DVD, they look just like captions from any other source. Some DVD players do not handle line 21 captions. The only way to be sure before buying a player is to take along a DVD to the store that you know has closed captioning on it, and see if it works.

Subtitles on a DVD are decoded and displayed by the DVD player. Typically, subtitles show up as edged text (light characters with a dark border or shadow) rather than text on a black box, and they usually use proportionally spaced fonts. DVD players allow for significantly more language choices, but are somewhat limited in color options.

If your TV set has captioning turned on, and you play a DVD with captioning, you'll see the captions automatically. If you prefer the look of subtitles, you'll need to turn off the captioning on your TV when you turn on the subtitles on the DVD player, or you'll get both of them on the screen at the same time, with the captions obscuring the subtitles.

If you use an external decoder, it needs to be hooked up between the DVD player and the TV, as shown with the VCR in figure 5-3.

Caption Readers and Decoders for Computers

Video cards that allow you to watch TV on your computer have been available for quite some time. The newest generation of these cards has a wide selection of capabilities, from live video capture to simultaneous multiple-channel viewing. Many of them also decode captions. Figure 5-6 shows such a card from ATI.

Figure 5-6: The ATI All-In-Wonder VE Card

The high-end cards don't stop at displaying captions on the TV picture, however. They can do quite a bit more with the captions, and when you're shopping for a TV video card, you'll want to look for some of these features:

Caption Display

The card shown in figure 5-6 reads only CC1 and TEXT1. While it's possible to do more (see "Custom Programming" below), that's a limitation you'll want to consider.

Some cards allow for traditional caption formats (text on the video picture, just like a TV set), while others display the text somewhere outside of the video picture, thus not obscuring any of the picture (see figure 5-7). ATI offers both options with its products. If you display the captions in a separate window, you can scroll through the last few minutes of text right in the caption window.

Figure 5-7: Captions in a Separate Window using ATI's Multimedia Center

Caption Capture

A card with capture capability allows you to store the captions on your computer for later review, making your own transcripts (ATI calls this "TV Magazine"). This has numerous applications, from letting you get a synopsis of a show that you missed to monitoring stations for compliance with FCC or CRTC captioning rules.

There are legal implications to this, however.[2] Just as it's illegal to make videotapes of a program and resell them, caption recording is for personal use only. You can't produce transcripts of TV programs this way and sell them without permission from the broadcaster. They own the captions, just as they own the audio and video of their material.

Capturing of caption data does not require an internal video card. External devices like the MagHubcap mentioned earlier in this chapter can capture captions as well, sending them to your computer using serial or USB ports. There are also devices designed for broadcast environments, which are discussed in Chapter 8 (Encoding Equipment).

---

[2] As stated in Chapter 4 (Captioning Law), I am not a lawyer and nothing stated in this book should be construed as legal advice. If you have any questions concerning ownership rights to broadcast captions, you should consult an attorney.

Caption Monitoring and Alarms

With the ability to capture captions in the computer comes the ability to take action on them. Some of the products allow users to enter a list of keywords. When one of the keywords is detected in the captions, the program can produce an audible or visible alert, begin saving captions, start recording video, or begin other pre-programmed tasks.

ATI's implementation of this capability is called Hotwords. In their Multimedia Center, you can specify combinations of words and their proximity to each other, and define the task(s) to perform whenever there is a hit.

Custom Programming

Programmers who wish to do more with line 21 information have more limited options. With external units like the MagHubcap, programs can just capture the raw data as it pours into the serial or USB port on the computer. With internal cards like ATI's, you need to have a better understanding of how Microsoft Windows systems handle video.

ATI does not supply an application programming interface (API) for its cards, referring people instead to Microsoft's DirectShow interface. There are tools provided with DirectShow that allow programmers to parse and interpret VBI data, and to render captions on a video image. Since Microsoft video specifications have changed several times over the last few years, you should get the latest information directly from Microsoft before you begin programming.

ViewCast, while supporting DirectShow like ATI does, also provides an API for programmers, which they call the Osprey Programming Interface (OPI). The OPI allows cross-platform development, which means the cards can be used in non-Windows environments. ViewCast offers drivers written for Linux, among other options.

6 TROUBLESHOOTING

Successful troubleshooting is all about eliminating possibilities one at a time, until there's only one answer left. As Sherlock Holmes said in *The Sign of the Four*, "Eliminate all other factors, and the one which remains must be the truth."

Never change more than one thing at a time when troubleshooting—if you succeed in fixing the problem, you won't know why. Similarly, don't draw conclusions based on highly dissimilar situations. If you watch *Gone with the Wind* on network television and don't see captions, but your cousin in Oshkosh rented the videotape and did see captions, that tells you nothing. If, on the other hand, you have a TV set in the living room and a TV set in the kitchen, both hooked to the same antenna, and one shows the captions and the other doesn't, you've localized the problem.

Consumer Troubleshooting

Captions Are Missing (Television)

1) Check other TV channels to see if captions appear there. If you find another channel with captions, go to step 5. If captions are missing on all channels, proceed to step 2.

2) Make sure that captions are enabled on your TV or decoder. This may be a button on the remote, or it may require using the on-screen menus. On sets that support more than one caption channel, make sure that the TV or decoder is set to CC1. If your signal is coming from an antenna, the TV or decoder is set to CC1, and you're still not seeing captions, go to step 4. If your signal is coming from cable TV or a satellite controller, proceed to step 3.

3) Play a videotape known to have captions. If the captions on the video appear, but you still can't see captions from TV, then there's a problem with your cable TV box or satellite controller. If you still don't see any captions, proceed to step 4.

4) The problem is most likely in the TV set or caption decoder. Try substituting a different television set with a built-in decoder to confirm this diagnosis.

5) If captions are missing from one channel, it may be that the show you're watching isn't captioned, or that there are problems with the captions at the TV station or network. Watch commercial breaks and other shows on that same channel. If nothing on that channel is captioned, but other channels are, then notify the station or network that their captions are missing. If only that one show was uncaptioned, it was probably not captioned in the first place.

Don't assume that because something is captioned once, it's captioned forever. For example, a movie may have captions on its release to video. A TV network then licenses the right to broadcast the movie. They will edit the movie, possibly starting from an uncaptioned master. Even if the master they're working from has captions, the captioning will probably be stripped out during the editing process. The edited movie must then be recaptioned.

Captions Are Missing (VCR)

1) Insert a videotape that is known to have good closed captions on it. If the captions show up, then your original tape is the problem. If they don't, proceed to step 2.

2) Is the picture clear? If you're seeing a very fuzzy picture, then the TV or decoder probably can't lock on to the captions. Solve the problem with the picture and the captions should show up. If the picture is clear, and you're still not seeing captions, proceed to step 3.

3) Make sure that captions are enabled on your TV or decoder. This may be a button on the remote, or it may require using the on-screen menus. On sets that support more than one caption channel, make sure that the TV or decoder is set to CC1. If that doesn't solve the problem, proceed to step 4.

4) If you have another TV set, hook it up to the VCR. If the second TV shows captions, and the first one still doesn't, then your problem is in the TV set or decoder. If not, the problem is with the VCR (this is very rare, so go back and be *sure* you're using a videotape that has good closed captions). If you don't have access to another TV set, you may need to take your VCR in to a dealer or a friend's house to test it.

Captions Are Missing (DVR)

If you're using a DVR (digital video recorder) like TiVo or ReplayTV, then the first question is whether you have *ever* seen captions in a program you've recorded with it.

A number of DVRs, especially early units, were not designed to properly handle Line 21 captions, and they strip all captioning data from the shows they record. Before spending a lot of time trying to troubleshoot your DVR captioning, make sure that your unit is capable of recording captions. The best way to do this is to watch a live show with captioning on it, record a bit, and then play it back. If the captions disappear on the playback, then your DVR can't handle captioning.

If your DVR can definitely handle captioning, then try these steps.

1) Make sure that captions are enabled on your TV or decoder. This may be a button on the remote, or it may require using the on-screen menus. On sets that support more than one caption channel, make sure that the TV or decoder is set to CC1. If that doesn't solve the problem, proceed to step 2.

2) If you have another TV set, hook it up to the DVR. If the second TV shows captions, and the first one still doesn't, then your problem is in the TV set or decoder. If not, the problem is with the DVR. If you don't have access to another TV set, you may need to take your DVR in to a dealer or a friend's house to test it.

Captions Are Missing (DVD)

To troubleshoot captioning on a DVD player, you must have a known starting point: a DVD that *definitely* has line 21 captions on it. Many DVDs are labeled with the "CC" symbol, but contain only subtitles. We'll refer to this DVD as the "known good" DVD.

1) Make sure you're playing the main feature on the DVD. Many DVDs have the main feature captioned and/or subtitled, but not the additional features, clips, specials, trailers, and so forth. If captions appear on the main feature, then the particular portion of the DVD you were watching is uncaptioned. Otherwise, proceed to step 2.

2) Remove the DVD in the player and replace it with the known good DVD. Play its main feature. If captions appear, then the DVD you were playing is uncaptioned. Otherwise, proceed to step 3.

3) Make sure that captions are enabled on your TV or decoder. This may be a button on the remote, or it may require using the on-screen menus. On sets that support more than one caption channel, make sure that the TV or decoder is set to CC1. If that doesn't solve the problem, proceed to step 4.

4) If there are any VCRs or other devices connected between the DVD player and the TV, remove them and plug the TV directly into the DVD player. Copy-protection systems often produce marginal TV signals, preventing the decoder from locking on the captions. If there are no other devices between the DVD player and the TV, and you still don't see captions on the known good DVD, proceed to step 5.

5) If you have another TV set, hook it up to the DVD player. If the second TV shows captions, and the first one still doesn't, then your problem is in the TV set or decoder. If not, the problem is with the DVD player. If you don't have access to another TV set, you may need to take your DVD player in to a dealer or a friend's house to test it.

Captions Are Doubled

If you are seeing every caption twice (usually with one superimposed over the other), then there are most likely two devices decoding the captions.

1) If both sets of captions are traditional white lettering on a black background, go to step 4. If one set is on the standard black background, and the other set is edged or shadowed letters with no background, proceed to step 2.

2) If you are playing a DVD, proceed to step 3. Otherwise, you are most likely seeing an open-captioned or subtitled movie that also has line 21 captions. Turn off the captioning in your TV set for the duration of the movie, and turn it back on afterwards.

3) You probably have a DVD that is both captioned and subtitled. The DVD player is displaying the subtitles (the edged or shadowed letters), and the TV or decoder is displaying the captions (the white letters on the black background). Turn off either the subtitles on the DVD or the captions on the TV.

4) Switch to a different TV station, or play a different videotape. If the problem goes away, then the program or video you were watching was probably open captioned. Turn off the captioning in your TV set for the duration of the movie, and turn it back on afterwards. If the problem persists, proceed to step 5.

5) You most likely have two different pieces of equipment that are decoding the captions. All TV sets manufactured since July of 1993 have decoders in them. Additionally, some consumer VCRs, such as the Hitachi VTFX8000E, have caption decoders. Check that only one caption decoder is turned on in your system.

Captions Are Scrambled

Everyone has a different idea of what constitutes "scrambled" captions, and you can tell a lot about what's wrong by looking closely at the caption text. These are the most common incarnations of the problem.

- **MISSING LETTERS:** Look for characters to always be missing in pairs. The space counts as a character, so if "THE DOG" showed as "THEOG" it would represent a pair of missing characters (the space and the D). This is usually an indication of poor reception, especially if you are also seeing blocks (as described in the next paragraph). When the picture quality isn't good enough for the decoder to lock on to line 21, the two characters contained in a frame will both be lost.

    Some of these drops can be rather entertaining. Jeff Hutchins, in his opening remarks at the first Caption Quality Initiative (CQI) conference in 2002, reported seeing a TV commercial where the dialog said that "one call can save you more on insurance." A dropped pair of characters changed it to read, "one call can save you moron insurance."

- **WHITE BLOCKS ("SQUARES"):** If letters are sometimes replaced by white or colored blocks, as in "THE ▮OG" it is an indication of poor reception. When one of the bits in a character is received incorrectly, it generates a parity error in the decoder, and most decoders display parity errors as solid-color blocks.

- **MISSPELLINGS AND WRONG WORDS I:** If text appears to be full of typos and mistakes (as opposed to the missing letters described above), there are several possible explanations. In a newscast, this could mean that the captions are being pulled from a prompter or newsroom system. Look for cues (e.g., "TOSS TO HENRY"), notes (e.g., "VTR SOT"), and phonetic spellings as telltale signs of prompter captions. For more about prompter-base captioning see Chapter 10 (Online Captioning Overview).

- **MISSPELLINGS AND WRONG WORDS II:** A second possible explanation for typos is that they're exactly that. The increased demand for captioning in recent years has caused some companies to put realtime captioners on the air before they're ready. This can lead to some rather odd-looking errors (known as bloopers or misstrokes) as explained in Chapter 11 (Realtime Stenocaptioning).

- **MISSPELLINGS AND WRONG WORDS III:** Finally, the garbling of captions caused by poor reception can be mistaken for typos. Watch for missing letters in pairs and for white (or solid-colored) blocks interspersed in the text, as described above.

- **FRAGMENTS OF CAPTIONS THAT DON'T MATCH THE AUDIO:** This frequently shows up in sports highlights segments or video montages in a newscast—

especially when they're taken from another station or network. The various pieces of video have captions on them, and when they're edited together, those snippets of caption text remain. The editors should either remove all of these captions, or (better yet) recaption the segment after it's built, but this doesn't always happen. What remains is a mishmash of bits of captions from various sources. Since live captioning can lag the broadcast by a few seconds, a montage of short clips may even have captions unrelated to the actual video bits used.

- **TOTAL GIBBERISH:** When you see words or letters repeated many times, seemingly random streams of characters, captions leaping about the screen, and arbitrary color changes, it may be a sign of signal compression. This most often shows up these days when a program with perfectly good captions (or no captions at all) contains a commercial full of gibberish captions. It shows that the commercial was compressed or otherwise edited after it was produced, with the result that line 21 was garbled.

Broadcast Troubleshooting

Captions Are Being Stripped

In the life of a video signal, from the camera to the headend or tower, there are numerous opportunities for the VBI to be regenerated or stripped. If your original signal has captions, but they aren't being broadcast, here are some of the places to look for the problem.

1) Check any caption encoders in the signal path to make sure they're not set to block upstream captions. If a realtime captioner neglected to put the encoder back into a mode that passes through existing data at the end of a broadcast, it will strip all captions from the signal.

2) Digital video effects (DVE) generators frequently regenerate the VBI. If you are shrinking the picture to make room for a crawl, merging two pictures for a side-by-side, running a picture-in-picture (PIP), or even placing a bug, the DVE may be removing the captions. One possible solution is to place a caption recovery decoder upstream of the DVE or use an integrated caption bridge, such as the EEG CB-411.

3) Check the settings on any timebase correctors (TBCs) in the signal path. Most can be set to regenerate all or part of the VBI.

7 LINE 21 TECHNICAL DETAILS

The Line 21 Waveform

All closed captioning and related data in an NTSC video signal is in line 21 of the VBI. The encoding system was designed to make the caption data as robust as possible, so that it can survive even in a poor reception area or on a VHS videotape. This required a tradeoff of bandwidth. More characters could have been placed in a frame—Teletext, for example, carries dramatically more information than Line 21—but the captions would not have been nearly as reliable.

Figure 7-1 shows the waveform for line 21.

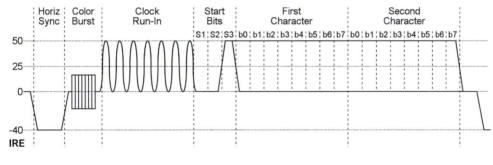

Figure 7-1: The Line 21 Waveform

The **Clock Run-In** allows the decoder to synchronize itself with the data to follow. The signal is 7 full cycles of a 0.5034965 MHz sine wave centered around the 25 IRE level, lasting 12.91 μs. The midpoint of the falling edge of the sine waves should be in phase with the transitions of the data bits and start bits. It should begin 10.5 µs after the start of horizontal sync. Decoders should be able to deal with at least a ±0.5 µs variation in the start of the clock run-in.

The **Start Bits** follow the same specifications as the data bits (described below), but will always have a value of 001. The rising edge of the third start bit happens 3.972 µs after the midpoint of the falling edge of the last cycle of the clock run-in.

The data itself consists of two non-return-to-zero (NRZ) encoded characters, each containing seven data bits (b0-b6) and one odd parity bit (b7). The high (one) level is 50±12 IRE, and the low (zero) level is –2 to +12 IRE. The rise/fall time for the bit transitions is 240 to 480 ns. Each data bit is 1.986 µs in length.

Each frame can carry additional captioning data in field 2, which is contained in video line 284. The waveform specifications are identical for the two fields. If only field 1 is being used, then encoder equipment can ignore field 2. If any information is inserted into field 2, then a valid field 1 must be generated as well, containing two NUL (zero) characters in each frame.

If there is no valid data in field 1, then decoder manufacturers are not required to check field 2.

If a decoder has detected valid data in field 1 and begun displaying captions, it should tolerate short lapses in the signal. If, however, there are 45 consecutive frames without valid data, then the decoder should erase all caption information on the screen. If two characters are received, where one has a parity error and the other doesn't, that counts as valid data for this purpose.

The Line 21 Character Set

The character set is based on 7-bit ASCII (American Standard Code for Information Interchange). Some changes were made to accommodate Spanish and French, which required the removal of some of the standard ASCII characters. Specifically, the basic line 21 character set does not include the asterisk (*), backslash (\ ), caret (^), underscore (_), grave accent (`), curly braces {}, vertical bar (|), or tilde (~). These were replaced mostly by accented letters, as shown in table 7-1. The modified characters are shown in boldface in the table.

All character codes in this book are given in hexadecimal.

Character 7F is a solid white (or colored) block. Most decoders display the solid block to indicate transmission problems, such as parity errors or framing errors.

Table 7-1: The Basic (One-Byte) Line 21 Character Set

Code	Symbol	Description	Code	Symbol	Description
20		space	50	P	uppercase P
21	!	exclamation mark	51	Q	uppercase Q
22	"	quotation mark	52	R	uppercase R
23	#	number (pound) sign	53	S	uppercase S
24	$	dollar sign	54	T	uppercase T
25	%	percent sign	55	U	uppercase U
26	&	ampersand	56	V	uppercase V
27	'	apostrophe	57	W	uppercase W
28	(	open parenthesis	58	X	uppercase X
29	)	close parenthesis	59	Y	uppercase Y
2A	**á**	**lowercase a, acute accent**	5A	Z	uppercase Z
2B	+	plus sign	5B	[	open square bracket
2C	,	comma	**5C**	**é**	**lowercase e, acute accent**
2D	-	hyphen (minus sign)	5D	]	close square bracket
2E	.	period	**5E**	**í**	**lowercase i, acute accent**
2F	/	slash	**5F**	**ó**	**lowercase o, acute accent**
30	0	zero	**60**	**ú**	**lowercase u, acute accent**
31	1	one	61	a	lowercase a
32	2	two	62	b	lowercase b
33	3	three	63	c	lowercase c
34	4	four	64	d	lowercase d
35	5	five	65	e	lowercase e
36	6	six	66	f	lowercase f
37	7	seven	67	g	lowercase g
38	8	eight	68	h	lowercase h
39	9	nine	69	i	lowercase i
3A	:	colon	6A	j	lowercase j
3B	;	semicolon	6B	k	lowercase k
3C	<	less-than sign	6C	l	lowercase l
3D	=	equal sign	6D	m	lowercase m
3E	>	greater-than sign	6E	n	lowercase n
3F	?	question mark	6F	o	lowercase o
40	@	at sign	70	p	lowercase p
41	A	uppercase A	71	q	lowercase q
42	B	uppercase B	72	r	lowercase r
43	C	uppercase C	73	s	lowercase s
44	D	uppercase D	74	t	lowercase t
45	E	uppercase E	75	u	lowercase u
46	F	uppercase F	76	v	lowercase v
47	G	uppercase G	77	w	lowercase w
48	H	uppercase H	78	x	lowercase x
49	I	uppercase I	79	y	lowercase y
4A	J	uppercase J	7A	z	lowercase z
4B	K	uppercase K	**7B**	**ç**	**lowercase c with cedilla**
4C	L	uppercase L	**7C**	**÷**	**division symbol**
4D	M	uppercase M	**7D**	**Ñ**	**uppercase N-tilde**
4E	N	uppercase N	**7E**	**ñ**	**lowercase n-tilde**
4F	O	uppercase O	**7F**	**█**	**solid block**

There is also a series of two-byte extended characters, shown in table 7-2, which was defined in the original line 21 specification. Other optional two-byte characters were added later for better language support, and these are discussed in Chapter 24 (Language Issues in Line 21)—see table 24-1 for a full list.

Table 7-2: The Extended (Two-Byte) Line 21 Character Set

Channel 1 Code	Channel 2 Code	Symbol	Description
11,30	19,30	®	registered trademark symbol
11,31	19,31	°	degree sign
11,32	19,32	½	1/2 symbol
11,33	19,33	¿	inverted (open) question mark
11,34	19,34	™	trademark symbol
11,35	19,35	¢	cents symbol
11,36	19,36	£	pounds sterling
11,37	19,37	♪	music note
11,38	19,38	à	lowercase a, grave accent
11,39	19,39		transparent space
11,3A	19,3A	è	lowercase e, grave accent
11,3B	19,3B	â	lowercase a, circumflex accent
11,3C	19,3C	ê	lowercase e, circumflex accent
11,3D	19,3D	î	lowercase i, circumflex accent
11,3E	19,3E	ô	lowercase o, circumflex accent
11,3F	19,3F	û	lowercase u, circumflex accent

When using two-byte characters, the first byte always indicates the data channel. A two-byte character in channel 1 (CC1, CC3, TEXT1, or TEXT3) always begins with 11, and in channel 2 (CC2, CC4, TEXT2, or TEXT4) it always begins with 19. For example, the text "98°F" would be represented by the bytes "39 38 11 31 46" in CC1, or by "39 38 19 31 46" in CC2.

In the original specification, "11,30" was a one-fourth (¼) symbol and "11,34" was a three-fourths (¾) symbol. These were replaced in 1992 by the registered trademark (®) and trademark (™) symbols. External decoders manufactured before 1993 and Zenith televisions with built-in decoders manufactured in 1992 will show the old characters.

The music note (11,37) is used to distinguish song lyrics from spoken words in captioning.

The transparent space (11,39) is used for positioning text. Since line 21 caption text always appears on a black background, a space character at the beginning or end of a row shows as an extension of the black box. The transparent space does not have a black background, which allows fine horizontal positioning of caption rows when using tab offsets or preamble address codes.

Text Attributes

In line 21 captions, the text can be made plain (Roman), italic, underlined, and colored. This is accomplished through a set of two-byte command codes, as shown in table 7-3.

Table 7-3: Mid-Row Text Attribute Codes

Channel 1 Code	Channel 2 Code	Attribute
11,20	19,20	White
11,21	19,21	White Underlined
11,22	19,22	Green
11,23	19,23	Green Underlined
11,24	19,24	Blue
11,25	19,25	Blue Underlined
11,26	19,26	Cyan
11,27	19,27	Cyan Underlined
11,28	19,28	Red
11,29	19,29	Red Underlined
11,2A	19,2A	Yellow
11,2B	19,2B	Yellow Underlined
11,2C	19,2C	Magenta
11,2D	19,2D	Magenta Underlined
11,2E	19,2E	Italic
11,2F	19,2F	Italic Underlined

These codes, known as mid-row text attribute codes, take up a space on the screen. This is not an issue as long as attributes are applied to entire words, but there is no way to make each letter of a word a different color, or to underline only a portion of a word. There is a method for applying attributes to the first word in a line without generating a leading space, by using preamble address codes (PACs), which we'll discuss later in this chapter.

All two-byte codes, including the special characters in table 7-2, should be frame-aligned, so that both bytes appear in the same frame. Two-byte commands whose first byte is in the range 10 to 1F may be transmitted twice to make the data stream more robust. If one of the codes is damaged by transmission errors or bad reception, the other may still pass on the command correctly. Decoders should ignore the second of two valid, identical commands in this range, so sending 11,2A,11,2A will generate only one blank space in the caption, not two.

There is no command code for underlining by itself. To turn underlining on or off, you must transmit either a color command or an italic command. The two italic codes (11,2E and 11,2F) do not change the color, so you can produce colored italics by transmitting first the code for the color and then the code for italics.

Here are a few examples of caption text, along with the string of bytes required to produce each of them.

STRAIGHT TEXT

53 54 52 41 49 47 48 54 20 54 45 58 54

ONE *ITALIC* WORD

4F 4E 45 11 2E 49 54 41 4C 49 43 11 20 57 4F 52 44   for channel 1
4F 4E 45 19 2E 49 54 41 4C 49 43 19 20 57 4F 52 44 for channel 2

In this example, there are no spaces between the words, as the mid-row codes show up as spaces. The command for white (11,20 or 19,20) is used to turn off the italics.

ITALIC, <u>UNDERLINE,</u> AND _BOTH_

11 2E 49 54 41 4C 49 43 2C 11 21 55 4E 44 45 52 4C 49 4E 45 2C 11 20 41 4E 44 11 2F 42 4F 54 48

This example only shows the byte stream for channel 1. To change it to channel 2, just substitute 19 for 11 in each of the four mid-row codes.

The first attribute (11,2E), which turns on italics, generates an extra space before the first word. Using PACs eliminates this problem, as we'll see a bit later. The second attribute (11,21) turns off the italics when it changes to white underlining. Both of the commas in this caption have the attributes of the preceding word, because changing attributes before the comma would generate a space there.

Caption Display Area

Caption text is displayed on the TV screen in a grid 15 rows high by 32 columns wide, as shown in figure 7-2. The grid comprises 80% of the width of the picture area, by 80% of the height of the picture area, leaving a 10% safe area on all four sides. This ensures that the captions will always be visible, even if the picture expands out into the area covered by the screen bezel. The area inside these boundaries is called the "safe title area."

When a caption is displayed, a blank space is placed at the beginning and end of each row. If a caption is a full 32 characters long, it will be displayed as 34 characters with the two added spaces. Column 0 and column 33 cannot be addressed in the encoder. They are used only for the blank spaces.

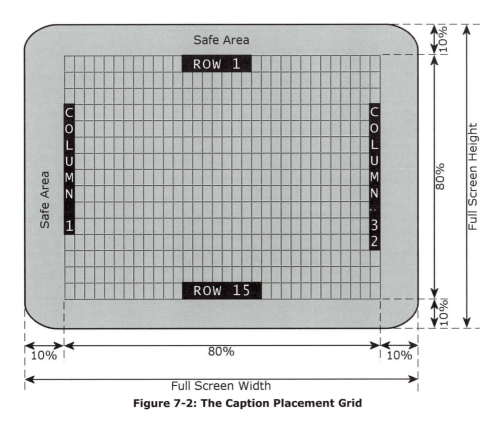

Figure 7-2: The Caption Placement Grid

Each grid cell takes up 26 interlaced scan lines, 13 from each field.

In the earliest decoders, the TeleCaption I and TeleCaption II from the National Captioning Institute, only the top four rows and bottom four rows of the screen could be used for captions. During the phase-over to full-screen use, there were workarounds for placement that allowed captions to show up properly even on older decoders. Since support for the TeleCaption I decoder officially ended in 1994 and support for the TeleCaption II ended in 2002, these workarounds are no longer required.

Determining the position of captions on the screen requires a set of miscellaneous command codes and a set of codes known as Preamble Address Codes (PACs). The miscellaneous codes, shown in table 7-4, are explained in the following sections that cover different caption styles.

Table 7-4: Miscellaneous Command Codes

Channel 1 Code	Channel 2 Code	Acronym	Description
14,20	1C,20	RCL	Resume Caption Loading
14,21	1C,21	BS	Backspace (erase previous character)
14,22	1C,22	AOF	Not used (formerly Alarm Off)
14,23	1C,23	AON	Not used (formerly Alarm On)
14,24	1C,24	DER	Delete to End of Row
14,25	1C,25	RU2	Roll-up, 2 rows
14,26	1C,26	RU3	Roll-up, 3 rows
14,27	1C,27	RU4	Roll-up, 4 rows
14,28	1C,28	FON	Flash On (heavily discouraged)
14,29	1C,29	RDC	Resume Direct Captioning
14,2A	1C,2A	TR	Text Restart
14,2B	1C,2B	RTD	Resume Text Display
14,2C	1C,2C	EDM	Erase Displayed Memory
14,2D	1C,2D	CR	Carriage Return (start new row)
14,2E	1C,2E	ENM	Erase Nondisplayed Memory
14,2F	1C,2F	EOC	End Of Caption (flip memories)
17,21	1F,21	TO1	Tab Offset, 1 column
17,22	1F,22	TO2	Tab Offset, 2 columns
17,23	1F,23	TO3	Tab Offset, 3 columns

Preamble Address Codes (PACs)

A PAC sets the cursor position and the text attributes at the same time, using only one frame (two bytes). The first byte of the PAC sets the data channel and provides half of the information required to determine the row (see table 7-5). The second byte sets the text attributes and provides the rest of the row information.

Table 7-5: The First Byte of a PAC

Channel 1 Code	Channel 2 Code	Row Number
11	19	1
11	19	2
12	1A	3
12	1A	4
15	1D	5
15	1D	6
16	1E	7
16	1E	8
17	1F	9
17	1F	10
10	18	11
13	1B	12
13	1B	13
14	1C	14
14	1C	15

The rather odd ordering of the command codes for the first byte of a PAC comes from the original TeleCaption decoders, which only supported the top four and bottom four rows. Command codes for rows five through eleven were added later, and the order wasn't changed in order to maintain compatibility with TeleCaption I and II decoders.

Each byte in table 7-5 (except for 10 and 18) is used for two different rows. The high-order bit of the second byte of the PAC determines which row, as shown in table 7-6.

Table 7-6: The Second Byte of a PAC

Row 1,3,5,7,9,11,12,14	Row 2,4,6,8,10,13,15	Attribute or Indent	
40	60	White	
41	61	White	Underlined
42	62	Green	
43	63	Green	Underlined
44	64	Blue	
45	65	Blue	Underlined
46	66	Cyan	
47	67	Cyan	Underlined
48	68	Red	
49	69	Red	Underlined
4A	6A	Yellow	
4B	6B	Yellow	Underlined
4C	6C	Magenta	
4D	6D	Magenta	Underlined
4E	6E	White Italics	
4F	6F	White Italics	Underlined
50	70	White Indent 0	
51	71	White Indent 0	Underlined
52	72	White Indent 4	
53	73	White Indent 4	Underlined
54	74	White Indent 8	
55	75	White Indent 8	Underlined
56	76	White Indent 12	
57	77	White Indent 12	Underlined
58	78	White Indent 16	
59	79	White Indent 16	Underlined
5A	7A	White Indent 20	
5B	7B	White Indent 20	Underlined
5C	7C	White Indent 24	
5D	7D	White Indent 24	Underlined
5E	7E	White Indent 28	
5F	7F	White Indent 28	Underlined

Let's look at a few examples to show how table 7-5 and table 7-6 are used to create a PAC.

Example 1: A caption in CC1 at row 1, column 1, with white text—**11,40**

Since we're using CC1, we use the Channel 1 code for row 1, which gives us 11 as the first byte. Row 1 is in the leftmost column of table 7-6. Since we're positioning the caption in column 1 (all the way at the left margin), we can use either the plain white code (40) or the white indent 0 code (50). They will both provide the same result.

Example 2: A caption in CC2 at row 15, column 4, with underlined yellow text—**1C,6B**

CC2 codes are found in the second column of table 7-5, so our first byte is 1C. Row 15 is found in the second column of table 7-6, so the second byte for yellow with underlining is 6B. There are no codes for indenting colored text, so we can either start the caption with three transparent spaces (19,39 since we're in channel 2—see table 7-2), or a tab offset command (see table 7-4). The TO3 command (1F,23 for channel 2) moves the cursor three spaces to the right without changing anything under the cursor.

Example 3: White text in T3 at row 15, column 1—**14,60**

T3 is in channel 1 of field 2, so the first byte is 14. Plain white text with no indent is 60, because row 15 is in the second column of table 7-6.

Decoder Memories and Caption Styles

Caption decoders have two separate memories, each one large enough for four rows of captions. At any given time, one of the memories is being shown on the TV screen and one is not. The visible memory is referred to as the "displayed memory" and the other is the "nondisplayed memory."

With roll-up captioning, all work is done in the displayed memory, and the viewer sees each character as it is transmitted.

With pop-on captioning, captions are sent to the nondisplayed memory, and when the caption is complete, a command is sent to flip the memories, which causes the caption to appear all at once.

Paint-on captioning is a hybrid method where captions are written to the displayed memory, but there is no scrolling.

If you attempt to send more than four rows to either memory without erasing in between, the decoder will erase the oldest row. This works well in roll-up captioning, but you should not rely on consistent behavior when more than four rows of pop-on or paint-on captions are sent.

There are separate erase commands for each of the memories (see table 7-4): Erase Displayed Memory (14,2C or 1C,2C) and Erase Nondisplayed Memory (14,2E or 1C,2E). Neither EDM nor ENM erases the memory in text mode. That is accomplished with Text Restart (14,2A or 1C,2A).

Roll-Up Captioning

Roll-up captions can be anywhere from two to four rows high and are written directly to the displayed memory. Text is added on the lowest row of the caption block, known as the base row, and the captions are scrolled up as each row is filled. Since each caption row is 13 scan lines high, most decoders scroll smoothly at a rate of one scan line per frame, thus completing the scroll in about 0.433 seconds. The recommendations in CEA-608-C allow for a scroll rate as fast as 0.2 seconds.

The top row of the roll-up caption block is either erased when the scrolling begins or allowed to scroll off as the row beneath it scrolls up. If another CR command is received in the middle of scrolling, the caption rows should jump to their final position rather than continuing to scroll.

Since viewers can change channels or turn their TV on in the middle of a show, it is important for each caption to begin with all of the commands necessary to generate it. Don't assume that the decoder already knows what your base row is or what color your captions are. Start each line of roll-up captioning with the following codes:

RU2, RU3, or RU4   Places the decoder in roll-up mode with appropriate number of rows

CR   Scrolls the caption display up one row and starts a fresh blank line

PAC   Sets the base row, indent, and text attributes

It is also important to use these three commands (in this order), because downstream encoders may be inserting other kinds of data, which are described in Chapter 18 (Other Line 21 Data), into line 21. For example, you may encode a videotape with captions in two languages on CC1 and CC3. When the tape is broadcast, the network and/or television station could insert XDS data in the blank spaces in field 2 and ITV links into field 1. By starting each of your captions with a full set of codes, you ensure that it will look like you intended it to.

For example, the following data stream would start captioning on CC1 in two-line roll-up at the bottom of the screen, and send a line of white text. Each additional line will begin with the same RU2, CR, and PAC, but will not require the EDM, as you don't want to erase what you've already displayed.

EDM	14 2C	- Erase anything that may already be on the screen
RU2	14 25	- Put the decoder in 2-line roll-up mode
CR	14 2D	- Scroll to start new line
PAC	14 60	- Set to row 15, column 1, white text
	...	- Transmit the first row of captions

If you want to indent the roll-up captions, you can use a combination of indent codes in the PAC, and either tab offsets or transparent spaces. PAC indents are in 4-column increments. Remember that the column numbering starts with 1, and the PAC indents in table 7-6 show the *number of columns* indented.

For example, if you wanted to place 3-line roll-up captions at the top of the screen, indented to column 8, with white text in CC1, you would use this series of codes for each line:

RU3	14 26	- Put the decoder in 3-line roll-up mode
CR	14 2D	- Scroll to start new line
PAC	14 52	- Set to row 3, column 5, white text
TO3	17 23	- Indent 3 more columns to column 8
	...	- Transmit the caption text

CAUTION: Always make sure that the base row is far enough down the screen to accommodate the desired number of rows of roll-up. In other words, 2-line roll-up should never be on row 1; 3-line should never be on rows 1 or 2; and 4-line should never be on rows 1 through 3. If you do put the base row too high on the screen, most decoders will push it down to let the caption fit, but this behavior is undefined in the specifications and results are unpredictable.

Word Wrapping

Caption decoders do not provide any word wrapping capabilities. The captions must be broken into rows before or during the encoding process. If a caption row is too long, each character after column 32 is filled will replace the character in column 32.

For example, let's look at what happens if you use an "indent 16" PAC to start your caption in column 17, and then transmit "THE QUICK BROWN FOX JUMPED OVER THE LAZY DOG". The first 16 characters will display correctly, and then column 32 on the decoder will flicker and change as each new character is received. When the entire caption has been received, the screen will show "THE QUICK BROWNG".

This behavior applies to text mode as well. When ITV links or content filter codes are placed in TEXT2, they are often preceded by 31 spaces or by an "indent 28" PAC and a TO3 to put the cursor in column 32. This way, if a viewer happens to turn on TEXT2, they will just see some flickering at the right edge of the screen rather than seeing the text of the ITV links or filter codes.

Backing Up and Making Corrections

Roll-up captioning is typically used in a realtime environment. In realtime, errors can occur that require backing up to make corrections.

For minor corrections, the easiest method is to use the backspace command (14,21 or 1C,21) to move the cursor left one position and erase what's there. For example, to send the word "CAT" in CC1 and then back up and replace it with the word "DOG," you would transmit the following:

43 41 54 14 21 14 21 14 21 44 4F 47

Decoders ignore a backspace sent when the cursor is in column 1.

Since a backspace (BS) command is two bytes long, each BS takes a full frame to transmit. A short correction like changing CAT to DOG would take 1/10 of a second to back up, and even less to retransmit. Longer corrections can be slow and distracting. Erasing 15 characters takes a full half second. Erasing and retransmitting a full 32-character line using BS commands would take a second and a half.

For these situations, you're better off repositioning the cursor using a PAC and a tab offset, and then using the delete to end of row (DER) command (14,24 or 1C,24). For example, assume you have transmitted the following caption on row 1 of CC1, in the left margin:

HOUSTON, WE SAVE A PROBLEM

To back up and change from "save" to "have" would require sending 14 BS commands followed by the corrected text. A much quicker method would be to send this command sequence:

PAC	14 76	- Set to row 15, column 12, white text (cursor on the space after "WE")
TO1	17 21	- Indent 1 more column to column 13 (cursor on the "S" in "SAVE")
DER	14 24	- Delete to end of row
	...	- Transmit the corrected text "HAVE A PROBLEM"

In this particular example, since we only have to move one column after the PAC, we could just as easily have used a single transparent space (11,39 or 19,39). In fact, since the character we're skipping over is a space, we could have saved a half a frame and re-sent the space.

Since the PAC has a resolution of 4 columns and there are tab offset commands for 1-3 columns, you can position anywhere in the row and delete to the end using only three commands, which takes a total of 1/10 of a second to transmit.

You should also use the DER method for correction if you have placed a character in column 32. The behavior of the BS command isn't well defined in column 32, and can produce inconsistent results.

You cannot back up after the captions have been scrolled to a new row. The only way to "unscroll" roll-up captions is to erase the entire display using an EDM command (14,2C or 1C,2C) and resend all of the lines that were showing. This process is not only slow (up to 2 seconds in 4-line roll-up with long lines), but distracting and confusing for viewers.

See Chapters 10-12 for more information about realtime captioning.

Moving Roll-Up Captions Around the Screen

In captioning of news and sports, you must contend with information being placed all around the periphery of the screen. Scores at the top, CG names at the bottom, bugs in the lower-right, and crawls at the bottom all compete with the captions for screen real estate.

Obviously, when information appears on the screen that is covered by the captions, you can erase the entire screen using an EDM command, and then start roll-up somewhere else. Viewers are usually at least a few words behind, though, so you'd be erasing text they hadn't read yet. A better choice is to move the roll-up to a different part of the screen without erasing it.

This uses the same method as backing up and correcting: transmit a PAC that sets the new base row and positions the cursor as close as possible to the desired column, and then send a tab offset (if required) to get to the exact column. You can then resume transmitting caption text right where you left off.

Pop-On Captioning

Unlike roll-up captions, which are visible as they are built, pop-on captions appear all at once to the viewer. This is accomplished by loading the caption into the nondisplayed memory, and then swapping memories to make the caption instantly appear.

To transmit a pop-on caption, use the following stream of commands:

RCL   Sets the decoder in pop-on mode, and prepares it to start loading data in the nondisplayed memory

ENM   Clears the nondisplayed memory

PAC   Sets the row, indent, and text attributes

Text   The text to be displayed on this row, which can include mid-row attributes

PAC/Text Repeat for a total of up to four rows

EDM   This is an optional step, which erases the displayed memory before displaying the caption. If the EDM is immediately followed by EOC, the display will flicker briefly between captions. Without an EDM, the old caption will disappear and the new one will appear at the same time. Some captioners prefer to have the flicker, as an indication to the viewer that the caption has changed, especially if the old and new captions are similar.

EOC   Swap the memories, causing the new caption to show

Paint-On Captioning

Paint-on captioning is rarely used except for special effects. It is a cross between roll-up and pop-on in many ways.

Like roll-up captions, paint-on captions are displayed as they are received by the decoder, so the viewer can watch them build. Like pop-on captions, paint-on captions do not scroll.

The primary use for paint-on captions is adding text to an existing caption without redrawing it. To send paint-on captions, use the following stream of commands:

RDC   Sets the decoder in paint-on mode, and prepares it to start loading data in the displayed memory

PAC   Sets the row, indent, and text attributes

Text   The text to be displayed on this row, which can include mid-row attributes

PAC/Text Repeat for a total of up to four rows

If the transmission of paint-on captions is interrupted by another type of data, then the RDC should be retransmitted.

Note that there is no swapping of memories, and erasing of memories is strictly optional.

Text Mode

Text mode is similar to roll-up, in that data is displayed as it comes in, and scrolls upward when a new line begins. Unlike captioning, though, text is rendered in a fixed black box, which can be anywhere from 7 to 15 rows high. Since Text mode uses the same placement grid as captioning (see figure 7-2), a 7-row text box covers roughly half the screen, and a 15-row box covers the whole screen.

When a decoder is in text mode, the first data received display on the top row of the text box. As each successive line comes in, it goes on the next line down. When the entire text box is full, it scrolls like roll-up captioning does.

Typically, text mode is used for information that is not synchronized to the program (ITV links and filter codes in TEXT2 are an exception). The text display is not cleared by EDM or ENM commands, nor is it erased automatically after some period of time.

The Resume Text Display (RTD) command is sent at the beginning of each stream of text data. Screen positioning information is not required, since the cursor cannot be moved from the line it occupies—when the decoder receives a PAC in text mode, the row information is ignored, and only the column changes.

The Text Restart (TR) command can be substituted for RTD. It does the same thing, except that the text box is cleared and the cursor placed in the leftmost column of the top row.

Some minor amount of editing can take place in text mode. The backspace character erases the prior character or mid-row code. The cursor column can be changed with a PAC, and data on the line rewritten or removed with a Delete to End of Row (DER).

8 ENCODING EQUIPMENT

The primary function of a caption encoder is to take a stream of captioning data and place it on line 21 of the vertical blanking interval (VBI). All encoders can handle this task. Beyond that, different models and manufacturers have different feature sets and different ways of handling tasks.

The list of equipment vendors in Appendix 1 provides a starting point in a search for captioning equipment, but selecting an encoder can be a complex task. In this chapter, we'll look at the basic functions of an encoder, and at the additional features that distinguish various models.

Encoder Modes

Just as important as what an encoder does to line 21 is what is *doesn't* do. Although different manufacturers use different terms for them, there are five basic modes of operation for an encoder.

Block Upstream Captions and Insert Raw Line 21 Data

In this mode, the encoder is accepting line 21 data and generating a fresh line 21 using that data. This is generally done on a field-by-field basis, so line 21 field 1 can be wiped and regenerated without affecting existing data (if any) on line 21 field 2 (video line 284).

Although encoders provide some buffering of incoming data, the software generating the data is responsible for timing, and shouldn't attempt to feed data to the encoder any faster than 2 characters per frame.

This mode is useful as a simple solution for preserving captions that would otherwise be destroyed by digital video effects (DVE) equipment. Figure 8-1 shows how a caption encoder in "raw" mode can be used for caption preservation.

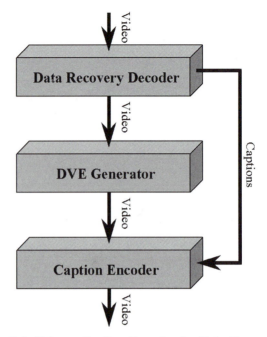

Figure 8-1: Using a Caption Encoder for Data Preservation

The data recovery decoder—see Chapter 9 (Decoding Equipment) for more on these—makes no change to the video at all. It just extracts the caption data from line 21 and passes it on. The caption encoder takes the modified, or even completely regenerated, video and reinserts the same line 21 data that was destroyed.

EEG refers to this mode as "pass-through" mode.

Block Upstream Captions and Insert Realtime ASCII Text

This is a simplified mode designed for realtime applications. Once the caption encoder is placed in this mode, all existing line 21 data is wiped, and new caption or text data is created from the incoming ASCII text. The encoder takes care of generating all line 21 commands and handles special characters automatically.

Pass Through Upstream Captions Unmodified

In this mode, typically known as transparent mode, the caption encoder does not change line 21 at all. It is passed through along with the rest of the video signal, as if the encoder wasn't there at all.

Pass Through Upstream Captions by Regenerating Line 21

This is similar to transparent mode, except that the encoder is extracting the line 21 data, and reinserting it on a "clean" line 21. This has the advantage of improving signal quality and increasing the reliability of the line 21 data. It has the disadvantage that it takes time to perform, and introduces a delay into the data path. Typically, the caption (and other) data will be delayed by about two frames. This is not an egregious delay unless there is a string of encoders in the video path, all of which are in this mode. Since delays are cumulative, a half-dozen encoders would delay the video by a noticeable amount—about 400 ms.

XDS Insertion

XDS-enabled encoders have a variety of methods for accepting packets and either inserting them immediately, repeating them at fixed intervals, inserting them on a "space-available" basis, or some combination of these.

Open Captioning and Character Generators

Any caption encoder that has a decoder built in can be used as a character generator for creating open captions. If the encoder and decoder are cross-coupled internally, just take your video from the "Decode Out" jack to get open captions. On some encoders, you'll need a short patch cable to connect the "Encoder Out" to the "Decoder In."

There are also devices that generate open captions without having encoding capabilities, so they cannot be used for closed captioning. Generally speaking, these are significantly less expensive than closed caption encoders.

One example is the MagHubcap from SoftTouch, which is pictured in figure 5-1 in Chapter 5 (Consumer Captioning Equipment). In addition to acting as a caption decoder, it can be connected to a captioning system and used to create open captions.

There are also rackmount devices that accomplish the same task, like EEG's DE241 CG or Link's PDR-870, which is shown in figure 8-2.

Figure 8-2: Link PDR-870 Character Generator

Open captioning can also be performed using traditional character generators, like the Chyron CODI. This has the advantage of creating very attractive output, but doesn't produce the cost savings of an open caption generator. If you are considering using a character generator like the CODI, check your captioning software first to make sure it is supported. Some captioning software does not support anything but line 21 devices.

For realtime use, your choices may be limited as well, since not all character generators support the roll-up format used by realtime captioning. Again, check all specs and interfaces carefully before selecting your equipment.

Encoder Form Factors

Most of the broadcast-quality encoders are rackmount units, usually less than four rack units (RU) in height. They take up very little space in an equipment rack, but are ungainly for portable applications. There are more portable options available, like the EEG EN370 DT desktop encoder shown in figure 8-3.

Figure 8-3: EEG EN370 DT Desktop Encoder

Desktop encoders are significantly lighter, and small enough to fit in a briefcase (10"×7¼"×1½"). The smaller size means fewer interconnection options on the back, and sometimes fewer features as well, but it can be an excellent choice for a captioner that frequently works on live events with limited equipment.

Encoder Interfaces

Encoders are typically connected to the computer using RS-232, although many models offer RS-422 as an option. Depending upon the manufacturer, the RS-232 port may have a standard DB9 connector, or an RJ-11 (6-pin modular telephone) connector. DB9 typically uses pin 2 for transmit and pin 3 for receive, while RJ-11 uses pins 3 and 4, respectively.

Some encoders with built-in decoders cross-link them internally, and others keep them separate. Figure 8-4 shows part of the back panel of an EEG EN470. If you wish to use the encoder to monitor the captions it's producing, then one of the encoder outputs would be connected with a short patch cable to the decoder input. One of the decoder outputs would go to the monitor.

Figure 8-4: Separate Encoder/Decoder Connections in an EEG EN470

There are a number of situations where this external connection approach can be useful. If, for example, captions are being inserted on video going to an uplink, the decoder can be connected to the downlink monitor to verify the integrity of the video through the path. Similarly, a switch could be installed in the line to allow the monitor to show decoded captions either on the video entering the encoder or the video leaving the encoder. This would allow verification of upstream caption data.

The caption data itself can be streamed to the encoder as a native line 21 byte stream with all command codes in place, or in a simplified realtime mode which allows programs to send straight ASCII text. These two modes are described briefly earlier in this chapter.

Using the realtime mode in an EEG EN470, all commands are preceded by a hex 01 byte. Enter control-A to generate the control code from a keyboard (in this book, we'll represent it as ^A). The command codes themselves are single ASCII characters. To enter realtime mode, use the command ^A2 optionally followed by the data channel, number of rows, and base row. For example, the command "^A2 CC3 2 2" would run two-line roll-up captions at the top of the screen in CC3. If the optional parameters are omitted, the encoder will default to three-line roll-up at the bottom of the screen in CC1, so "^A2 CC1 3 15" is equivalent to just "^A2" (all commands must be followed by hex 0C—carriage return).

Once the encoder is in realtime mode, all you have to do is send printable ASCII text with a carriage return at the end of each row. Sending ^C exits realtime mode.

Realtime caption sources that have the potential to generate data too fast for line 21 should support the XON/XOFF protocol to prevent buffer overflow. Most encoders have input buffers of 1,000 characters or so, which would take around 15 seconds to encode into line 21, so if you hit the buffer maximum, you're sending data much too fast anyway.

DTV Encoders (Servers) and Transcoders

The term "caption encoder" has been used for the devices that insert captions in the VBI since captioning first began. A terminology problem cropped up in the DTV world, however, since "encoder" is used to refer to the device that encodes the video into an MPEG stream. For this reason, DTV caption encoders are often referred to as "caption servers" to remove the confusion inherent in calling two different machines encoders.

As shown in Chapter 16 (DTV Captioning), the CEA-708 standard for captioning digital television is much more complex and feature-rich than line 21 (CEA-608) captioning. The sophistication of CEA-708 captioning allows for better control over the captions' appearance, both at the broadcaster's end and at the consumer's end.

All of these capabilities come at a cost, however. Few captioning programs support native 708 captioning, especially the advanced features. Creating and tuning the captions is more work than simple 608 captions, at least at this point in time.

Additionally, there's a huge library of analog programming that has to be recaptioned when it is converted to DTV if it is to take advantage of 708 capabilities.

Although several manufacturers started producing 708-compliant equipment soon after the standard was finalized, sales of these products have been slow. Most broadcasters requiring DTV captioning have been purchasing transcoders instead, which take line 21 captions as their input, and produce 708 captions.

Figure 8-5: EEG EN520 Closed Caption Server/Transcoder

Transcoding is usually built into native DTV caption encoders, like the EEG EN520, shown in figure 8-5. It can accept native 708 caption data from a DTV captioning system, 608 data from a line 21 captioning system, or raw caption data from a previously encoded analog broadcast.

Some of the transcoding devices, like the Ultech DTV-708 shown in figure 8-6, even have the ability to convert timecoded line 21 caption files on floppy into 708-compatible captions and feed them to a DTV encoder.

Figure 8-6: Ultech DTV-708 DTV Closed Caption Server/Transcoder

Unfortunately, there is no single standard for line 21 caption data files, as we'll see in Chapter 13 (Offline and Nonlinear Captioning). If you are shopping for an encoder that can encode directly from floppy (as opposed to being connected directly to a computer with encoding software), then check format compatibility with your captioning software.

XDS Encoders

XDS encoding offers a different challenge than straight caption encoding. There are XDS packets that apply to a broadcast network (e.g., network name), local station (e.g., call letters), the current program (e.g., current program name), upcoming programs (e.g., future program name), general information (e.g., time of day), and public service announcements (e.g., NWS warnings).

Some of this information is encoded by the network and some by the local station. The local time zone packet, for example, may not be placed on a nationally broadcast signal—only on a signal destined for a single time zone. The station, on the other hand, may not have enough information to insert packets relating to upcoming programming, NWS alerts, or even content advisories on the local program.

A local broadcaster must be able to designate certain classes of packets that are preserved from the upstream signal, and others that will be inserted locally.

Typically, XDS encoding isn't a standalone function. It is included in high-end caption encoders and combo units that perform other functions. The technically minded can program an encoder like the EEG EN470 directly through the serial port to block and insert various packets, but the process is far easier through a program that offers a graphical user interface (GUI) like EEG's XDS XPress, shown in figure 8-7.

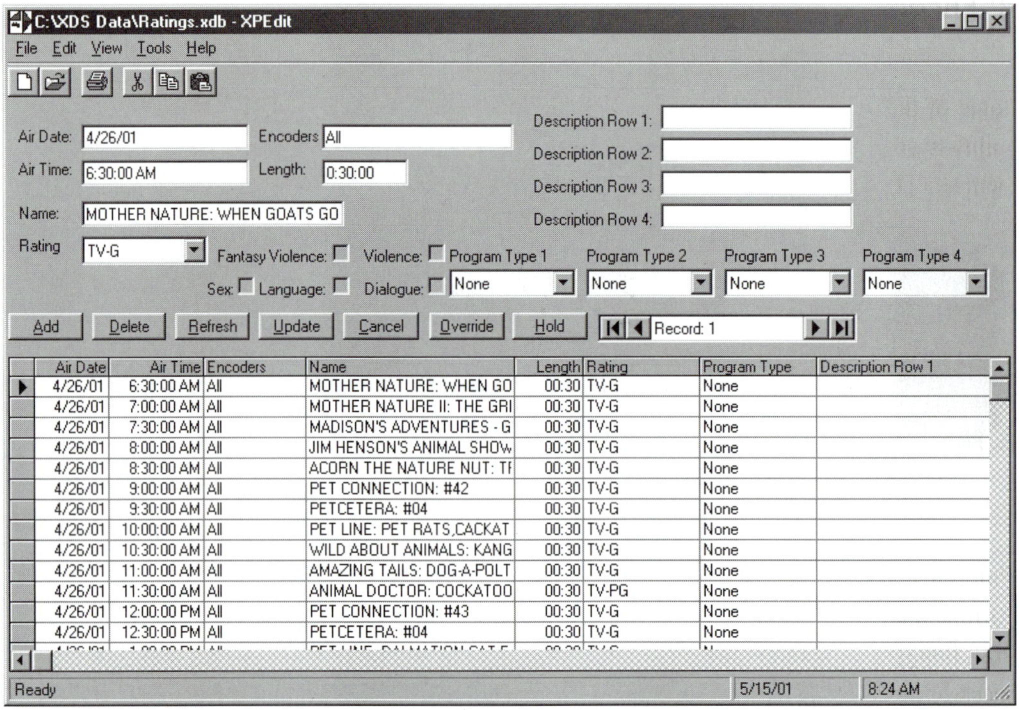

Figure 8-7: EEG's XDS Scheduling Software

When using any software that generates time-of-day packets, make sure that you have a procedure in place for keeping the PCs clock accurate. The clocks in computers are notoriously inconsistent, often losing or gaining as much as a second a day. If the computer has an Internet connection, there are programs available that can set the clock to an accurate standard like the National Institute of Standards and Technology atomic clocks. For details, see

```
http://www.boulder.nist.gov/timefreq/service/time-computer.html
```

Evertz goes a step farther, as shown in figure 8-8, offering XDS/V-Chip encoding combined with their logo inserter, so that when the V-Chip rating is being broadcast, the appropriate logo is displayed on the video as well. Their MetaCast2 software handles scheduling for multiple events and logo insertions.

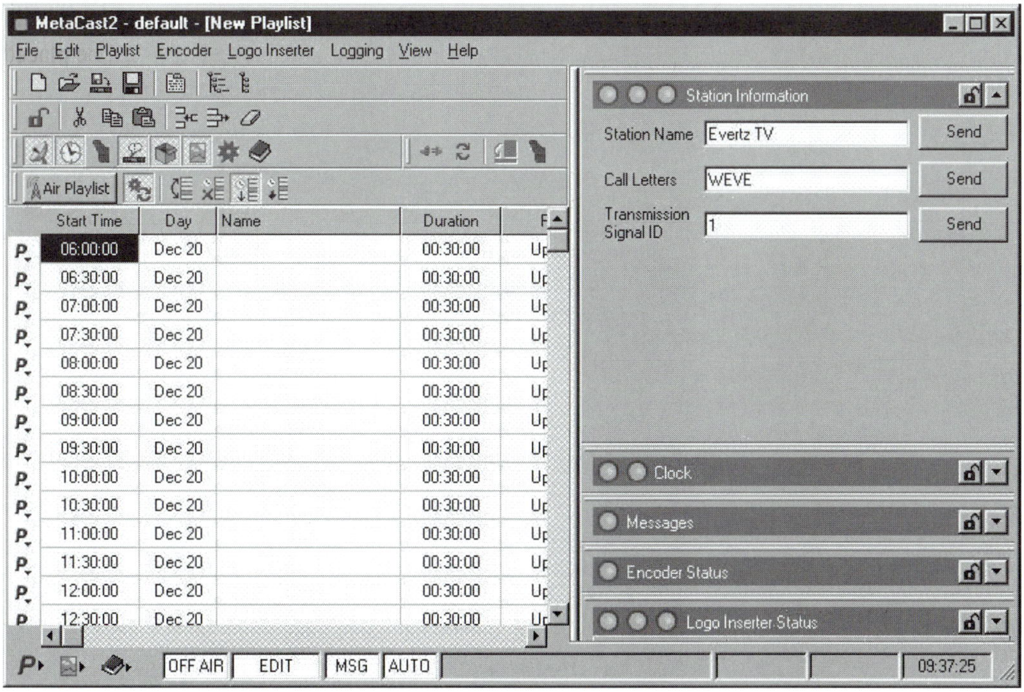

Figure 8-8: Evertz MetaCast2 XDS/V-Chip/Logo Insertion Software

Caption Bridges and Relocation

Figure 8-1 shows an equipment configuration for preserving line 21 data when the signal is passing through devices that regenerate or mangle the VBI. There is a simpler solution as well, known as a caption bridge.

A caption bridge accepts two video inputs—the original (source) video, and the edited (master) video. Line 21 is simply extracted from the original video and inserted into the edited video with no modification at all.

Another option available in newer caption bridges is caption relocation, which can either be done manually or by using a GPI trigger, as shown in figure 8-9.

The most common requirement for caption relocation is with emergency alert crawls. These crawls are placed at the bottom of the screen, which is the most common location for captioning. A viewer with their caption decoder turned on will often not be able to read the emergency crawl because it is covered by the captions.

A bridge with relocation capability has a defined "caption keep-out" zone (typically the bottom two caption rows, which cover video lines 212 to 239). When activated either manually or with the GPI trigger, caption data from the source video is analyzed, and captions that would be placed in the caption keep-out zone are moved out of the way.

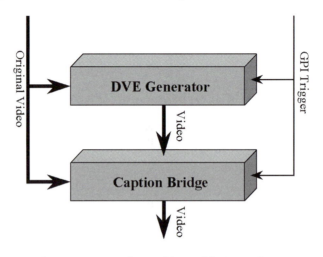

Figure 8-9: Caption Bridge with GPI Trigger

During realtime captioning, relocation should not be necessary, as the captioner can move the captions around the screen easily as they are generated. There are still quite a few situations where an automatic approach like the caption bridge with relocation is required, as the captioner doesn't know that the captions need to be moved.

- In many cases, remote captions can't actually see the video for what they're captioning. If a TV station in Atlanta is using a captioner in San Francisco, that captioner will be working from audio only unless the station is on a satellite feed accessible to the captioner. In this situation, the captioner has no idea that a crawl has appeared on the screen. The same configuration can ensure that such captions don't cover graphics as well.

- When captioning a national feed, the captioner has no way of knowing when a local station puts up an emergency crawl. A caption bridge with relocation can move the captions for that one station's broadcast without affecting the national feed at all.

- Bridges can be triggered before a crawl actually starts, thus moving the captions early and assuring that even the first word isn't covered. Live captioners, on the other hand, won't know about a crawl until it appears on their monitors. The lag between the start of the crawl and the caption relocation can be long enough for most viewers to miss the first word or two of the crawl.

Handling Multiple Lines and Fields

Handling more than one caption language at a time can be a tricky issue in live events. This requires more than one realtime captioner, each with a separate online captioning system. In the past, custom solutions have been required to merge the captions from the two systems into a single caption stream.

In 1996, when captioning firm Waite & Associates was given the opportunity to caption the Canadian Parliament simultaneously in English and French as part of Caption Awareness Week, this problem had to be solved on a short timeline. With U.N.-style translation, it was easy to get English audio to one captioner and French audio to another. Producing the two streams of captions was straightforward as well.

The difficulty lay in the destination of the streams. English went into CC1 and French into CC2. Both, therefore, needed to be in field 1. If two encoders were used, one stream would destroy the other. A software engineer by the name of David Blanchette developed a custom software package that interleaved the two streams into a single encoder, thus solving the problem. As neat and tidy as it was, the solution still had problems. One of them was the requirement for a third computer, which had to have three serial ports.

In the years since then, it has been recommended that the second language be placed not in CC2, but CC3. This solves potential bandwidth problems in field 1, but also solves the problem of one caption stream being destroyed by the other. Most encoders, when writing into one field, leave the other untouched. This means that if one encoder handled the English in CC1 and another, downstream from it, handled the French in CC3, the two processes would be completely independent of one another, and the result would be clean bilingual captioning.

Today, the solution is even easier than that. Encoders like the EEG EN470 offer multiple data ports, so that two captioning systems can be connected to the same encoder. The ports have independently controlled access rights, so that one can be set to allow writing to field 1 *only* and another to field 2 *only*. Even if the captioning system attempts to put data in the wrong field, the encoder will block it.

Since most high-end encoders include built-in modems, this can work even when the two realtime captioners are physically separated. As long as they are each near a telephone line, one can be connected directly to the encoder and the other dialed in over the phone.

Software Encoding

One product takes a unique approach to caption encoding: MacCaption. This Macintosh-based offline system from Computer Prompting & Captioning is discussed in Chapter 13 (Offline and Nonlinear Captioning), but their encoding system is more appropriate for this chapter.

MacCaption is a nonlinear system, meaning that it works with video stored on the Mac's hard disk. Unlike most nonlinear captioning programs, which work from a low-resolution copy of the video, MacCaption works directly from original digital video. When the caption editing process is complete, the final video is rendered from the Mac, which generates line 21 as it creates the video images, thus obviating the need for a hardware encoder.

9 DECODING EQUIPMENT

Consumer vs. Broadcast Decoders

In the early days of caption decoders, there was a clear line between the consumer products (e.g., the TeleCaption set-top boxes) and broadcast-quality products such as those that EEG manufactured. After the passage of the Television Decoder Circuitry Act (TDCA), new models of broadcast decoders continued to be developed, but the consumer products began to disappear.

Today, NCI no longer manufactures, refurbishes, or repairs TeleCaption decoders. Specialty products like the Teknova multilingual caption decoder appeared and then faded away. With decoders embedded in every television set, there is little market for set-top decoders unless they have something significant to offer.

The few remaining set-top decoders are described in Chapter 5 (Consumer Captioning Equipment).

Most of the manufacturers discussed in Chapter 8 (Encoding Equipment) make decoders as well as encoders, or at least have decoding capability built in to their decoders.

One of the biggest visible differences between set-top decoders and built-in decoders is that many of the set-top and professional units don't display colored captions.

Decoder Chips

Several companies manufacture CEA-608-compatible decoder chips for use in television sets.

The Zilog Z86129 is typical of the offerings. In an 18-pin package, either through-hole (DIP) or surface mount (SOIC), it has a line 21 decoder (for both captions and V-Chip) and on-screen display (OSD) built in. It can decode and display all four caption channels and all four text channels, and display XDS data on the screen using the OSD as well. In addition to the standard CEA-608 display options, it can show drop-shadowed text without the black background, or change the background color to blue.

Another chip in that product family, the Z86130, can be used for data recovery, extracting raw line 21 data, and feeding it out a serial port.

These chips take composite video and sync as input, and send out red, green, blue, and box (OSD) timing) signals, enabling the caption display to be integrated directly into the video path.

The chip manufacturers offer application notes and sample circuits showing how their products can be integrated into a TV, along with data sheets and programming manuals.

Do It Yourself

There's no real black magic to reading and decoding line 21 caption data. The process was kept intentionally simple, and the majority of the work can be done with a few off-the-shelf parts.

Eric Smith built his own decoder based on the Microchip Technology PIC16C622 chip, which you can pick up for about $4.00, and an Élantec EL4581C sync separator. He has a Web site that includes a schematic of his project, along with full source code for the EPROM in the PIC chip, which is an 8-bit microcontroller. His board uses a total of only four chips, one of which is eliminated in his newest design. For more details about Smith's project, see:

`http://www.brouhaha.com/~eric/pic/caption.html`

Smith built his project in 1995, when dedicated caption chips were fairly new. Someone repeating that process today could use a PIC chip or other dedicated microcontroller with custom code, or just use a chip like the Z86130 along with a microcomputer or microcontroller to process the information.

One of the applications that several electronics hobbyists have experimented with is a simple "mute on commercial" product. During live shows such as news and sports, captions are almost always roll-up. When pop-on captions appear, it's an almost-sure sign of a commercial. If you're willing to either tear apart your TV or mutilate a remote control, you can make a simple box that mutes the sound when it sees a pop-on caption, and turns the sound back on when it sees roll-up.

Of course, this is a far-from-perfect approach. Many commercials are still uncaptioned, and there's usually a lag of a few seconds before realtime captions resume coming out of a commercial break.

Still, it's an entertaining project that can provide a few minutes of silence here and there when everyone's watching the game.

Data Recovery Decoders

Data recovery decoders extract information from line 21 and send it to a computer. They range from external devices, like the MagHubcap (see figure 5-1) and the EEG DR221 to plug-in cards for a PC like the Adrienne PCI-21/RDR and the ATI All-in-Wonder (see figure 5-6).

While consumers' primary use for a data recovery decoder is capturing transcripts of shows, broadcasters have a wider variety of applications.

Caption Monitoring

A data recovery decoder and a very simple program are all that's needed to provide a log of when data on line 21 is present and when it's not. Norpak takes the process much farther, however, with its WHAZ-it software and line of data recovery cards.

Computers can be configured with one PCI card to monitor a single channel, or connected to one or more external chassis to monitor as many as 60 channels at a time. WHAZ-it sorts out and logs the streams to an SQL database for analysis. This way, the system can be used for compliance logging, and also for live monitoring. The software is capable of generating alerts based on a wide variety of conditions. For example, it could generate an alert if there is nothing in CC1 for more than five minutes, or if there is no V-Chip data for more than three seconds. It understands individual XDS packet types, so it can also watch for specific types of data, such as station identification or time-of-day packets.

This kind of system is designed for broadcast environments, and it has extensive interconnect options with the rest of the station's equipment. An individual or small watchdog group trying to keep an eye on compliance[1] doesn't need anything nearly this complex.

 A cheap computer can be configured with a data recovery decoder—or even a few of them—quite inexpensively. The software could be as simple as a program that scans the incoming data for certain trigger commands to determine the presence of captions. At its simplest, the presence of any data at all in line 21 could be accepted as evidence that there is captioning. A bit of basic interpretation of the data could sort it out by data type.

---

[1]   The FCC relies heavily on consumer complaints to keep track of compliance with captioning requirements, despite the addition of their random audit policy described in Chapter 4 (Captioning Law).

For example, commands where the first byte is 1C and the second byte is between 20 and 2F (inclusive) are evidence of the presence of CC2 data (if found in field 1) or CC4 data (if found in field 2). Table 7-4 lists the commands, which could be used to further sort things out.

Simulcasting

For a broadcaster that simulcasts TV programs on the Internet, it can be troublesome finding caption service providers that can simultaneously feed line 21 captions to the broadcast signal and an online format such as SMIL/RealText to the Internet transmission.

Additionally, each broadcast requires getting IP addresses and other pertinent information to the caption service provider and assuring that the connection is made properly.

An easier solution is to just hire caption service providers to feed realtime captions for the broadcast signal. Use a data recovery decoder to capture their data from the broadcast feed, and have it automatically reformatted and transmitted on the Internet.

This can be accomplished by writing some custom code of your own, or using a commercial package like CSpeech, which can interpret line 21 captions and reformat them into RealText/SMIL format to send to a RealOne player.

Writing your own code for a project like this is straightforward for the most part, but there are a few situations that can be tricky, like properly handling backspacing. There needs to be a lag in the retransmitted caption data to allow for recognizing and processing backspaces. Also, not all captioning software uses straightforward backspacing for realtime corrections. When a long word or phrase is being removed, the program may reposition the cursor to the beginning of the word and use a DER (delete to end of row) command, a process which is described in Chapter 7 (Line 21 Technical Details).

Producing Transcripts for Searchable Video Archives

If you are producing searchable video archives, closed caption text is the perfect way to generate the search keys. Many caption service providers are willing to provide transcripts of their work, which are generally inexpensive, but these do not have the time links needed for clip-based archives.

A data recovery decoder can provide the full transcript from line 21, and either a timecode reader (when SMPTE timecodes are present) or a time-of-day clock synchronized to the start of the clip can be used to generate time offsets into the video.

Video clips synchronized to transcripts have been produced in the court reporting business since the early 1990s. Companies like Stenograph (Discovery Video ZX) and Cheetah Systems

(VideoView) sold products that allowed precise playback of clips from court or deposition based on selected text. An attorney could search the transcript, select a block of text, and choose "play" to see the video corresponding with the selected text.

Those systems of a decade ago required a videotape machine with computer control and a computer system with a timecode reader. They were expensive, and slow to find the video, as their seek speed was limited to what the VTR could do. As they developed in sophistication, those systems added laserdisc capability, and later MPEG from CD-ROM or hard disk.

Today's video archive systems draw from the same basic technologies, although they are now database-driven and can handle far larger libraries of video. Some can even synchronize the transcript to the video using speech recognition, although this isn't as reliable as simply extracting a timecoded transcript from the captions using a data recovery decoder.

Recaptioning an Edited Show

When a program is edited, caption data is mangled at the cut points. Recaptioning the show from scratch is a waste of time and money. There are two approaches to the recaptioning process.

If line 21 has survived the editing process, the video can be run through a data recovery decoder connected to an offline captioning system after the edits are complete. All of the timing will be correct, or very close to it, and the captioner will only have to look for edit points and correct captions on both sides of them. Once the cleanup is complete, the video can be recaptioned.

If line 21 has either been wiped or hopelessly mangled, then the pre-edit video can be captured. A captioner can then watch the show looking for edit points where the captions no longer match, and make corrections there.

Sometimes the process gets more complex than that. For example, when video is compressed, it is typically done through selective frame removal. Even if compression is the only edit performed, the caption timing will start out correct and grow gradually farther and farther off as the show runs.

Some offline captioning systems have built-in handling for compression. They apply the same compression process to the captions that's applied to the video. It can leave things a few frames off here and there, because "smart" video compression isn't purely linear. Scenes with heavy action have fewer frames removed and scenes with little change from frame to frame have more removed. Still, it balances out over the duration of the show, and the few tweaks required by the captioner are still far easier than a full recaptioning job.

10 ONLINE CAPTIONING OVERVIEW

Online captioning is performed live during a broadcast or event. This does not necessarily mean that it is done without advance preparation, or even that the captions are not completely written out beforehand. On the contrary, scripted captioning (known as live display) uses scripts that are prepared in advance, and fed out by the captioner during the event.

Working with Scripts

Script files for an online captioning system are typically ASCII text files with embedded formatting codes. Typically, they are streamed out in roll-up mode, especially when interspersed with realtime stenocaptioning or voice writing (see next two chapters).

Usually, when watching a broadcast, it's easy to see whether the captions are coming from a script or from realtime. Realtime captions flow out a word at a time, while scripted captions tend to flow out a line at a time.

Scripts that are sent out in roll-up mode are typically not word wrapped before the broadcast. This way, positioning macros can be used to change caption positioning and line length, and the script will be dynamically formatted to match.

Scripts from Newsroom Computers

One of the most obvious situations for the use of scripts is TV news. Much of the newscast is pre-scripted anyway, with the talent reading from a prompter. Why not just feed those scripts out as captions? Certainly, it has been done, and in some cases it is still being done. The concept is good, but the implementations tend to have problems.

- Prompter scripts aren't written for the public at large. Generally, scripts from a newsroom computer are full of cues, timing notes, phonetic spellings of names, and other information that is meaningless or confusing to the average viewer (see figure 10-1). Also, these scripts are often not proofread for spelling accuracy.

- Many segments of a newscast are often not scripted, such as weather, taped segments, and live remotes.

- Banter between newscasters is not captioned, which may not seem like an important part of the news, but often includes discussion of issues relating to the story being covered.

- Timing is a significant issue. Text on the prompter will often roll ahead to let the talent see what's coming up, or to skip over tapes and live remotes.

With the FCC requiring more and more hours of programming to be captioned, using newsroom scripts seems like an obvious move. Complaints from the deaf community, however, caused the FCC to intervene. Because of the problems listed above and others, the FCC ruled in 1998 that newscasts captioned using only the prompter text do not count toward the required number of captioning hours for the four major networks (ABC, CBS, FOX, and NBC), their affiliates in the top 25 TV markets, and networks that reach at least half of all homes with cable TV or satellite receivers. See Chapter 4 (Captioning Law) for more about this.

This ruling does not mean the prompter scripts are discarded. On the contrary, realtime captioners that are given access to the station's newsroom computer download the scripts before a show and intersperse them with the realtime captioning. Using edited and cleaned-up prompter scripts ensures correct spellings of proper names and prevents "typos" (known to stenocaptioners as "misstrokes").

Typically, the process begins with the stenocaptioner downloading the scripts from the newsroom computer, and loading them into an editing program of some sort. Figure 10-1 shows a script conversion and editing program that I wrote for Bay Area Captioning.[1]

---

[1] ScriptConverter is based on a DOS program called BScript that I wrote in 1993. It was completely rewritten in 1997 as ScriptConverter. Since that time, Bay Area Captioning has been acquired by VITAC, along with the rights to both programs.

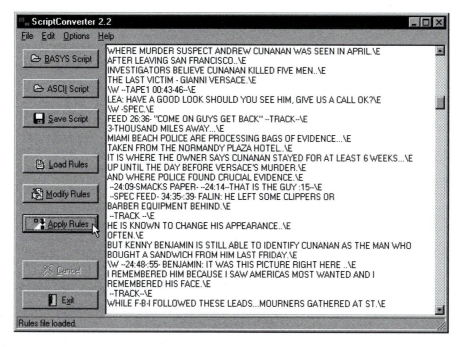

Figure 10-1: Manipulating Scripts in ScriptConverter

As the script is loaded, the ScriptConverter program adds end-of-line tags (\E) after end-of-sentence punctuation marks, and adds \W tags to lines that appear to be cues. Lines preceded by the \W tag generate an audible warning to the captioner and are not output as captions. Although the specific tags mentioned here (\E, \W, etc.) were created by Cheetah Systems for their CAPtivator Online software, several other systems can read and interpret them.

The next step is to load a set of editing and conversion rules. Some captioners do this step in a program like WordPerfect or Microsoft Word, using macros to perform multiple search-and-replace operations. The rules perform functions like:

- Removing spaces before punctuation marks.

- Converting strings of periods and dashes to a maximum of one or two.

- Condensing multiple spaces down to one—there should never be more than one space in a row in line 21 captions unless transparent spaces are being used for positioning.

- Removing spaces at ends of lines.

- Cleaning up common phonetic spellings. Scripts are written for the talent to read easily and quickly, and often contain words like tonite, week-end, thru, and gonna.

- Correcting trademarks and names of newscasts and segments.

- Cleaning up acronyms. For easier reading (especially in an all-caps environment), scripts may contain dashes in acronyms (like the F-B-I on the bottom line in figure 10-1).

- Fixing formatting of numbers, times, and dates.

These rules can be edited by the captioner, and tailored to each specific network, station, or newscast.

Once the scripts have been prepared, the captioner will load them into the captioning system. The system can display the rundown (also known as the story queue), as shown in figure 10-2.

Figure 10-2: Handling the Story Queue in CAPtivator Online

Although the CAPtivator Online software illustrated in figure 10-2 is an older DOS program, the concepts of story queue manipulation remain the same. News directors may change the rundown at any time, especially to accommodate breaking news stories. Online captioning systems must have a quick and easy mechanism for jumping from story to story, and for changing the order of the rundown.

Typically, a single keystroke is all that's required to jump to the next or previous story, or to feed the next line of script as a caption. More elaborate functions, such as editing the script files from within the captioning software, rebreaking lines, searching up and down through the scripts, and deleting individual words before sending, vary from one software package to the next.

Interspersing Scripts with Realtime

When a realtime captioner is feeding scripts, the newscasters may depart from what the prompter says at any moment. Should that occur, the captioner immediately begins verbatim realtime captioning. In most systems, the transition is seamless, and occurs without any kind of switching taking place. Realtime captions always override any other source of captioning.

The warning tag (\W) mentioned earlier is one way for a captioner to be prepared for the transition to realtime. For example, when the script shows a toss to a field reporter or playing of an untranscribed tape, the captioner can throw a warning line in. When that script is being fed, the warning line will appear in the preview window (in the lower right corner in figure 10-2), and the captioner can get ready to switch to realtime.

Stenocaptioners may wish to avoid jumping back and forth between the QWERTY keyboard and the steno keyboard by defining a steno stroke to feed script lines. If the macro capabilities of the captioning software allow it, a stenocaptioner can perform all of the script manipulation from the steno keyboard.

Standard Scripts

Scripting is still useful outside of the news environment. Perhaps the best example is song lyrics. Since the 9-11 terrorist attacks in the U.S., the national anthem has been telecast much more frequently, not only at sporting events, but at other public meetings. While most captioners already know the lyrics to *The Star Spangled Banner*, why take a chance on a misstroke?

Song lyrics can be formatted into individual files (each containing a story slug for easy access), complete with music notes and appropriate line breaks. For details on how to format lyrics, see Chapter 3 (Captioning Styles and Conventions).

As more and more government proceedings are televised, captioners face another challenge: people talk faster when they're reading out loud. Many government organizations read ordinances, motions, and proposals aloud before taking a vote. They can do so at a pace that a stenocaptioner or voice writer simply can't keep up with. The captioner can alleviate this problem by getting copies in advance of documents to be discussed, and entering them as script files. This transforms the high stress of realtiming someone who is speaking at over 300 words per minute into the easy task of feeding out a script.

The Ultimate Script

In captioning of religious programming and church services, lyrics are even more important. Entire hymnals can be preloaded into the captioning system, so that song lyrics will be at the captioner's fingertips.

There is one document, however, that is quoted frequently and at length in church services. I refer, of course, to the Bible. When first faced with captioning a Bible reading, even the best realtime captioners quail. The old English words and the profusion of proper names make it an extremely challenging job.

Aside from its length, however, the Bible need not be treated any differently than any other script file. It doesn't even have to be typed. Since the copyright on the King James Bible expired a few hundred years ago, there are many sources for the text in electronic form, many of them free. Other versions of the Bible may be harder to get, but the chances are you can get your hands on whichever one you need.

All of this, of course, applies equally to the Bible, the Torah, the Qur'an, the Book of Mormon, or the Holy books of any other religion or sect.

To prepare the Bible as a script, I started by searching the Internet for a good copy of the King James version and downloading it. Project Gutenberg (`www.gutenberg.org`) is usually a good source for such documents, but their copy of the Bible lacked italics and some of the other formatting I wanted.

From there, I wrote a simple filtering program and a series of word processor macros that inserted appropriate italic codes for the captioning software, highlighted the chapter and verse numbers, and split each chapter of each book into its own file, naming them appropriately.

Loading all 1,100+ files would be a burden on any captioning program, and could be difficult to maneuver through during the captioning. If possible, find out what will be discussed in advance and what chapters are bookmarked in the speaker's Bible, and preload only those scripts.

If you are interested in setting up the Bible as a set of script files for your captioning system, you can begin with the version that's available on `www.CaptionCentral.com`, which has all of the formatting as HTML tags. Your captioning software may be able to read this directly, or you can change the files into your system's format with some simple text search-and-replace in a word processor or editing program. To download these scripts, go to:

`www.captioncentral.com/resources/scripts`

These Bible scripts are free and come with no warranties or technical support whatsoever.

Autofeed

There are times, especially during live events, where nobody is speaking, but there is information that can be presented in captioning. For example, before the event begins, captions on the video projection system could be showing the starting time, the name of the first speaker, and the subject of the seminar. At conventions or trade shows with concurrent sessions, this also ensures that people have found the correct room. Similarly, during breaks, captions might display a schedule for the event, breaking news, or changes in the agenda.

Captioning is legally required for emergency broadcasts, as described in Chapter 4 (Captioning Law). If a realtime captioner is not available, a description of the emergency and its status can be typed into an online system and set to repeat automatically so that deaf and hard-of-hearing viewers know what's going on until realtime captioning can be provided.

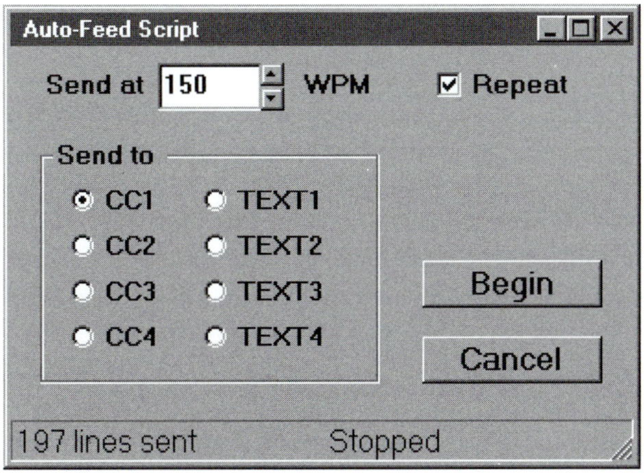

Figure 10-3: Automatically Feeding a Script as Captions

Figure 10-3 shows an autofeed screen from one of my test programs, which is similar to that found in commercial programs with autofeed capabilities. The transmission rate shown seems to be a comfortable level, which conforms with the findings in Carl Jensema's study of caption speeds,[2] which found 145 words per minute (WPM) to be a common preference.

Some systems can autofeed a script in the background while realtime is being performed. This would allow a summary of an emergency situation to run continually in TEXT1 with realtime captioning running in CC1. Viewers coming in late could be directed to read TEXT1 to catch up with the situation.

---

[2]   "Viewer Reaction to Different Captioned Television Speeds," by Carl Jensema. Institute for Disabilities Research and Training, Inc. June 1997.

"Typed Realtime"

Sometimes, especially during a nonscheduled breaking news story, a realtime stenocaptioner or voice writer simply isn't available. This leaves broadcasters with a dilemma. They can omit captions entirely, use a looping summary as described above, or use the "typed realtime" capability offered by most online systems.

To use this feature on most systems, you simply place a reasonably fast typist at the keyboard, and summarize what's being said. Even though typists can't keep up with spoken English, they can communicate the gist of the story by paraphrasing as they go. While this isn't an acceptable alternative to realtime captioning,[3] it is certainly better than providing nothing at all.

Stock Captions

There are captions that are used on a regular basis, such as the credits at the end of a show or a funding notice. Some of these can be heavily formatted. Even at the end of a show captioned entirely in realtime using plain white left-justified roll-up captions, the credits will often appear as a centered pop-on caption at the top of the screen in several different colors.

This is accomplished through the creation of stock captions, which are essentially very short scripts with a few significant differences. First, stock captions do not change the default display settings. A captioner can be writing 3-line roll-up captions, invoke a stock caption that clears the screen and pops on a caption like [applause], and the next realtime will return to 3-line roll-up mode.

Secondly, stock captions do not change the story queuing. They appear when invoked and then go away without affecting the scripts at all.

Online Captioning Software

Over the years since personal computers were introduced, we've seen "word processors" that consisted of everything from highly sophisticated productivity-enhancing writing tools to bare-bones programs barely more capable than Microsoft Windows Notepad. The same phenomenon has been true in online (or realtime) captioning software.

At the bottom end of the scale have been some computer-aided transcription (CAT) programs with a simple command added for output to a caption encoder. All they actually do is output control-A, the digit 2, and a carriage return, and then stream out realtime ASCII text, word wrapped to 32 columns. Chapter 8 (Encoding Equipment) describes this interface approach, which sets the

---

[3]   See Chapter 4 (Captioning Law) for a discussion of legal mandates regarding realtime captioning compared to other forms of captioning on live newscasts.

encoder to 3-line roll-up captioning at the bottom of the screen. There is no further control over the encoder.

Such programs are captioning software in the same sense that Notepad is a word processor. If your needs are extremely basic, then this approach is adequate—but barely.

At the other end of the spectrum are full-blown professional online captioning systems representing years of development time and a variety of integrated technologies. There are online systems for every need and every budget.

Purchasing Online Captioning Software

New stenocaptioners or voice writers getting into the business should do a careful analysis of systems before making a purchase decision. There are captioning service providers that mandate specific software tools for their employees and contractors, and others that provide the programs for their people.

Several of the larger captioning service providers have developed proprietary software, or are in the process of doing so at press time. The National Captioning Institute, for example, has developed their own realtime software for their employees to use. Since realtime software costs thousands of dollars, it makes sense to take advantage of the tools provided by your employer rather than buying your own.

Online captioning systems have traditionally been very specialized. They would handle only one type of input (e.g., steno or speech) and a limited number of outputs (e.g., line 21, Teletext, CEA-708, or SMIL). While this is still true to some extent, software vendors are broadening their capabilities, and it is common with newer software to see a single program for both voice writers and stenocaptioners, and to see programs that can handle multiple output formats simultaneously.

As an example, ProCAT and Advantage Software have been firmly entrenched in the stenocaptioning and court reporting markets for many years. Both of them have added speech recognition capabilities for voice writers to their captioning products (CaptiVision and AccuCAP, respectively).

Software license transfer fees are common in this industry, meaning that if you change your mind after purchasing a particular program, you may be required to pay significant fees (often hundreds of dollars) to transfer the software license to someone else, which limits how much of your original investment you can recover by selling your "used" software.

System Requirements and Configurations

The majority of online captioning software runs under Microsoft Windows and will work on just about any new computer. The demands placed on the processor by stenocaptioning systems are modest by today's standards, although, as with any realtime software, you should be careful how many other programs are running at the same time. Voice writing systems, on the other hand, require fairly significant amounts of RAM and processor speed to power the speech recognition engines at high speed. Be sure to check on hardware requirements with the software vendor before purchasing equipment.

Since the fundamental requirements of line 21 captioning haven't changed significantly in the last decade, there is still DOS-based online captioning software in use today. Captioners who have invested thousands of dollars in software are understandably reluctant to throw it away and purchase something new. These DOS-based software packages have (marginally) adequate capabilities even now, but they are disappearing because of incompatibility with modern computers. As Microsoft Windows moves forward, its DOS compatibility deteriorates with each passing generation, to the point where it is very difficult to get a DOS captioning system to run reliably on a new Windows-based computer.

Experiments have been done with realtime captioning software on other platforms, but none has succeeded as of yet. Because virtually all court reporting software is Windows-based, and the majority of stenocaptioners start out as court reporters, it is difficult for a system based on any other operating system to establish a foothold.[4]

Generally, in online captioning, the software is the single largest expense, costing far more than the computer. A remote captioner, working over phone lines, needs only a modem for output, as the broadcaster will supply an encoder with a dial-up port. For input, stenocaptioners will require a steno keyboard, which will connect to the computer using either a serial port or a USB port—USB interfaces in steno keyboards are a fairly recent innovation. Voice writers will require a microphone/mask, and sometimes a hardware accelerator, depending on the system they're using.

No other hardware is required, unless a captioner will be working on-site and providing an encoder or character generator.

In a live broadcast, there can be a lot going on at once. With script files loaded, realtime running, dictionaries being modified, and the screen showing WYSIWYG simulated caption output and various status windows, the screen can get quite dense, as you can see in figure 10-4, which shows Advantage Software's AccuCAP system.

---

[4] This is not true, however, of offline captioning software. Other platforms are discussed in more detail in Chapter 13 (Offline and Nonlinear Captioning).

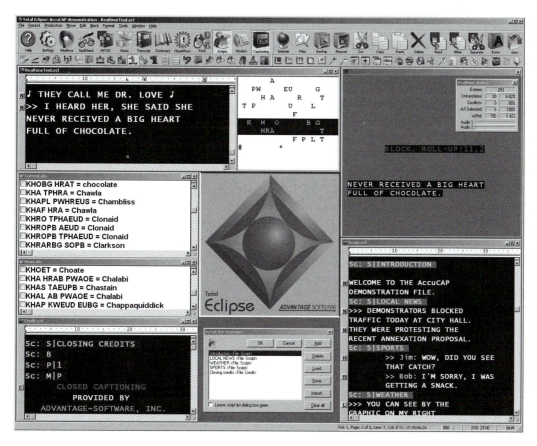

Figure 10-4: The AccuCAP Screen with Scripts and Realtime Active

A high-resolution display is a useful addition to your system, as it can handle more information at once, and the smoother text is easier on the eyes when putting in long sessions in front of the computer.

Software Features

Standards Support

By definition, any line 21 captioning system must be compliant with CEA-608, which is the standard for analog (NTSC) captioning in North America. That isn't the only possible form of output, however. Depending on your future plans for the system, some of the following may be useful as well:

- **CEA-708** is the standard for native DTV captioning. It has not been a high priority for software developers, since transcoders allow CEA-608 captions to be upconverted for DTV broadcasts, but this approach does not allow captioners to use the advanced features of CEA-708. As the systems continue to develop, expect native DTV support to become commonplace in realtime captioning software.

- **Teletext** is used throughout much of the world outside North America, and there is a published standard for North American Teletext as well as World Standard Teletext. If you intend to do any captioning in Europe or Australia, Teletext is a must-have.

- **SMIL, RealText, and SAMI**, discussed at length in Chapter 19 (Captions in Internet Streaming and Computer Media), are the standard protocols for captioning streaming media on the Internet. Although there are numerous proprietary protocols and chat systems allowing streaming realtime text on the Web, anyone serious about Internet video captioning should support SMIL, SAMI, or both. Note that SMIL is well suited for streaming realtime, as it uses a separate file for the text (RealText), but it is more complex to use SAMI in realtime.

Support for multiple simultaneous output streams is a growing trend in online captioning systems. Why put converters (or multiple captioners) in place if a single system can simultaneously produce captions in two or three different formats?

If you plan to use this feature, check with your software vendor to make sure that each output stream can be formatted independently. For example, line 21 captions allow up to 32 characters per line, while Teletext allows 40, large LED display signs may allow 80, and SAMI captions word wrap independently on the target systems, with adjustable window and font sizes.

Since some venues traditionally use all caps and others are in mixed-case, it's important for the system to be able to capitalize output independently on each stream.

Telephone Dialers

Dialing a telephone number using a modem is hardly a new concept. Telecommunications programs and Internet service providers (ISPs) have been offering dialers for many years. There are some special considerations to dialers in online captioning systems, however.

- **Speed** is of the essence. Freelance captioners must often change numbers in a hurry, sometimes disconnecting from one encoder and reconnecting to another in the space of a commercial. If it takes an assortment of menus and dialogs, they won't be able to connect in time.

- **Searching** the phone number list must be easy, too. With an ISP, you use the same number (or small group of interchangeable numbers) almost all the time. Freelance captioners often have dozens—or even hundreds—of encoder numbers on file. Saved lists or hierarchical structures (e.g., folders) make this much easier.

- **Clear status display** ensures that you know when you're connected. It should be obvious from a glance at the screen whether you are dialed up or not. Stenocaptioners can't stop writing realtime to press a key to see the connection status.

- **Robust connections** are important. When the line is flaky, or there are transmission/parity errors, the software should do everything it can to maintain the connection anyway. Getting some information through is better than losing the connection entirely, especially in an emergency situation where all phone lines in an area are tied up—once you disconnect, you'll have trouble getting connected again.

- **Automatic reconnect** can save valuable seconds. If the line disconnects, the system automatically redials and re-establishes the connection without user intervention. This ensures the minimum possible loss of realtime caption data.

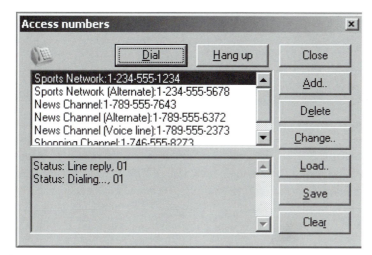

Figure 10-5: AccuCAP Modem Dialer

The dialer shown in figure 10-5 is fairly typical. The three buttons near the top right (add, delete, change) allow manipulation of individual telephone numbers. The three buttons below those (load, save, clear) allow for manipulation of phone number lists, or "phone books." All of the phone numbers relating to a particular station can be grouped on one list, including those that aren't dialed using the modem (like the voice line in the figure). This provides a central reference point for the captioner.

The CaptiVision system from ProCAT creates profiles for each station, network, or job, as shown in figure 10-6. This includes everything from encoder type to the IP address and port for Internet connections.

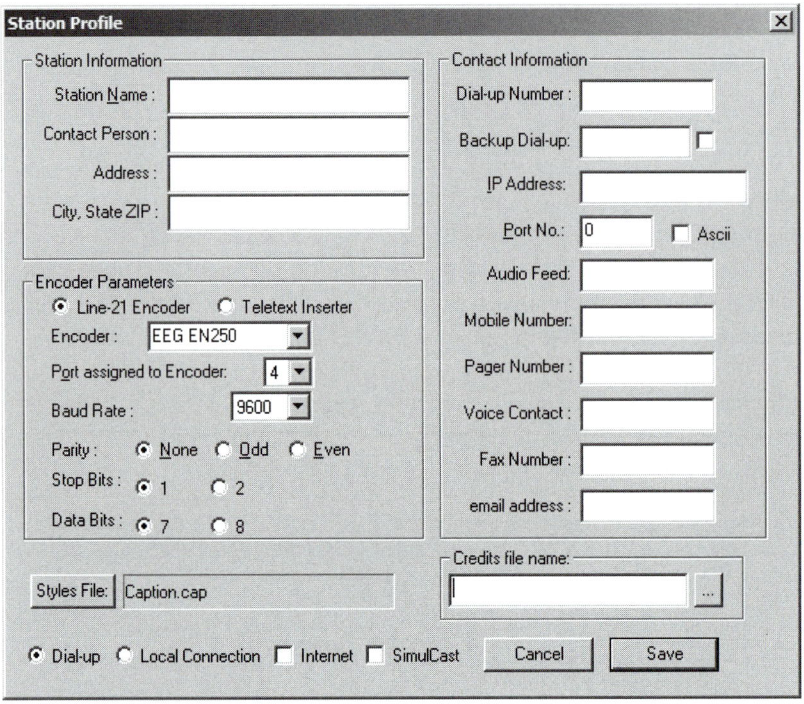

Figure 10-6: CaptiVision Station Profile and Connection Manager

Modem support may be done through direct interface to the modem, or through Microsoft Windows' Telephony Application Program Interface (TAPI). Each method has its advantages, although using TAPI means that virtually all new modems will be supported by the captioning system with no modification to the program. If any other programs on the computer use the modem, make sure the captioning system remembers settings and reapplies them with each session.

Device Support

A captioner who intends to purchase an encoder and work only onsite, using only that encoder, has no worries about device support beyond buying an encoder that the software supports. For everyone else, a comprehensive list of supported devices is important.

Before a job, a realtime captioner will be given a telephone number for an encoder and its model number. If you are working freelance, or working for an agency with multiple clients, you may be dialed into an Evertz encoder for one broadcast, and a Norpak encoder for the next. Changing encoders in the output should be quick and easy and should not require any knowledge of compatibility. When frantically getting ready for a live event, you have more to worry about than remembering whether you select "EEG EN270" when you're using an Ultech Insertacap. Each should be listed separately on an easily accessible device menu.

This function can be combined with modem dialing into a profile. Presumably, each time you dial a particular encoder number, the same model encoder will be at the other end. If the modem dialer stores that information along with the phone number, you don't have to remember to change device parameters when you call. Some systems take this even farther, allowing other parameters, such as default caption format and position, to be stored in the profile as well.

Several systems offer the ability to send command codes in ASCII or hexadecimal directly to the encoder. This allows technically minded individuals to manually control new or obscure encoders without waiting for their software vendor to make program changes.

Another output option offered by a couple of vendors is TCP/IP. This allows the exact same data stream that would go to an encoder to be sent over the Internet to a specified IP address and port.

Multiple Language Support

Even if you intend to work only in English, the software you choose should have basic multilingual capabilities to cover situations that may come up in the future.

- **All caption data channels** (CC1-CC4) should be supported, and all four text data channels, too, although they're rarely used.

- **Accented letters** should be available both in realtime and in scripts. Again, even if you only write English, you may be called upon to feed key phrases, song lyrics, quotes, or words in another language.

Some of the systems, especially those designed outside the United States, are built for multilingual applications. Figure 10-7, for example, shows the dictation screen from AudioScribe's SpeechCAP system, which was designed primarily for Spanish- and Italian-language markets.

In some systems, the software is built to process non-English languages. In others, the entire user interface (UI) can be presented in various languages. At least two systems offer Spanish UIs, and others are available as well.

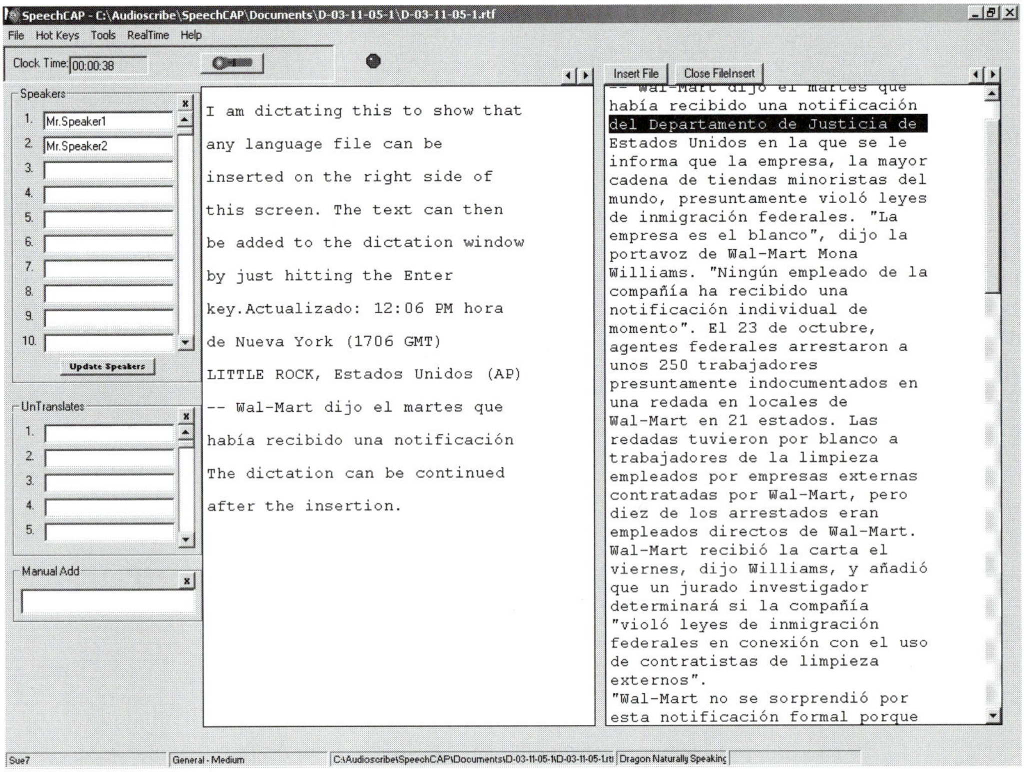

Figure 10-7: SpeechCAP Multilingual Caption Output

The large pane on the right in figure 10-7 contains a prepared script file, and the center pane is realtime text from the speech engine (Dragon NaturallySpeaking, in this case). Unlike a stenocaptioning system, which avoids mouse use because the realtimer's hands are always on the steno keyboard, this voice writing system makes use of the mouse to select a block of text from the window on the right, and the Enter key to copy it into the dictation, which is then streamed out to the encoder.

Script Manipulation and Editing

As discussed earlier in the chapter, script handling is an issue even in environments that are mostly realtime. Any online captioning system should be able to load scripts, change the story order (rundown, in news parlance), skip around easily, and swap between feeding scripts and feeding realtime.

Some systems have integrated script editors, and others require you to use an external editor or word processor to create the scripts. When evaluating systems, look at the ease of making fast changes while you're on-the-air and at the import capabilities.

Some systems can import scripts directly from newsroom computer systems, while others require the scripts to be downloaded and run through a converter like the one shown in figure 10-1. Either approach works, but if you intend to pull scripts right up until air time, it can be more convenient to fetch them directly rather than going through an extra step.

Most online captioning software allows for embedded commands in the scripts that change positions, styles (pop-on, roll-up, or paint-on), and formats (e.g., italics or colored text). Some also offer screen blanking and warning signals. These commands allow for the creation of stock files like credits.

All systems allow the scripts to be loaded and manipulated through menus or keyboard commands. Most also allow at least some of these functions to be performed through steno or voice macros, described in more detail later in this chapter.

File Save/Export

Generally, captioners don't need to prepare transcripts. There are cases, however, when you'll need to be able to save the text you're generating.

When a broadcaster is posting transcript text from an event to a Web site, they often want text quickly—sometimes even at intervals during a broadcast. The system should be able to save plain text in ASCII format, formatted text (preserving attributes), or a fully formatted and word wrapped file.

Stenocaptioners often perform "post-mortems" on broadcasts, looking for errors and missing dictionary entries. This requires saving both the text and the steno that generated it. Sometimes the captioning system provides an easy way to do this, and sometimes you'll need to save it in a format that a CAT system can read.

Timecodes and Refeeds

In addition to saving the plain text for other applications, national broadcasters often require a transcript for later refeeds of the same show in other time zones. If you can save a fully formatted transcript, then it's easy to hand-time and feed out in the next broadcast.

Going beyond that, many online systems can save a timestamped file, either using SMPTE timecodes (if available) or time offsets calculated using the time-of-day clock in the computer. Then, when the refeed is broadcast, the captions only need to be synchronized once, and they'll run through the show, including even the encoder commands when entering commercials. Typically, there are commands to tweak the synchronization by stepping back or ahead by small intervals.

Steno/Voice Macros

During a live broadcast, stenocaptioners are working with both hands on the steno keyboard. It breaks the flow and slows them down if they have to reach up to the computer's QWERTY keyboard to change caption positions or send a clear-screen (EDM) command to the encoder.

Something as simple as moving the captions can require a string of commands to change the base row, the line length, the number of caption rows, and the indent. The software should allow you to define formats and assign steno stroke(s) to them, as described under "Caption Positioning" in Chapter 11 (Realtime Stenocaptioning).

Some systems have much more sophisticated macro capabilities, allowing full control of the system from the steno keyboard, even to the point of dialing encoders through the modem or adding entries to the dictionary.

This capability is not nearly as important to voice writers, as they have their hands free as they caption.

Non-Caption Data

To date, few online captioning programs deal with extended data services (XDS), ITV links, or V-Chip content advisories. This information is usually encoded through a different program, sometimes one connected to the same encoder through a different port.

Translation Dictionaries

In realtime stenocaptioning, the translation dictionary is the core of the process. The next chapter discusses dictionary concepts and interchange formats. Any stenocaptioning software should be able to import and export dictionaries in RTF/CRE format so that you can easily move your dictionary to another system if required.

Selection

Captioners often use multiple dictionaries, including "job" dictionaries that are specific to one event or session. The software should make it quick and easy to select which dictionaries are being used in any given realtime session, and to set the order of precedence (if an entry appears in more than one dictionary, which is used?).

Editing

Stenocaptioners must perform constant maintenance on their translation dictionaries. A full-featured dictionary editor should be able to perform all of the tasks on the following list.

- Changing the steno and/or English for an entry.

- Adding entries, preferably offering the option of entering steno either from a steno keyboard or a QWERTY keyboard.

- Deleting entries, blocks of entries, or classes of entries.

- Performing a global change (search-and-replace) in the English. This might be used, for example, if a captioner has placed multiple entries in the dictionary for a proper name and needs to change the spelling in all of them at once.

- Moving one or more entries to a different dictionary. Some systems do this with cut and paste, some use a "move" command, and others have merge and selective merge capabilities.

- Searching in both the English text and the steno.

- Search for conflicts.

- Sorting entries and/or viewing selectively. For example, it should be easy to review only prefixes, or only punctuation, or only speaker IDs. Sorting by the English text is a more natural way to find entries, but sorting by steno makes it easier to spot conflicts and potential word-boundary problems.

- Printing or saving just the English text. This capability is used when a captioner has been working on a particular event or show and wants to share the special terminology from a job dictionary with another captioner.

Adding Entries on the Fly

When a stenocaptioner encounters a word that isn't in the translation dictionary, it is often a word that will be repeated during the broadcast or event—a proper name, perhaps. It's easy to wait until the next commercial break and enter the word in the dictionary, but it may have been mentioned several times by then, and live events may not have commercial breaks.

Most stenocaptioning systems allow some method for adding dictionary definitions on the fly. In some cases, it requires a "start new entry" command, followed by the spelled-out word and the steno stroke(s) that will be used to represent it, and then a "finished" command. Given that the stenocaptioner has to spell out the word anyway using a fingerspelling alphabet, this adds a minimum of three strokes to the process—one each for the commands and one for the new entry.

A shorter approach, used by Advantage Software in their AccuCAP software, allows users to define a stroke that says, "Remember the last thing I fingerspelled," and another to call it forth. Later, when there's time, the word can be transferred to a dictionary.

11 REALTIME STENOCAPTIONING

Stenotype Theory

Although it's not unusual for a highly skilled typist to reach speeds in excess of 100 wpm (words per minute) on a standard QWERTY keyboard, it's almost impossible to keep up with spoken English, which regularly reaches speeds of 250 wpm. Even the widely touted Dvorak keyboard, which rearranges the keys for more efficient typing, isn't up to the task.

To achieve the speed and accuracy required for realtime transcription, stenocaptioners use the keyboards and writing theories used by court reporters. In fact, most stenocaptioners begin their careers as court reporters. The stenotype keyboard, unlike QWERTY or Dvorak keyboards, has only 23 keys, and allows more than one key to be pressed at a time (known as "chording").

Realtime stenocaptioners must regularly work at sustained speeds of over 225 words per minute with accuracy of 99% or better.

Chording allows stenocaptioners to write an entire syllable, word, or even phrase with a single hand motion, known as a stroke. The layout of a typical steno keyboard[1] is shown in figure 11-1. The key labels shown in the figure, however, don't appear on actual steno keyboards. The theory is that if you have to take the time to look at the key, you can't write fast enough to keep up.

---

[1] All of the examples in this book use the Stenograph/Stenotype keyboard design prevalent in North America. Other machines, such as the Grandjean from France and the Palantype from the U.K., offer similar functionality, but have different keyboard layouts.

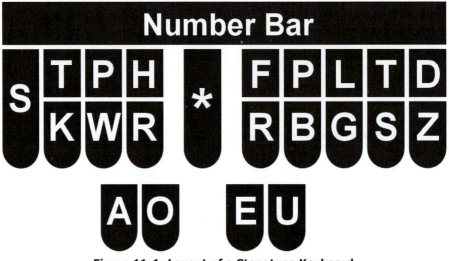

Figure 11-1: Layout of a Stenotype Keyboard

Home position for a stenocaptioner's hands places the fingertips on the cracks between the rows of consonant keys, and the thumbs over the vowel keys. The seven keys under the left fingers (STKPWHR) are used for initial consonants, and the ten keys under the right fingers (FRPBLGTSDZ) are for final consonants.

The theory is phonetic in nature, so (with certain exceptions) words are written the way they sound, rather than the way they are spelled. The computer takes care of the translation from raw steno into correctly spelled English (or other language) text.

Since there aren't enough keys to provide all of the possible starting and ending consonants, combinations of keys represent different letters. The left forefinger, for example, can write an H by moving slightly up from home position, an R by moving slightly down, or an L by pressing the H and R together. Even when writing an L, the steno paper or computer listing will show the HR key combination.

Vowels are written differently depending on their sound as well. For a short vowel sound, the key is pressed by itself. A long vowel sound is generated by pressing a vowel key along with the two vowels on the other hand (e.g., A is a short A sound and AEU is a long A). The E and U keys together generate the short I, and all four vowel keys at the same time generate a long I. Table 11-1 shows the key combinations for all of the initial, final, and vowel sounds.

Table 11-1: Steno Keyboard Letter Combinations

Letter or Sound	Initial (left hand)	Vowel (thumbs)	Final (right hand)
short A		A	
long A		A EU	
B	PW		B
C	K or S		
CH	KH		FP
D	TK		D
short E		E	
long E		AO E	
F	TP		F
G	TKPW		G
H	H		
short I		EU	
long I		AO EU	
J	SKWR		PBLG
K	K		BG
L	HR		L
M	PH		PL
N	TPH		PB
short O		O	
long O		O E	
OO		AO	
P	P		P
Q	KW		
R	R		R
S	S		S
T	T		T
short U		U	
long U		AO U	
V	SR		F or *F
W	W		
X			BGS
Y	KWR		
Z	S or SE		Z

There are actually dozens of different stenotype theories, and stenocaptioners tend to modify their theories to suit their particular writing styles. This particular arrangement of keys is based on the most common theories, and most court reporters could read it.

The asterisk key, in the middle of the keyboard, has several uses. By itself, it is used as a backspace, erasing the previous stroke. In combination with other keys, it can change a sound or resolve a homonym problem (which we'll discuss in a moment). As an example, some stenocaptioners will use the asterisk to change a final F sound into a final V, which differentiates words like leaf (written HRAOEF) and leave (written HRA*OEF).

Fingerspelling

The keys on a steno keyboard can be used to spell out words one letter at a time, as with a QWERTY keyboard, and stenocaptioners do have to do this at times when new or oddly spelled words come up in the middle of a broadcast.

Fingerspelling, as this process is called, consists of pressing key combinations that represent a single letter. There are various ways of writing fingerspelling alphabets. One common method uses the letter (as shown in table 11-1) along with a period (-FPLT). Thus, to write BAT, a stenocaptioner would stroke PWFPLT/AFPLT/TFPLT. Another common method uses the letter along with an asterisk.

Stenocaptioners often create multiple fingerspelling alphabets. One runs all the letters together (e.g., ABC), one places periods after each letter (e.g., A.B.C.), and one places dashes between letters (e.g., A-B-C). This way, a captioner can write sentences like, "My name is Smyth, spelled S-M-Y-T-H, and I work for the F.B.I."

Some stenocaptioners take it even farther, creating different fingerspelling alphabets for upper- and lowercase letters.

Captioning systems have different ways of handling fingerspelling. Some require each alphabet to be defined separately. In this case, perhaps writing the letters with an asterisk would run them together and writing them with -FPLT would put periods after each one. Other systems define different modes, and a stenocaptioner with a single fingerspelling alphabet could write a command stroke to switch between "squished" letters and letters with periods.

Writing Numbers

One of the obvious missing pieces on a stenotype keyboard is numbers. Many stenocaptioners write numbers by using the large bar across the top of the keyboard (known as the "number bar") as a shift key, which transforms various other keys on the keyboard from letters to numbers. If the arrangement of number keys in figure 11-2 looks odd to you, remember home position of the fingers. Other stenocaptioners write out their numbers as words, but the software takes care of properly representing the numbers as words or figures—whichever is appropriate in each situation.

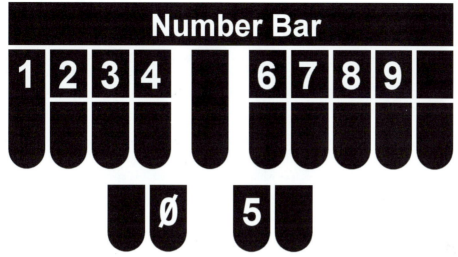

Figure 11-2: Writing Numbers on a Stenotype Keyboard

To write the number two, for example, the stenocaptioner brings the ring finger of the left hand up from its normal position to the crack between the number bar and the initial T. The finger presses down both keys at once, generating a 2 rather than a T. The numbers are arranged as they are so that each finger—including the thumbs—has one digit (no pun intended).

Multidigit numbers can be written in a single stroke, as long as all of the digits are in ascending order. You can press down the number bar along with THFL to write the number 2468 in a single stroke. Writing the number 8642, on the other hand, would require four separate strokes to keep the digits in the correct order.

Some realtime captioning software includes sophisticated number formatting code, which makes clear writing of numbers far easier for the stenocaptioner. As an example, the stenocaptioner can define a stroke meaning "format the previous number as currency." When the captioning software detects that a number is being written, it holds the digits until a nonnumber stroke is received, giving it a chance to format the number as a whole (and ensuring that the number isn't broken up between lines). If the stenocaptioner writes the currency stroke after writing 1234, the captioning system will display $1,234, assuming the system is set for U.S. currency.

Punctuation and Speaker Identification

To write punctuation, stenocaptioners abandon phonetic concepts and move to keyboard patterns. For example, moving the right hand slightly up from home position produces FPLT, steno for a period in many theories. Moving slightly down instead produces RBGS, which is steno for a comma. Stroking the period twice produces a colon. Stroking a period followed by a comma (FPLT/RBGS) produces a semicolon.

The left hand is commonly used for speaker identification, although many stenocaptioners have their own methods. As an example, the upper four keys on the left hand written along with the left-hand vowels (STPHAO) might indicate a change of speaker, which shows on the captions as a new caption row beginning with the >> symbol.

Part of what makes stenocaptioning difficult is that you can't simply write what you hear. You must insert all punctuation and formatting, including things like quotation marks or italics for the name of a newspaper. You must detect when somebody different is speaking and indicate that in the captions.

Control and Editing Strokes

In addition to strokes that produce text on the TV screen, stenocaptioners can define strokes that control the encoder or decoder. These range from a "blank" stroke that removes all caption text from the TV display, to formatting strokes that change the position of the captions on the screen.

Television commercials are typically captioned in a studio using pop-on style. When a stenocaptioner is writing realtime, the caption encoder is blocking upstream captions to prevent a jumble of old and new text. When a show stops for a commercial break, the captioner must tell the encoder to pass through upstream captions so that the commercials will be properly captioned. This is often done with a "pass-through" stroke defined on the steno keyboard, so that the captioner does not have to reach over to the computer keyboard or mouse.

Conflict Resolution

When two or more words or phrases are written the same, but spelled differently, stenocaptioners call it a conflict. For example, using the straight phonetic rules described earlier, the words two, to, and too would be written alike. This is known as a homonym conflict.

A word boundary conflict involves the interactions between multiple strokes. For example, look at the following two sentences:

- That song is **on side** B of your cassette tape.

- That was a penalty, so he'll take an **onside** kick.

Depending on context, "on side" can be one word or two. An even more common problem is "maybe" vs. "may be." Word boundary problems can be even more insidious, however. There are syllables that can be used at either the beginning or the end of a word, and stenocaptioners must write them differently to avoid situations like this one:

- I did my **car research** yesterday.

- I did my **carry search** yesterday.

In this example, the steno for KAR/RAOE/SER/FP could translate as either "car research" or "carry search." To resolve this conflict, the stenocaptioner would typically come up with an alternate way to write the "re" prefix, possibly using an asterisk. We'll explore this concept a bit farther later in the chapter when we look at translation dictionaries.

Automatic Conflict Resolution

When court reporters moved from manual translation of their steno notes to computer-aided transcription (CAT) systems, conflicts became a much greater issue. Even though "been" and "bin" sound the same, it is generally clear from context which one you mean. A court reporter or transcriber can similarly interpret the notes without really thinking about it.

Computers, on the other hand, are more rigid and inflexible. The advent of CAT brought great changes to the way steno theories were taught, and it didn't take long for "computer-compatible" and "conflict-free" theories to arrive. The way to avoid homonym problems was to write the words differently on the steno keyboard.

This, however, is easier said than done. Court reporters and stenocaptioners need to deal with issues of words that sound the same, but also with similar prefixes and suffixes, and with word boundary problems. Developers of realtime court reporting and stenocaptioning software stepped in with automated tools to resolve these conflict problems.

Since the first primitive tools for automatic conflict resolution (ACR) emerged, vendors have promoted them as artificial intelligence. In fact, they were just lookup tables or simple expert systems. One company even goes so far as to call theirs "true" artificial intelligence. Another vendor told me that he knows his ACR system isn't artificial intelligence,[2] but since everyone else calls it that in their marketing materials, he has to as well. When shopping for software, it is important to set aside the hype and the terminology, and look at what the products actually *do* rather than what the vendor calls it.

---

[2]   Clearly, an automatic conflict resolution system isn't going to be passing the Turing Test (the classic artificial intelligence benchmark) anytime soon.

ACR Basics

The most fundamental criteria for ACR are sentence position and surrounding parts of speech. For example, let's look at the "been/bin" conflict described above. For purposes of illustration, we'll assume that the stenocaptioner writes both of these words as PWEUPB.

If PWEUPB is preceded by an article (e.g., a, an, or the), the word is probably "bin." You might say "Toss that in the bin," but never "Toss that in the been." The same is true if it is preceded by a verb ("Discard bin 4," but not "Discard been 4").

If PWEUPB is preceded by a noun or adjective, it's probably "been." You would refer to "the parts bin" or "the blue bin."

Some systems have ACR rules built in for common conflicts. The first conflict to be dealt with automatically wasn't actually a homonym. Many early reporters learned to write "a" and "an" the same way. CAT and captioning systems as early as the 1980s were algorithmically resolving the conflict as "a" when the following word began with a consonant and "an" when it began with a vowel. This grew more sophisticated in the early '90s until it was virtually perfect.

Some systems learn as they go (which seems like artificial intelligence magic but is actually a weighted decision table). If you manually resolve the "red/read" conflict to be "read" whenever followed by an article (e.g., "He read the book"), the system will adopt this as a rule. By recording and analyzing every manual selection of a conflict, the realtime software can eventually intuit how that conflict is resolved. This does not require the program to actually parse and understand the sentence, although it may look like it to a casual observer.

ACR has made it significantly easier for stenocaptioners to solve the majority of their conflict problems, but no ACR system is perfect. Our language is just too complex. At first glance, you might think that PWEUPB at the beginning or end of a sentence will always be "bin." Certainly it applies to "Bin 4 needs cleaned" or "Toss this in the bin." That flips around, however, when you are asking questions, such as "Been waiting long?" or "Where have you been?"

Even a seemingly firm rule, such as the "red/read" rule described above, may have exceptions, like the sentence "I painted it red the first time and blue the second." Although ACR systems continue to improve, they are still prone to errors from time to time, and they simply can't substitute for human intelligence. For this reason, stenocaptioners are constantly on the alert for problem conflicts and looking for ways to improve their writing style.

Obscenities in Captioning

As a general rule, any dialog that's audible in the sound track is written in the captions. Words are only "bleeped" from the captions if they are bleeped out of the audio as well.

Stenocaptioners must, then, be prepared to write almost anything, especially when captioning live shows on cable channels that don't censor their content. At the same time, remembering that a slight misfingering on the stenotype keyboard can dramatically change a word or phrase, they must ensure that they will never write one of George Carlin's "Seven Words You Can Never Say on TV" by accident.[3]

Even on a standard QWERTY keyboard, words like sit, batch, carp, and funk are just a slip of the finger away from something embarrassing. On a stenotype keyboard, there are many more ways to accidentally write something you shouldn't. To avoid this problem, most stenocaptioners define the straight phonetic translation of an obscene word to be either something innocuous, or a blank space. The obscenities themselves are usually written with an asterisk, "double stroked" (written twice in succession), or otherwise modified to make it hard to write them by accident.

For more information about obscenities in captioning, including commercial filtering systems and rating systems, see Chapter 18 (Other Line 21 Data).

Stenotype Keyboards

Upon hearing that stenotype keyboards typically cost thousands of dollars, most people's first reaction is shock. "I can buy a QWERTY keyboard for my computer for $19.95 at the local electronics store! Why does the leading stenotype keyboard cost almost $5,000?"

Part of the reason is that steno keyboards are highly adjustable to suit the touch of the individual writer. The "throw" on the keys (the distance they travel when pressed) is considerably longer than a QWERTY keyboard. The more expensive keyboards allow the sensitivity to be adjusted on a key-by-key basis, so that stenocaptioners can compensate for a weak finger or one that tends to press too hard. For example, the index finger is typically much stronger than the little finger, so the keys will be set to require less pressure for the little finger than the index finger.

---

[3]   This is a reference to a comedy routine from George Carlin's 1972 album, "Class Clown." In the interest of propriety, we won't list the words here.

Figure 11-3: The Stenograph Stentura Keyboard

Another part of the reason for the cost of steno machines is that most are designed to be capable of use without a computer. Court reporters often take their battery-powered steno keyboards on a deposition or into a courtroom, write for an entire day, and then load the steno notes into their computer later. Steno keyboards may contain RAM memories, floppy diskette drives, flash memory cards, or combinations of the three, capable of storing more than a full day's work.

The batteries in these machines are designed to power the keyboard for far longer than a typical notebook computer. Court reporters are sometimes required to work where there is no convenient power outlet, running from battery for six to eight hours at a stretch. Again, these batteries add cost to the steno keyboards.

Also, unlike a QWERTY keyboard, the majority of steno keyboards include a printing mechanism for producing a paper record of the steno notes.

```
    P   RA      F              }   (new line) >>
    P   RA      F
  T       H
                  EU        S      this
              A       PB           is
    KP    A        P  L            an
                   P  L        }   example
              F
        P H           PB           of
  S       H A         PB       D   machine
    T  P   R                       shorthand
              A                    from
  ST              E   PB           a
            O  E               }   steno
      K       AO E
        PW    AO      R      D  }  keyboard
        W
        P   A  EU   P              with
              E    R           }   paper
                  F  P  L  T        (period)
```

Figure 11-4: Paper Notes from a Steno Keyboard

Computer keyboards are typically placed on a table, which is not the ideal ergonomic height for typing. Carpal tunnel syndrome and related types of repetitive strain injury (RSI) are a serious occupational hazard for court reporters and stenocaptioners, so steno keyboards are usually placed on a tripod. The Stenograph tripod connection has become the industry standard, and virtually all steno machines use the same tripod mount.

Finally, there is the issue of mass production. It is far more expensive to produce something a few thousand at a time than a few million. In a typical year, 4,000 to 5,000 new stenotype keyboards are manufactured and sold.[4] In that same year, tens or even hundreds of millions of QWERTY keyboards will be built. The economies of scale allow engineering costs to be spread out over these huge quantities, and prices are driven down.

The astute reader will have noticed, however, that many of these features are not required for a stenocaptioner. Unlike court reporters, captioners rarely find themselves with a need for batteries, paper notes, or storage devices in the keyboard. They are virtually always cabled to a computer, with numerous other electronics surrounding them. There are, indeed, a few keyboards designed specifically for captioners and CART reporters, with lower prices and fewer of these features, but

---

[4]   According to Stenograph Corporation, they produce 3,500 to 4,500 per year. This includes the models that are modified and resold by other companies, such as ProCAT. My estimate is that roughly 500 are made each year by manufacturers that do not use Stenograph parts, although this number appears to be growing.

the economies of scale are once again working against them, since the number of new stenocaptioners purchasing equipment each year is in the hundreds, not the tens of thousands.

The History of Steno Keyboards

The concept of a stenotype machine goes back well over a century. The first American patent for a stenotype machine was issued to Miles M. Bartholomew in 1879. Bartholomew's keyboard, manufactured by the United States Stenograph Corporation, still produced only one letter per stroke, using its ten keys to create a stream of dots and dashes, but it was shortly thereafter that George Kerr Anderson invented a machine that would produce a word per stroke. Anderson's machine, the Anderson Shorthand Typewriter, made the news in 1897 when it was used to transcribe President McKinley's inaugural address.

It was the Ireland Stenotype, developed by Ward Stone Ireland, that really cemented the stenotype machine's place in the courts. The machine was produced by the Universal Stenotype Company, owned by Ireland, and bears a remarkable resemblance to today's steno keyboards. In 1914, at the National Shorthand Reporters Association[5] annual convention, reporters using Ireland's machine beat out the practitioners of pen shorthand (people using Gregg and Pittman methods) in the speed contests. Ireland's steno keyboard, whose keyboard layout is still in use today, defined the modern stenocaptioner's equipment.

In the 1960s, steno keyboards were first connected to computers, and the concept of realtime translation was born. By the 1980s, Stenograph, Xscribe, BaronData, and a variety of smaller companies manufactured steno keyboards with various memory devices and realtime interfaces, ranging from digital data cassettes to flash memory cards.

In the 1980s, a court reporter-cum-inventor by the name of Jerry Lefler developed a steno writing theory called Digitext that could be expressed algorithmically, requiring a steno-to-English dictionary only for handling exceptions to his basic rules. In 1987, he created a steno keyboard that performed its own translation, not requiring a computer.

Several varieties of Lefler's machine were sold over the ensuing years, and the concept went mainstream when Stenograph put translation capability into its Stentura line of steno machines in 1992. This was also an era of consolidation, as Stenograph purchased its largest rivals, Xscribe and BaronData, and discontinued production of their products (Xscribe's Stenoram & Vision keyboards and BaronData's Transcriptor line).

In the '80s and early '90s, several companies produced "paperless" steno keyboards, designed for captioning or high-speed text entry applications. Digitext, StenoCAT, and AdvoCAT all sold

---

[5] In 1991, NSRA changed its name to the National Court Reporters Association. NCRA still holds speed contests, and now has realtime contests as well, testing accuracy of realtime translation without allowing after-the-fact editing.

paperless machines, and Stenograph made a brief foray into the paperless world as well. The stenocaptioning market was still young, and high-speed text entry never broke into high volume, so all of these machines disappeared from the market.

In 1994, my brother, Bill Robson, and I designed and built the Gemini writer, an ergonomic paperless keyboard split into two parts and mounted on a fully articulating tripod mount that allowed independent movement of the two halves for natural hand placement. Figure 11-5 shows a Gemini mounted on an early version of the tripod. Its primary market was captioners, and court reporters with wrist and hand problems. It is sold by Robson Technologies.

Figure 11-5: The Gemini Keyboard

The last few years have seen the real coming of age for paperless machines. Stenograph introduced two new models, the élan Mira and the élan Cybra. Word Technologies introduced the Trèal. This also marked the start of the transition from RS-232 serial interfaces to USB connections for steno keyboards.

Stacking

Another major difference between QWERTY-style keyboards and steno keyboards is the mechanism for detecting that a key has been pressed. Most QWERTY keyboards trigger on the downstroke. As soon as the key has been pressed far enough, a signal is fired off to the computer.

Steno keyboards, on the other hand, trigger on the upstroke. Since the keyboards are designed for chording, you can press two, three, or all 23 keys at the same time. Press them down in any order, and when you *release* the keys, the computer will be notified. While this mechanism is integral to machine shorthand, it also causes a side effect that is the bane of many stenocaptioners' existence: stacking.

Stacking typically occurs when a stroke utilizing only one hand is immediately followed by a stroke utilizing only the other hand. Say, for example, that a stenocaptioner is writing the word "to" (steno TO, using only the left hand), followed by a period (steno FPLT, using only the right hand). If the right hand begins its downward movement before the left hand comes completely off of the keyboard, then the steno machine will read them as a single stroke (TOFPLT, which would most likely be meaningless gibberish).

Stacking can lead to some bizarre bloopers. People unfamiliar with steno theory can't understand how the stenocaptioner could write such a thing. During the Winter Olympics, announcers were discussing a member of the American women's luge team, whose brother competed in the same sport. The announcer began a sentence with "Her brother, also a luger who…"

In steno, "luger" is written as HRAOUPBLG/ER (being phonetically based, the word uses the J ending rather than the G ending) and "who" is written as WHO. The stenocaptioner stacked the second stroke of luger on top of the who, writing HRAOUPBLG/WHOER. The sentence that came out on televisions around the world began, "Her brother, also a luge whore…"

Producing this horrible blooper didn't require a single misfingering. It was only a matter of timing, with the stenocaptioner bringing the right hand up a little too slowly or starting the left hand down a little too quickly.

A number of today's modern steno keyboards have adjustments designed to reduce stacking, but there is no way to completely eliminate the phenomenon.

Antistacking designs range from adjustable trigger points like the Gemini to Stenograph's stroking pattern analysis algorithm in their élan Cybra machine.

Realtime Interfaces

The traditional interface between a steno keyboard and a computer is a serial cable connected to the COM port on the computer. Transmission uses the RS-232 standard, typically set to 9,600 to 38,400 bits per second. Since stenocaptioners rarely hit speeds higher than bursts of five or six strokes per second, this speed is adequate for most uses.

There are two general categories of realtime steno keyboard interface: instant and polled. Instant steno interfaces fire off each stroke to the computer as it is written. Polled interfaces require the computer to query the steno keyboard periodically to see if there is any new steno to transmit. When there is, the steno keyboard sends the new stroke(s) as a packet.

All of the Stenograph and Xscribe machines use polled interfaces. BaronData and RTI machines use instant.

The actual transmission of the steno is typically done as a bitmap. Since there are 23 keys on the machine, a stroke can be transmitted in as few as three bytes.

There is no industry standard protocol, but since the BaronData Transcriptor series and the Xscribe product line have been discontinued, the Stenograph protocol is by far the most common. In the 1990s, Stenograph licensed the protocol to several software companies and sold their machines through them as OEMs. According to a Stenograph spokesman, the company is no longer licensing or distributing interface protocols for any of their machines.

The interfaces are not overly complex, and can be reverse-engineered using a protocol analyzer and a functional system. This process is easier with some systems than others. The Xscribe protocol, for example, includes a complex system of compressing stroke data and a nonstandard checksum algorithm, which took me weeks to reverse-engineer. BaronData's protocol used a four-byte bitmap (six keys per byte) which divided the keyboard into quadrants. The data stream was compressed by transmitting only those quadrant bytes in which keys were depressed.

Stenograph's Stentura/SmartWriter protocol, on the other hand, uses no compression, and is very straightforward to use.

Translation Dictionaries

A translation dictionary consists of matched pairs of steno and English[6] entries, and the software uses a "longest match" lookup system to perform the translation. When translating in realtime, there is no look-ahead capability, so the software must sometimes hold back strokes to determine when there is a longer match.

Table 11-2: Sample Steno-English Translation Dictionary Fragment

Steno	English
KAT	cat
KAT/SUP	catsup
KAT/A/HROG/D	cataloged
MOUS	mouse
MOUS/TRAP	mousetrap
A	a

---

[6]   Translation dictionaries can theoretically convert steno into any language, and this same basic technology is used for English, French, Spanish, and various other languages. Rather than falling back on some awkward phrase like "steno-to-natural-language," however, we'll just say English.

For example, assume a translation dictionary contains the entries shown in table 11-2. If a realtime system receives the steno stroke KAT, it doesn't know whether you are writing "cat," or this is the first stroke of "catalog" or "catsup." It will hold back that stroke and wait to see what comes next.

If the next stroke is A, the system still doesn't know whether you have written "cat a" (as in "he's my cat a lot of the time") or you're partway through the word "cataloged."

If the third stroke is MOUS, the software will see that there are no dictionary entries beginning with KAT/A/MOUS, so it will translate "cat a" and output it. The MOUS may be the word "mouse" or it may be the start of "mousetrap," so the software won't translate that third stroke.

If, on the other hand, the third stroke is HROG, then the program must *still* wait. Even though there's only one possibility in the dictionary, you may write a completely different fourth stroke. For example, you may be writing "cataloging" without having entered it in your dictionary before.

For a court reporter new to stenocaptioning, this can sometimes be puzzling. Many steno theories use the stroke FPLT to mean a period, FPLT/FPLT to mean a colon (since it has two dots), and FPLT/FPLT/FPLT to mean an ellipsis. When the stenocaptioner writes the period at the end of a sentence, the software will hold back the stroke, waiting to see if it will turn into a colon or ellipsis.

For this reason, most stenocaptioning systems have a "force" stroke—a steno stroke defined to release all held-back steno and force it to be translated.

Backing Up and Making Corrections

When flying along at over 200 words per minute, even the best stenocaptioner can make typos—or misstrokes, as they're called in steno theory. The asterisk key on the steno keyboard is the correction key. Unlike the backspace on a computer keyboard, which takes out the last *letter* written, the asterisk key on a steno keyboard takes out the last *stroke*.

In a court reporting environment, there's no great problem with a word appearing on the screen, and then disappearing when the court reporter "asterisks" it out. It can be distracting to see text go away and get replaced by something else, but it's an infrequent-enough occurrence that nobody really worries about it.

In stenocaptioning, on the other hand, it can be a problem. Most realtime stenocaptioning is done in the roll-up mode, where the text appears as it is written, and when a row of text is filled, everything smoothly scrolls up and a new row is begun. If a word shows up in the middle of a row, it can be erased—although this takes longer than it would on a computer screen. If the word forces the screen to scroll because a row was filled, however, there is no way to "unscroll" the screen and correct the word.[7] This problem is even more noticeable when a dictionary entry contains a whole phrase rather than just a word. Many stenocaptioners use briefs (shortened, non-phonetic steno entries) for phrases like "House of Representatives" or "*New York Times.*" Phrases like this can generate a lot of text, possibly filling more than one row.

Stenocaptioning software, therefore, usually has a programmable built-in delay. Captioners may set this to anywhere from a few tenths of a second on up to a second or more. All steno strokes are held for this defined delay time to give the stenocaptioner a chance to stroke the asterisk and make corrections. Thus, as long as the stenocaptioner realizes there was a misstroke and fixes it quickly, it will never be translated and will never appear on the television set.

Typically, when a misstroke is translated and transmitted, so that it appears on the TV and can't be erased, then the stenocaptioner will simply "dash it out" and keep going. This might appear on the TV like this: **THE GOVERNOR WAS UNAVAILABLE FUR--FOR COMMENT.** Some captioning companies are now encouraging their stenocaptioners to simply keep writing and ignore the error in those cases, feeling that the correction is likely to just further confuse viewers.

Prefixes and Suffixes

There is another situation where the software can end up removing and regenerating text, even though the stenocaptioner didn't misstroke or correct anything—when using suffixes.

Stenocaptioners typically have dictionary entries for suffixes like "-ment," as in "enforcement" or "attainment." After writing the word "enforce," it takes only a slight pause (as long as the built-in delay is set) before the word appears on the screen. If it comes close to the end of the row, and then the stenocaptioner writes the "-ment" ending, there won't be room for it on the line.

Some stenocaptioning software has an option to hyphenate the word and break it before the suffix. The far more common solution in this case is to erase the word, scroll down a row, and rewrite the word with the suffix attached. Yet another solution is to hold the word in the translation buffer until the next entry is translated to see whether or not it's a suffix.

Most stenocaptioning software has "smart" handling of word endings that minimizes the number of dictionary entries required to handle common suffixes. The "-ment" ending used in the prior example rarely changes the spelling of the root word, but "-ing," "-ed," "-s," and others can make significant changes (e.g., run+ing $\rightarrow$ running; die+ing $\rightarrow$ dying; pay+ed $\rightarrow$ paid; fly+s $\rightarrow$ flies).

A set of predefined rules can be used as an algorithm for spelling changes when suffixes are added, and exceptions can be placed in a translation dictionary.

---

[7] Well, actually, there is, but the process is so awkward, time-consuming, and messy-looking that it's not worth doing.

By using dictionary definitions for common prefixes (e.g., un-, re-, non-, bi-) and suffixes (e.g., -ed, -es, -ing, -ment, -er), a stenocaptioner can enter a new root word in the translation dictionary and have all of the derived words available immediately.

Punctuation and Special Characters

Since the steno keyboard contains only letter keys and the number shift (plus the handy and morphological asterisk key), stenocaptioners must select steno strokes to represent punctuation and special characters.

Table 11-3: Punctuation in a Translation Dictionary

Punctuation	Symbol	Behavior
Period	.	No space before, start new line after,[8] cap next word.
Decimal point	.	No space before when preceded by a digit, otherwise one space before. No space after when followed by a digit, otherwise one space after.
Question mark	?	No space before, start new line after, cap next word.
Inverse question mark	¿	Start new line before, no space after, cap next word (used in Spanish).
Exclamation point	!	No space before, start new line after, cap next word.
Inverse exclamation	¡	Start new line before, no space after, cap next word (used in Spanish). Since the line 21 character set doesn't have an inverse exclamation, use a lowercase "i."
Comma	,	No space before, one space after.
Semicolon	;	No space before, one space after.
Quotation marks	"	Most systems treat these as "smart." The first one stroked acts as an open quote and the next one is a closing quote. Punctuation following the closing quote may or may not be moved inside the quotes, depending on the software.
Parenthesis	( )	Like the quotes, some systems allow users to define a single "paren" stroke, and the software determines whether it's an opening paren (preceded by a space) or a closing paren (followed by a space).
Brackets	[ ]	Systems may or may not have smart bracket handling.
Angle brackets	< >	Treated as individual symbols.
Braces	{ }	The line 21 character set does not include braces (see table 7-1 for details).

---

[8] There are some cases where end-of-sentence punctuation (e.g., period, exclamation point, question mark) does not start a new line, and in those cases, it is always followed by *one* space in stenocaptioning, not two as in court reporting.

Most punctuation marks require some special action on the part of the software, so they have to have special definitions in the translation dictionaries. Table 11-3 shows the behavior of some typical stenocaptioning punctuation definitions.

Punctuation also raises one of same issues we explored earlier in the discussion of backing up and making corrections. What happens when a row is completely full, and the captioner adds a punctuation mark?

The captioning software can remove the last word, scroll up a row, rewrite the word, and then add the punctuation mark, but this is slow and messy looking. Even using the DER method described in Chapter 7 (Line 21 Technical Details), this process can take ¼ to ½ second.

A common solution to this problem is for the software to allow the line length to be extended by one character when needed for punctuation. Obviously, this only works if the captions are not already extending into the rightmost column on the screen. For this reason, you'll often see captioners defining the maximum line length as 31 rather than 32 characters. Most lines will end on or before the 31st column, but on those occasions where a row is full (31 characters) and a punctuation mark is added, the punctuation mark will appear in the 32nd column.

Character Attributes

Stenocaptioners usually don't worry much about underlining and italics (line 21 captions do not allow for boldface text), but there are situations where they are definitely called for. When defining briefs for names of newspapers, for example, it's easy to include the italic codes to produce *New York Times* rather than New York Times.

Color, although an integral part of Teletext captioning (or subtitling, as it's known in Great Britain), is rarely used in line 21 captioning except in the caption credits at the end of the program. Again, it is easy to include in a dictionary entry, but difficult to remember and apply codes to change colors on the fly when writing at speeds in excess of 200 words per minute.

The most common use of color during a program is speaker identification. The speaker ID itself may be in a different color (to make it stand out from the text), or the text may be a different color for each of the primary speakers in a program. The latter, while used frequently in the U.K., is almost unheard-of in the U.S.).

Capitalization

In the beginning, virtually all line 21 captioning was done in all capital letters. There has been a trend in recent years (largely attributable to the more attractive fonts in recent decoder chips) toward captioning in mixed-case.

Translation dictionaries are usually built in mixed-case for flexibility. It is far easier to convert mixed-case text into all-caps than it is to convert in the other direction. Realtime captioning software has a setting for all-caps vs. mixed-case.

Even in mixed-case captioning, however, there are some situations that call for the use of lowercase letters. Examples are McDONALD, 49ers, and eBAY. Translation dictionaries have a token that overrides the automatic conversion of lowercase letters into uppercase during all-caps translation. In an "Mc" name, that token would be applied only to the "c," allowing the rest of the letters to capitalize automatically.

The other common situation calling for lowercase letters is accent marks. The only accented vowels in the line 21 character set (see table 7-1) are lowercase. In all-caps captioning, the captioner is left with the choice of removing accent marks from vowels (the standard practice in Parisian French), or leaving the accented vowels in lowercase. This produces some odd-looking captions (e.g., HE WILL RESUME NEGOTIATION BY SENDING HIS RéSUMé), but preserves the accents.

Caption Positioning

Some caption formats (e.g., pop-on vs. roll-up, number of rows) are usually set for an entire program. Others (e.g., position on screen, line width) can change during the program.

Along with presenting the dialog accurately and in a timely fashion, a primary goal of captioning is to make it clear who is speaking and avoid covering anything critical on the screen. In offline captioning, speaker identification is often provided by using caption position, as explained in Chapter 14 (Caption Placement Strategies). With online captioning, which is typically roll-up, it would be highly distracting—and almost impossible for the stenocaptioner—to keep changing the position to reflect who is speaking. Speaker ID is typically handled in stenocaptioning by inserting the speaker's name at the beginning of a line.

Caption positioning in realtime is still a significant concern in an environment where extraneous information is being regularly placed on the screen, such as a newscast or a sporting event. Titles frequently appear at the bottom of the screen, as well as crawls and bugs. At the top of the screen, you'll see scores and status information about the game. Not only does this information appear and disappear during the broadcast, but it changes positions as well. The captioner is responsible for keeping the captions from covering any of it.

During college football broadcasts, for example, ESPN changes the location of the score box depending on which team has possession of the ball. Every time possession changes, the score box jumps to the other side of the screen, and the captioner must move the captions to compensate.

Rather than try to change the line length, vertical position, horizontal position, and number of rows individually, captioners typically predefine a set of positions and assign them to keys on the QWERTY keyboard (the number pad is a typical location for this), strokes on the steno keyboard, or both. This can be done using macros or as a built-in feature of the captioning program.

Table 11-4 shows some typical position macros. The rows are numbered from 1 (at the top) to 15 (at the bottom). See the discussion earlier in this chapter about punctuation for an explanation of why line lengths are set to 31 instead of 32.

Table 11-4: Typical Predefined Caption Positions

Description	Base Row	Column Indent	Line Length	# of Rows
Bottom, standard	15	0	31	2 or 3
Bottom, with a bug	15	0	27	2 or 3
Bottom, with a crawl or title	13 or 14	0	31	2
Top, with score box on left	2	4	27	2
Top, with score box on right	2	0	27	2

The subject of positioning is covered in greater depth in Chapter 14 (Caption Placement Strategies).

System Control

Some steno strokes don't generate text or formatting information, but control the encoder or decoder. The most frequently used control stroke is probably the "force" stroke, which causes all strokes held back in the input buffer to be immediately translated.

Another common control stroke is called "clear screen" or "erase screen." It wipes all captions from the TV screen. This is usually used when there's a long pause in the dialog or when something appears on the screen that the captions are covering. For example, if a full-screen block of text appears (a table, perhaps), which the newscaster is reading, the captioner will erase the captions and let the viewer read the table rather than providing exactly the same text as captions partially obscuring it.

Sometimes, the video being captioned already has captions on it. This occurs, for example, when a newscast is showing highlights from an earlier sporting event, or replaying footage from an earlier newscast. As long as captions are being generated in realtime, the encoder is set to block these upstream captions, replacing them with the new ones.

Television commercials, however, are not recaptioned by a live stenocaptioner. The captions on the commercials are very carefully placed and timed, and should not be replaced by live captioning. To leave them alone, the captioner must instruct the encoder to pass through upstream captions without modification. The command is usually combined with an erase screen (EDM) command when going into a commercial break. This removes the last of the stenocaptioner's text from the screen and allows previously created captions through.

Phonetic Translation

Sometimes, a word will come up that just isn't in the dictionary, whether it's due to a misstroke or because the word was never entered. These are known as untranslates. Displaying raw steno for an untranslate is more likely to confuse readers than help them. As an example, if my first name (Gary) wasn't in a steno dictionary, and the stenocaptioner wrote TKPWA/RAOE, the result would be incomprehensible to anyone unfamiliar with steno theory.

Realtime captioning systems, therefore, use a phonetic lookup table to convert untranslates into something hopefully more readable. Unlike translation dictionaries, phonetic lookup tables use *portions* of steno strokes to guess at the spelling, based on something like table 11-1. Again using my first name as an example, the TKPW in the first stroke would turn into a G and the A would remain unchanged. In the second stroke, the R would be unchanged, and the AOE would be translated as a long E, probably spelled EE. The viewers may not see the correctly spelled name GARY, but GA REE is a lot closer than TKPWA RAOE.

Dictionary Exchange Formats (RTF/CRE)

Obviously, a stenocaptioner's translation dictionary is a critical component of his or her work. In the early days of realtime stenocaptioning and court reporting, captioners could spend years developing a dictionary, and then be faced with the daunting task of recreating much of that work if they switched software vendors.

Each vendor had to write dictionary translators that could read competitors' formats, with varying degrees of success. All of the formats were proprietary and none of the specifications was published. Xscribe, the leader in realtime closed captioning at the time, proposed a dictionary interchange format, but it was found inadequate to the task, as it handled only words, and not formatting or control entries.

In the early 1990s, the presidents of three court reporting software companies met to discuss possible solutions. Greg Seely of Advantage Software, B. Robert Bakva of ProCAT, and I (then representing Cheetah Systems) decided to write a standard for exchanging documents between disparate court reporting and captioning software packages. We chose Microsoft's Rich Text Format (RTF) as a starting point, and assigned software engineers from all three companies to extend RTF for court reporting: T.J. Crowder from Cheetah, Jeremy Thorne from Advantage, and

Alex Freylicher from ProCAT. Crowder wrote up what they developed as the RTF/CRE (Court Reporting Extensions) specification document.

In addition to handling translation dictionaries, RTF/CRE allows for interchange of text documents and steno shorthand files between the systems. When the standard was finalized in October of 1995, vendors set forth writing import and export software. Soon, court reporters and stenocaptioners were able to move freely between software packages.

One of the fundamental design criteria of RTF/CRE was that extensions would not cause problems with existing RTF converters such as the ones built into Microsoft Word. Steno data is embedded in "ignored" groups, so that if an RTF/CRE file is loaded into a word processor with an RTF reader, the steno will simply be discarded. All of the CRE control words begin with "cx" to avoid possible conflicts with later extensions by other groups.

Similarly, RTF/CRE importers should ignore anything they haven't been programmed to recognize. Exporters may or may not include font tables, style sheets, and so forth.

Steno is represented in RTF/CRE files using a letter or symbol for each key, and *must* be entered in order: STKPWHRAO*EUFRPBLGTSDZ. The number bar is represented by the # symbol, and may be placed at the beginning or end of the stroke. Multiple steno strokes are separated by slashes.

When a stroke does not contain vowels or an asterisk, its representation can be ambiguous. SR, for example, could represent the initial S with either the initial R or final R. To avoid this problem, use the dash to separate initial and final consonants. Thus, SR means S with the initial R, and S-R means S with final R. To be completely safe, I recommend inserting a dash in every stroke that has final consonants without having vowels or asterisk. This means generating some unnecessary dashes (as in the stroke -FPLT, which would not be ambiguous without the dash), but it's a safe and easy algorithm to follow.

The annotated RTF/CRE dictionary in figure 11-6 should provide a basic understanding of the file structure.

The full RTF/CRE specification can be downloaded at

`www.captioncentral.com/resources/rtfcre`

```
{\rtf1\pc
{\*\cxrev100}    ← revision of the RTF/CRE spec to which this document was generated
{\*\cxdict}    ← type of RTF/CRE file (a dictionary, in this case)
{\*\cxsystem DictTest Rev 1.2 by G. Robson}    ← program that built this file
{\*\cxs -T/SHAU}the shah    ← two strokes of steno for "the shah"
{\*\cxs EL/PWAR/A/TKAEU}Elbaradei
{\*\cxs ORD/TPHAPBS}ordnance
{\*\cxs OE/PHAPB}Oman
{\*\cxs AL/KAEUD/A}Al\~Qaeda    ← the "\~" is a non-breaking space
{\*\cxs AL/KAOEUD/A}Al\~Qaeda
{\*\cxs AOU/TKAEU}Uday
{\*\cxs AOEU/RABG/KWREU}Iraqi    ← if the stenocaptioner misstrokes, it will still translate
{\*\cxs AOEU/RABG/SKWREU}Iraqi    ← this is the correct steno
{\*\cxs PWOS/RA}Basra    ← two different pronunciations, same translation
{\*\cxs PWAS/RA}Basra
{\*\cxs SKWRURB/SKWRURB}George\~W. Bush    ← a "brief" for a name
}
```

Figure 11-6: Annotated Sample of an RTF/CRE Translation Dictionary

NOTE TO PROGRAMMERS: The lists of steno/English pairs in an RTF/CRE dictionary are not necessarily in any particular order, and sorting them for any particular application is your responsibility.

Bloopers

Since stenocaptioners produce entire words, syllables, or phrases with a single stroke, a slight misfingering can produce unexpected and highly amusing results. This is exacerbated by the way combinations of keys produce a single letter. A captioner's finger only has to move a fraction of an inch to produce an L instead of an H or R.

The bloopers I'm listing here are funny (at least I think they are), but they also explain something about how steno shorthand works. All of these actually happened. They aren't urban legends or exaggerated mis-tellings. I've either seen these myself, or heard them directly from the stenocaptioners that blooped them.

The bloopers are grouped by what caused them. Each shows the wrong word(s) *in italics* with the word(s) that should have been there [in brackets].

Note to the sensitive reader: Some of these bloopers are sexual, some are suggestive, and some are just plain weird. If you are easily offended, you may wish to skip the rest of this chapter.

Words That Aren't in the Translation Dictionary

This can happen with new words, which sportscasters, marketing people, and scientists delight in creating on a regular basis. It can also come up with words that just aren't mentioned in conversation very often. Additionally, when court reporters change professions and move into stenocaptioning, they find that the vocabulary of a television broadcast can be quite different than what they've encountered in court.

Sometimes, a quick glance will tell the informed viewer what was meant, as when the name of former Senator and Presidential hopeful Carol Moseley Braun came out as Carol Mostly Brown, or when the sponsor of an event was shown as "butt wiser" instead of Budweiser.

Perhaps the best-known blooper to those in the field is the one written by Marty Block, who was the first person to write realtime captions on a live broadcast. In a newscast, one of the lead stories was the death of well-known piano player Arthur Rubinstein. In all his years as a court reporter, Marty had never written the word "pianist" before. Typically, when a stenocaptioner writes words ending in ST, they omit the T, since the keys are in the wrong order. This led to the caption:

The world-famous *penis*, Arthur Rubinstein, died tonight.

A few other examples along those same lines:

I'd like to introduce the *bitch hop's* [Bishop's] regional director...

Give generously and the lord will bless you with *a bun dance* [abundance].

Coming up later tonight, some new *stud disease* [studies] that will affect elderly men in Florida.

Conflict Trouble

Some of these examples are homonyms, and some show words that don't quite sound alike, but are written alike on a steno keyboard. Rarely, for example, do stenocaptioners distinguish between a final S sound and a final Z sound.

Up next, Joey Buttafuoco and his torrid *tail* [tale].

We can park the bikes and put the *lox* [locks] on them.

Men with *sauce* [saws] climb the branches the kids once did.

Of course, sometimes this will happen even when the words aren't quite homonyms, but they are very close. That is what happened with these gems:

Next up: Dining out with Pavarotti. What kind of a *male* [meal] does a large star consume?

Female anchor: What's that smell?
Male anchor: It's my *colon* [cologne].

I've been a *liar* [lawyer] all my life. It's what I do for a living, and I enjoy it.

Word Boundary Problems

The homonym problem is exacerbated when you realize that combinations of words can form homonyms, depending on where you break the words apart. Court reporters and stenocaptioners call such word combinations word-boundary problems, like when a courtroom reporter didn't have "acidic" in her dictionary, and the realtime transcript referred to an "acid dick solution." Ouch!

A perfect broadcast example of a word-boundary problem was when a sportscaster was interviewing San Francisco 49er football player Jerry Rice. When asked what kind of person quarterback Steve Young was, Rice responded by saying:

He's a *fungi* [fun guy] to be around.

When former San Francisco Mayor Frank Jordan spoke, this was the result:

I thank each and every one of you for allowing me to participate in the *grandpa raid* [grand parade] of San Francisco history.

Realtime translation of steno shorthand into English is complex. When a steno stroke, or strokes, appears that the computer doesn't recognize, it does its best to fit something to it. Sometimes the combination of strokes for a long, unrecognized word actually makes sense (to the computer, anyway) when split apart into several shorter words. That's what happened here:

This whole situation is *lewd crows* [ludicrous].

Phoenix, bludgeoned by pigeon lovers, has decided not to *piss on* [poison] the pigeons.

There was *areola salt* [a real assault].

I think *urine tract* [you're on track] with that one.

And in this embarrassing exchange:

Question: And they worked as –
Answer: *Asshole sale* [As wholesale] producers.

Misstrokes

As we mentioned earlier, it takes only a slight slip of the finger to dramatically change the meaning of a word or sentence.

A misstroke doubling as a double entendre showed up on my wife, Kathy's, first newscast. It was the night Audrey Hepburn died. She missed the P key in one of the words, and the captioning software obligingly "fixed" the spelling to match what she wrote:

Audrey Hepburn has *laid* [played] with some of Hollywood's greatest leading men.

Another happened after I'd been involved in setting up captioning at a large church. The day of the first captioned service came, and the captioner was understandably nervous. Her text was on a gigantic projection screen, and there were over 1,000 people in the congregation. A group of us stood behind her watching as the preacher spoke, and out came this caption:

...and now, let us *sin* [sing] together.

Here are a few more from various stenocaptioners:

Now, John has the *nudes* [news] for us.

...*fartly* [partly] cloudy skies.

Erection [election] night coverage

President Clinton addresses the *nag* [nation] at 6:00.

Tom Watson, flirting with the leaderboard, nice *butt* [putt] at the 7th.

And a great basketball player, out for two weeks with an *anal* [ankle] injury.

We were able to sit down with members of the A's who *wormed* [worked] under Walter Haas Junior.

George is *wilted* [wild] and crazy...

...a *bowel* [bowl] of fruit.

A shot of Ken Harrelson, the former *White Sex* [White Sox] announcer.

A 1:00 *sickoff* [kickoff] in San Diego, Sunday.

The Braves won, too, so it comes down to a *thigh breaker* [tie-breaker] Monday night if necessary.

And there's the *jello* [yellow] flag.

I've been in New York before, but I've never *squatted* [skated] in this rink.

It turned out to be a *stink* [sting] operation by police.

President Clinton hopes it will provide a basis for new *regular layings* [regulations] as well as voluntary standards.

He had just exchanged rings and *vowels*[9] [vows] with his new bride.

A low voter *tushout* [turnout] is expected.

Jordan becoming the *sexed* [sixth] nation to make formal peace with Israel.

Now you can go to McDonald's and order *flies* [fries] and a Coke.

His future is *sobriety* [so bright], he had to wear shades.

The next step is culling out the *dumb cats* [duplicates].

This will be the best weekend for aspen *screwing* [viewing].

Good morning. I'm David *Heartburn* [Hartman].

That is unacceptable and stunning coming from a *syphilised* (civilized) democracy.

The whole Mideast is such an incredible place. I like to think of it as a *hole* [home].

Rot [Rod] Stuart will be with us today.

He denied the *wrong dong* [wrongdoing], but the question persisted.

---

[9]   You don't suppose this fellow was marrying Vanna White, do you?

Look at this *cross-sexual* [cross-sectional] diagram.

That was the *sexy thought* [section I thought] I was referring to this morning.

You have *aunts* [ants] in your pants?

Icky lab rat [I can elaborate].

Sometimes you just have to tell the *prick* [public] to wait.

Correcting Misstrokes

A stenocaptioner's options for backing up and correcting errors are limited in broadcast captioning. Once the caption decoder moves on to a new line, the blooper is there forever (or at least until it scrolls off or the screen is cleared). For that reason, many stenocaptioners will simply write a dash followed by the correct word. Most of the time, that's a good thing. Sometimes, it can make the blooper even funnier. How about this exchange from a British newscast where a news reporter was planted outside 10 Downing Street awaiting an important announcement:

Anchor: So what's going on there now? Any sign yet?

Reporter: No, the *sex* – session has been going on for 15 minutes now and still no sign...

In another case, the stenocaptioner knew that he'd be realtiming a doctor from the Department of Corrections. He loaded up his medical translation dictionary, in which some common medical words are defined several ways to avoid errors. In this case, he got a whopper of a double blooper out of it:

I'm with the Maryland Department of *erections* [Corrections], and I'm here this evening to talk about services available in the *penile* [penal] system...

Drops

Sometimes, especially when writing at high speed, a stenocaptioner can miss an entire stroke, which drops either a whole word or a part of a word. This leads to fun like these:

Hell [hello], David. Getting tired of seeing me this morning?

A large *shrimp* [shrimp boat] carrying a half ton of marijuana was seized earlier today.

Briefs

When a particular word or phrase comes up a lot, stenocaptioners often create a brief form for it. When two briefs are too much alike, it doesn't take much of a slip to produce hilarious results. A brief for Nelson Mandela that was a tad too similar to a brief for a prominent (at the time) figure skater led to the captions in one newscast announcing that Nancy Kerrigan had just become President of South Africa!

One captioner told me that he was preparing for a newscast, and came up with a new brief for a phrase that was to be used repeatedly. Unfortunately, he didn't get it defined properly. Thanks to the phonetic translator, it came out:

> Prince Andrew and the *dork* [Duchess of York] have now boarded the plane...

Similarly, a captioner got tired of writing out the phrase "President Clinton," and came up with a shorthand stroke of "plic," which is PHREUK in steno. Dropping the H resulted in her President Clinton brief translating as "prick."

Stacking

Stacking, as we described earlier in this chapter, is when two strokes are piled on top of each other. This can result in errors like the "luge whore" that was discussed at the time. Another good one happened in a live government meeting, when captioner Jack Boenau managed to stack a comma (steno RBGS) onto the prior stroke. When a group of high-ranking officials were invited into the room, he wrote:

> >> CHAIRMAN: *Jerks* [Gentlemen,] please come in.

And sometimes the resulting blooper can be even more appropriate than the original text:

> The Giants say goodbye to exhibition baseball: *Spraining* [spring training] is over.

12   REALTIME VOICE WRITING

Speech recognition is one of the most misunderstood areas of captioning. Newcomers to the field can't understand why stenocaptioners are still employed when speech recognition has advanced so far in recent years. Stenocaptioners who participated in speech recognition experiments in the '90s wonder how anybody could ever believe that this technology could work. As usual, the truth lies somewhere in between.

First, we need to define some terminology.

Speech recognition is the computerized translation of voice to text. Products such as IBM's ViaVoice and Dragon's NaturallySpeaking are inexpensive programs that require only a microphone and a personal computer.

Voice recognition is a related technology used in the security industry for identifying a person by their voice prints (i.e., software that recognizes voices). The terms "speech recognition" and "voice recognition" are *not* interchangeable, and voice recognition technology is currently not used in the captioning business. Unfortunately, the distinction has blurred significantly of late, and even companies in the speech recognition business will call their products "voice recognition software" from time to time.

Speaker-dependent speech recognition is trained to a specific person's voice. Most commercial speech recognition products today require a training period when the software is first installed where the system can learn the user's voice.

Speaker-independent speech recognition can be used without any training period, working with multiple people simultaneously.

Voice writing, which used to be called mask reporting, uses a person trained as an "echo." Voice writers, usually wearing sound-blocking masks containing microphones, repeat everything they hear, inserting voice codes for punctuation, speaker identification, and formatting. They use a speaker-dependent speech recognition system trained to their voice, which can produce output in realtime.

Why Voice Writing?

If you're going to use speech recognition software anyway, why not just hook up the TV audio directly into the computer and let 'er rip? What good does this voice writer person do, anyway?

I asked this exact question of software developers at a speech recognition conference, but couched slightly differently. How long will it be before speaker-independent speech recognition software is capable of producing realtime transcription of multiple speakers in a noisy environment, such as an interview on a football field after a big game or a live remote at an accident scene during a rainstorm with people yelling and sirens going? Oh, and by the way, the system must punctuate the sentences correctly, identify the speakers, and make sure the transcription is at least 98% accurate with a lag of no more than three seconds.

Most engineers responded with something along the lines of "not in the near future" or "not in our lifetimes." The most optimistic time estimate I heard was 10-20 years.

On the other hand, if a *person* is hearing and interpreting that interview, it is possible to transcribe it at high speeds with high accuracy using either machine shorthand (stenocaptioning) or speech recognition (voice writing).

Voice Writing vs. Stenocaptioning

Voice writers and stenocaptioners each have trade associations to fight for their cause. The National Court Reporters Association (NCRA) champions stenotype, and the National Verbatim Reporters Association (NVRA) champions voice writing.

Each association has a plethora of information and materials showing why their method is the better of the two. For the most part, they focus on their strengths, but there is certainly conflicting information available.

In reality, NCRA and NVRA are promoting two different means to the same end. At this point, it is undeniable that both stenocaptioners and voice writers are capable of producing high-quality realtime at normal speaking rates.

Marty Block has a unique understanding of both sides of the issue. He was the first person to ever write realtime for a live broadcast, at the National Captioning Institute in 1982. He went on to become one of the foremost proponents of stenocaptioning, including a term as president of NCRA. He was one of the founders of VITAC, from which he has since retired. Now, however, Block is the CEO of Voice to Text, LLC, a company that produces a speech-based captioning software package called ISIS.

He made this switch largely because he believes that there will not be enough trained and qualified stenocaptioners to meet the demands of the captioning mandates discussed in Chapter 4 (Captioning Law), and he didn't feel the voice writing products on the market at the time were focused on captioning. In late 2003, I asked him whether stenocaptioners and voice writers are now equivalent in speed and accuracy.

Block responded that (in his opinion) the average stenocaptioner and the average voice writer now have equivalent speed and accuracy, but the precision of stenocaptioning means that the very top stenocaptioners are more accurate than the very top voice writers, and it will probably remain that way for quite some time.

Jim Bouck, the first voice writer ever to pass the Realtime Verbatim Reporter (RVR) certification, agrees. He did point out, however, that developments in voice writing methodologies and products will allow increasing accuracy as time goes on. "So while I agree with Marty Block," Bouck said, "I must also say that I believe the very top voice writers will be sharing the realtime stage with the very top steno writers sooner rather than later."

As of mid-2003, I was unable to find a single regularly scheduled (daily or weekly) show that was being captioned by voice writers in English. Everyone agrees that the technology has been proven, and it's only a matter of time before speech-based captioning systems are more broadly deployed.

Steno-based realtime is a considerably more mature technology than voice-based realtime. With the availability of high-quality speech engines such as IBM's ViaVoice, it is easier to add speech recognition capability to an online captioning system than it is to add full online captioning capabilities to a speech recognition program. Voice writing systems for captioning are coming from a variety of sources.

- Companies producing Computer-Aided Transcription (CAT) software for voice writing are moving into captioning. AudioScribe has already released their SpeechCAP software, and StenoScribe has announced their intention to sell captioning software.

- Producers of stenocaptioning systems are adding speech input capabilities to their existing products. This has already been done by ProCAT (CaptiVision) and Advantage Software (AccuCap), and others are working on it at this writing.

- A number of companies known for their offline captioning software are now offering online systems with speech input capability.

- At least one captioning hardware manufacturer (Ultech) is now producing online captioning software for voice writers (Caption Mic).

- And, finally, brand-new companies like Block's Voice to Text are entering the market with new speech-based captioning systems like ISIS.

This list represents differing backgrounds, points of view, and approaches to captioning. Some have more experience with captioning than others, and some have more experience with speech recognition.

Equipment

Stenocaptioners and voice writers require similar equipment, except for the input device. The microphone, whether masked or not, is a critical component of a voice writing system. A poor-quality mike will have a marked effect upon the accuracy of the caption text. Some standalone speech recognition software includes a microphone as part of a headset. These generally produce excellent results, as the software is designed to work with that particular mike.

Generally speaking, voice writers require faster computers than stenocaptioners and use prodigious amounts of random access memory (RAM) when processing continuous speech in realtime. While stenocaptioners can purchase a middle-of-the-line computer and be perfectly comfortable with it, voice writers should invest in a fast processor—even a dual processor—and the maximum feasible amount of RAM.

Language Issues

One area where voice writing has an advantage over stenocaptioning at this time is non-English languages. Steno theories have been developing in the U.S. for a century—computerized theories for decades. Voice writing, by comparison, is quite new. Although a great deal of research and development money is poured into speech recognition every year, most of the applications have different requirements than voice writing, and only recently has the focus of that development turned to realtime.

Realtime translation of steno writing in other languages, on the other hand, has received far less R&D money and effort. There is a relatively small number of stenocaptioners in North America that can write clean, accurate realtime in Spanish or French, and there are none that I'm aware of writing in languages like Chinese or Japanese.

Speech recognition research in these languages, however, has been extensive, and it's much easier to adapt a speech recognition system to a new language than to adapt steno theory to a new language.

This means that voice writing for non-English languages is likely to gain acceptance faster, as there are fewer available alternatives. Indeed, several of the aforementioned systems have multilingual capabilities already. AudioScribe is focusing on markets requiring the Spanish and Italian languages. Voice to Text has already translated not only the speech engine, but the entire ISIS user interface (UI) into Spanish, allowing users to switch between Spanish and English in the UI and the speech engine independently.

Lag Times

When a sound is transformed into caption text, it must be processed and recognized by the captioner, entered into the computer either by steno or speech, processed by the computer, output as caption data, encoded into the VBI, broadcast, decoded, and then displayed.

There are many factors that can affect the transcription speed, but three seconds is a fairly good average approximation for stenocaptioners.

When I first began researching speech-based captioning systems in the 1990s, I tried out a product at the National Association of Broadcasters (NAB) convention from a company called Blue Feather. Understandably, the accuracy was significantly impaired by the environment, so I ignored the accuracy of the text. What I found shocking and utterly unacceptable was the lag time. After a word was spoken into the microphone, an average of over 20 seconds passed before it appeared on the screen as a caption. When speaking quickly, I timed lags as high as 40 seconds. With today's fast-paced news shows, an entire story could be missed going into a commercial.

Thankfully, that problem has been dealt with in modern systems, where the lag time is comparable to stenocaptioning. When dictation begins, there may be an additional couple of seconds of delay as the system "gets its bearings," but after a moment it will settle in and stay several words back in the translation—just far enough to have contextual clues to aid recognition.

The Training Process

Before a new voice writer can begin work, both the person and the speech recognition engine must undergo training—which begins with a "getting to know you" process.

The aspiring voice writer takes microphone in hand (or desk stand, or mask) and begins dictating prepared material that is presented by the speech recognition program. This material varies, but generally includes some general text and some carefully designed tongue twisters.

Since the system knows in advance what will be said, it can match the voice to what it expects and begin to tune itself to the individual speaker. With early systems, certain types of voices were harder to pick up than others. I was told repeatedly in the mid-90s that deeper voices like mine were harder to recognize than higher-pitched voices and that the systems had an easier time with women than men. Modern systems, however, seem to have eliminated that problem, and speech recognition specialists I've spoken to in the last year report little or no difference in recognition quality between the genders.

When you first pick up the mike, the system's accuracy is generally quite low—80% to 90% is common. As you go through the initial training, accuracy improves rather quickly, until a plateau is reached, at which point it's time for the next phase. Typically, the plateau is reached during the first day of training, but sometimes a steady increase can be seen for some time afterwards as the system becomes more and more familiar with your voice.

Since people tend to pronounce words differently when speaking more quickly or more slowly, it is important to train the system at typical speaking speeds. Bouck feels that the highest accuracy levels are in a window between 150 and 225 wpm. Speaking either faster or slower will cause the accuracy to decrease.

Training the Speaker

Once the speech engine has been partially trained to understand you, you need to start adjusting your speech patterns for the speech engine. If there are words that are consistently mistranslated, you'll need to pronounce them a bit differently, enunciate them more carefully, or be more careful about not slurring them into the next word.

This is a process that will continue throughout a voice writer's entire career. Just as stenocaptioners watch for common errors and adjust their writing style to eliminate them, voice writers keep an eye on their transcription accuracy and tune themselves to the system even as the system tunes itself to them.

Building Vocabulary

Speech engines come with significant vocabularies of 100,000 to 250,000 words. As large as they are, they are still generic. A captioner doing local newscasts must add a plethora of terminology to the vocabulary, including names of towns and districts, prominent people, geographic features, streets, and local businesses.

Like voice training, vocabulary building will continue as long as the voice writer works. New words and phrases are constantly added to our language, and new people come into prominence.

No matter how much time and effort a voice writer spends on preparation, there is bound to come a situation where a new word comes up in the middle of a broadcast or event. A stenocaptioner would simply use a fingerspelling alphabet to write out the new word, as explained in Chapter 11 (Realtime Stenocaptioning). It works much the same way with voice writers.

Voice writers develop ways of spelling words out loud that are recognized by the captioning system. They can also enter words into the dictionary as they work. This process is difficult for stenocaptioners, as both hands are occupied with the steno keyboard, but voice writers have both hands free while dictating, allowing them to type in new vocabulary using the QWERTY keyboard. Voice writers, however, generally have to add their new words during breaks, as it often involves temporarily shutting down realtime input. They can, however, use other methods for temporarily adding words, such as a voice macro that calls forth the text definition for recent untranslates.

Dealing with Homonyms

Voice writing software includes sophisticated contextual analysis to resolve homonym issues. Sometimes, however, there are words that the system just can't identify reliably, just like conflicts for a stenocaptioner.

One way for voice writers to resolve these manually is to pronounce one of the words differently. To the speech engine, one of them becomes a completely different word. This solution is clean and reliable, but it requires the voice writer to change how they say a word. This is a difficult thing to accomplish, as anyone who has moved to a different part of the country knows. Accents and subtleties of pronunciation tend to stick with us.

According to Bouck, this is becoming less and less of a problem. When asked about homonyms, he said,

> The newer versions of the speech engines are hugely superior to the ones I began on when it comes to correctly distinguishing between homonyms. Vocabulary building does much to resolve the problem also. I do not pronounce them differently unless I see a problem occurring repeatedly during a particular realtime session, but I would say that the software and vocabulary building apply them correctly over 90 percent of the time.

Linda Drake, 2003 president of NVRA, agrees. She said there are very few cases where she has to modify the pronunciation of a word to fix a homonym. Frequently, she uses phrasing instead. Combinations of words become a single entry in the vocabulary, with the correctly spelled homonym as part of the group. It can take longer to enter the numerous combinations and variations that may come up, but since it doesn't require a change in how the voice writer speaks, the dictation process itself doesn't have to change.

Punctuation and Speaker Identification

Voice writers do not simply "parrot" exactly what they hear. They must process it and add additional information. Each punctuation mark must be inserted, using a spoken code word. It is not enough to caption what is said: it is also important to note who said it.

Speaker identification is handled by voice writers in much the same way it is handled by stenocaptioners. Instead of stroking a particular combination of keys to form a steno symbol representing a particular speaker, the voice writer uses a spoken combination of sounds, a "voice symbol," if you will.

Prior to a particular event or broadcast, a voice writer will find out who the primary speakers are and use the captioning software to assign the voice symbols for first speaker, second speaker, and so on, to actual names. In some cases, special voice symbols will be created to represent specific individuals.

It is not the symbol itself that is critical, but the voice writer's ability to remember it, and say it so that it can't be confused with another word or phrase. Having a speaker identification appear instead as a word is much more confusing to the viewer than a simple substitution of one word for another.

Speech Recognition Engines

For speech recognition to gain wide acceptance, it must be implemented in a wide variety of systems and situations. To this end, companies that have developed speech recognition software offer their products two ways.

- **Consumer products** are designed for speech recognition neophytes to plug in and run. They may include only the speech recognition software itself, with the ability to feed its results into other programs, or include full-blown applications of their own, such as word processors.

- **Speech engines** include only the code for the core speech recognition functions themselves, along with an application programming interface (API) that can be used by computer programmers to tightly integrate the speech recognition functionality into their own code.

There are speech-based captioning systems that use both types of products, and both have their advantages. By using the consumer product for input, a voice writing system keeps itself isolated from the specific speech recognition company. If they need to switch vendors, or if a new technological advance comes along, they can easily adapt to it.

Using the speech engine's API directly, however, makes for faster and more efficient processing of realtime text at the expense of being tied to a particular vendor. The output from the speech engine is handed directly to the captioning system—along with some useful parametric information not available from consumer applications—without having to go through several layers of operating system buffering. Microsoft Windows, for example, allows one program to feed text to another through a well-defined system, but it carries significant overhead.

The two most commonly used speech recognition engines as of this writing are IBM ViaVoice and Dragon NaturallySpeaking. Both have their adherents and detractors in the voice world, but the majority of voice writers would find it difficult or impossible to tell which one is at the heart of any given captioning system.

Most of the limiting factors of a voice writing system are in the speech engine and the computer hardware, both of which are used by multiple vendors. If there is a breakthrough in speech recognition or personal computer technology, it is likely to be adopted by all of the captioning software companies at virtually the same time. This means that, with some exceptions, the differences between systems are centered more around usability and non-realtime features than they are around the actual accuracy of the speech recognition.

History of Voice Writing

Voice writing, previously known as Stenomask reporting, was originally developed by a court reporter and it had nothing to do with speech recognition systems.

In the days before computer-aided transcription (CAT), court reporting was traditionally a multi-step process. First, a court reporter would take down the proceedings. The reporter might use pen shorthand (either the Gregg or the Pittman system) or a shorthand ("steno") machine. At the end of the day, the result was a stack of paper unintelligible to all but other court reporters on the same system.

The next phase of the process consisted of the court reporter dictating those notes into a tape recorder, carefully enunciating the words and inserting all appropriate punctuation. These tapes were sent to a transcriber, who used a tape recorder with a start/stop foot pedal and typed out what had been dictated. Later advances in technology included tape recorders that could slow down the voice without dramatically affecting the pitch, which meant a fast typist required less starting and stopping of the tape.

Still, the process required several hours of dictating and transcribing for every hour spent in the courtroom or deposition suite.

In the 1940s, a Gregg shorthand reporter in Chicago by the name of Horace Webb thought that there had to be a way to eliminate some of that required time. His goal was to dictate into the tape recorder during the proceedings themselves, eliminating the shorthand step entirely.

The sound of someone echoing every word you say can be very distracting. Webb obviously couldn't just sit in the room with a microphone and speak, or he would disrupt proceedings. So Webb set forth to figure a way to mask the sound of his voice without affecting the quality of the recording.

He tried a variety of "Stenomasks," ranging from cigar boxes to tin cans, and all of them had the same problems. The microphone would be picking up the dictation clearly and accurately until Webb wrapped something around it, at which point the recording turned completely unintelligible. On top of that, the sound of his voice wasn't well silenced outside the "Stenomask" either.

As we've heard from many other inventors, Webb went to an expert—an acoustical engineer— who told him that the problem was unsolvable. The sound would always bounce around inside the mask and the echoes would distort the sound to the point of making it unusable. Webb didn't understand the technical explanation he was given, so he went back to work trying to solve the problem.

He noticed that when the mike was at the far end of the mask, the recording was total gibberish. As the mike was moved closer and closer to his lips, the recording quality improved. When it was almost touching his lips, he could almost understand the recording. A couple of years into the process by now, Webb continued experimenting, and found that the quality improved still more when some rags were stuffed into the bottom of the mask.

The rags were the key to the process. By baffling the sound, they prevented the echoes that were distorting the recordings beyond recognition. The sound of his voice would hit the mike only once, and then be absorbed by his baffling, which served the dual purpose of making it nearly inaudible to other people in the room. He thought of this as providing a "tortuous path" for the sound from his lips to the outside of the mask.

Excited now that he was getting close, Webb bought a rubber facepiece that had originally been designed for the Air Force, and a Royal Chef coffeepot that looked like the right shape. He removed the handle from the coffeepot, reshaped it, attached the facepiece and microphone, and looked for appropriate baffling material. Finally, he found what he referred to as a "sanitary disposable tortuous path," and the first Stenomask was born.

Webb's first real-life test of the device was in Senate committee hearings, where he determined that the process worked, but acceptance was glacially slow. Webb and his partner, Harold Steinman, incorporated, trademarked the name Stenomask, and set up a machine shop to produce masks. They hired a machinist named Frank Kenny who was unfamiliar with court reporting, but learned the process as he worked on manufacturing for them.

At the height of World War II, Kenny was drafted into the Navy and went to sea. When his ship was in for repairs in Rhode Island, he met a base executive officer named Captain Mott, who had been directed by the Navy to research court reporting methods and recommend one for the navy to adopt. Kenny told him about the Stenomask and set up a meeting between Mott and Webb. The Navy ended up adopting the Stenomask as its court reporting system of choice.

The base technology of Stenomask reporting changed little over the next few decades. Digital tape recorders improved quality and made typing of the dictation easier. Mask designs were improved. But the core system remained the same until two other factors converged to provide the next advance.

Speech recognition technology is nothing new. Engineers have been working on it for decades. The biggest challenge they faced, however, was continuous speech recognition.

Fast computers could pick up isolated groups of phonemes and assemble them into words that were recognized with reasonable accuracy in the late 80s and early 90s. By that time, telephone companies were already introducing speech recognition in their systems in limited form ("Press zero or say 'yes' to accept the charges"). But this is a very different problem from understanding normal human speech, where words are run together, often eliminating entire sounds or syllables.

An analysis algorithm known as the Hidden Markov Model (HMM) had been introduced to speech recognition research by then and was showing great promise. As continuous speech recognition systems improved, however, they were limited by the available processing power of the day's computers. Even with hardware accelerators performing specialized calculations, it required either multi-CPU parallel processing systems or computers much too large for a court reporter to carry around.

At the same time, however, computers were becoming simultaneously faster and less expensive. Gordon Moore, co-founder of Intel, observed in 1965 that the density of integrated circuits was doubling every year, allowing twice as many transistors as the year before. He predicted that the trend would continue into the foreseeable future, and his prophecy became known as "Moore's Law." Although the doubling period has slowed to about 18 months rather than a year, it has indeed held, and it is this increase in circuit density that has been largely responsible for driving the size and price of computers down over the years while simultaneously driving the speed up.

In the late 1990s, improvements in speech recognition technology, coupled with fast, powerful personal computers, made realtime translation for Stenomask reporters feasible. The technology was renamed voice writing, and companies began designing systems around it. NVRA designed the Realtime Verbatim Reporter (RVR) certification, and in 1999, Jim Bouck became the first certified RVR.

Where will it go from here? In the court reporting field, states that have traditionally allowed only pen and machine-based reporters are experimenting with voice writer certifications. Many states already use voice writers as court reporters.

Most of the voice writers working in the captioning field today (including nearly half of the RVRs as of this writing) are using their skills to create the scripts for offline captioning systems. While many voice writers have expressed interest in realtime captioning, little is being done. That should change in the future. As the huge demand for captioning creates more and more jobs in the field, both steno-based and voice-based court reporters are being drawn to make the switchover.

13 OFFLINE AND NONLINEAR CAPTIONING

Online and offline captioning are as different as live and prerecorded television programs. Offline captioning provides time to hand-craft, research, synchronize, position, and format the captions. Typically, online (realtime) captions are provided as roll-up text with minimal formatting, and they change position only to keep from covering important information on the screen. Offline captions, on the other hand, are typically pop-on, with speaker identification implied by the position.

Linear vs. Nonlinear

Traditional linear offline captioning, using external videotape recorders (VTRs) synchronized to the software by timecodes, is being replaced by nonlinear captioning, just as tape-based video editing systems are becoming less common.

In both cases, the captioner is rarely working with original video.

Linear offline captioners are typically provided with a timecoded dub on VHS, SVHS, or ¾" U-Matic tape. Even though the tape has SMPTE timecodes in VITC or LTC format—see Chapter 15 (Caption Timing) for details—captioners often request that the timecode be burned into the video as well, so that it shows up in the corner of the screen.

Once the captioning is completed, only the caption file need be sent to the video producer. The producer can make a new captioned master or submaster using encoding software or a hardware encoder capable of reading the timecoded captions. This task is often handed off to duplication facilities, where there is equipment capable of dealing with just about any video format.

With nonlinear captioning, the process is similar, except that the timecoded dub is actually a video file in MPEG (or similar) format. Since it's a digital file, the video can be sent to the captioner through the Internet or a wide-area network (WAN) in far less time than it takes to overnight a tape.

The final encoding dub step can be skipped with direct-to-air encoding systems, where the captioning software is connected to an encoder at broadcast time and the captions are added as the show is broadcast. There is no generational loss with this approach, and there is no captioned master tape produced.

Final encoding is also eliminated as a final step when captioning material that's being edited in a nonlinear editing (NLE) system. The captions can be added to the video during the process of cutting the master tape from an Avid system. The same applies with the MacCaption system, seen in figure 13-1, which generates line 21 as the video is output from the Macintosh.

Figure 13-1: The MacCaption Nonlinear System

The screen layout of MacCaption shows elements common to all nonlinear captioning systems. The video display on the screen has What-You-See-Is-What-You-Get (WYSIWYG) captioning on it, or near-WYSIWYG in this case. In the video display in figure 13-1, the mandatory space at the beginning and end of each row of a line 21 caption isn't shown. This problem shows up on quite a few nonlinear captioning systems.

All systems show the captions, as figure 13-1 shows down the right side of the screen, although the position varies, and the type of information shown varies. In this example, you see the caption text along with a display time (in-time) and a set of editing buttons. Other systems show reading rate information, erase times (out-times), position, format, and various other pertinent data. Some, like MacCaption, show this extra information only for the current caption. Others show it for all captions.

The current timecode in the video is always shown somewhere on the screen, as is the current caption number. Systems vary widely in how much video control is shown and how many functions are placed in toolbars versus menus. This is configurable in many of the systems, allowing them to be tailored to each user's preference.

System Configurations

Analog offline captioning systems require different types of equipment depending on the software vendor. Figure 13-2 shows a typical configuration.

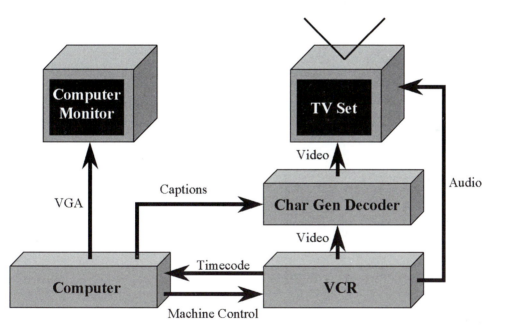

Figure 13-2: Typical Analog Offline Captioning System Configuration

The TV set is used to view the video, with captions generated by the character generator decoder. Audio runs straight from the VCR to the TV (or possibly to headphones—common in office environments). The computer receives the timecodes from the VCR either on a video line (for VITC) or an audio line (for LTC).

There are many variations on the theme. For example, the CAPtivator Offline software from Cheetah International uses a video card in the computer that allows the video to be displayed on the TV screen with simulated WYSIWYG captions, much as most nonlinear systems do. This means the TV and character generator decoder are not required, except for producing a check tape or checking fine positioning decisions.

For tape decks with integrated timecode controllers, the single machine control line can be used for transmitting timecodes to the computer as well.

Hardware configurations are much simpler with nonlinear captioning systems, where the video digitizing, caption editing, and caption encoding typically happen on three different systems.

The caption editing system itself often consists of nothing more than a Windows or Macintosh computer. No external equipment is required at all.

VTR Control

Strictly speaking, an analog offline captioning system doesn't need VTR control at all. With the VTR sitting on the desk, captioners can reach up to its control panel or use a remote jog/shuttle control to run the deck, and the computer can read the timecodes to figure out where the tape is positioned.

Computer control over the VTR allows for capabilities like "back up and play," where the play button rewinds a couple of seconds first to allow the sound to come up and the captioner to hear an entire sentence or utterance. Similarly, with VTR control, a captioner can select a caption and tell the VTR to seek to that caption's display time.

For those more comfortable with a jog/shuttle control or foot pedal than they are with a keyboard or mouse, there are external controls available that can be attached to the PC, and a number of captioning systems allow them as alternate user interface devices.

File Manipulation

Importing Captions

The first task an offline captioner is faced with is producing a transcript. Often, even if a script is provided, it is outdated—not reflecting the final edits to the video. Most of the time, no script is available.

All captioning systems allow users to type captions directly into the program, either splitting them appropriately as you go or allowing the computer to do it. Most, however, offer alternate ways of producing the text.

Several systems allow for direct connection to speech recognition engines like IBM ViaVoice or Dragon NaturallySpeaking. Others allow importing captions in a variety of formats, allowing users to do their word processing wherever they're most comfortable, in programs like Microsoft Word or Star Office.

```
*DropFrame
*WIDTH 32

** Caption Number 1
*PopOn
*T 00:00:00:03
*BottomUp
*F1  *C1
*Cf16
He's got a huge list of credits
I gotta go through.\E

** Caption Number 2
*T 00:00:01:21
Let me think.
Okay-what is it?\E

** Caption Number 3
*T 00:00:03:03
He's from Ottowa:
\AI\B.J. Woodbury\E

** Caption Number 4
*T 00:00:06:09
\AI\[clapping & cheering]\E

** Caption Number 5
*T 00:00:22:09
I don't know, eh?\E

** Caption Number 6
*T 00:00:31:15
*E 00:00:37:18
How is everyone today?\E
```

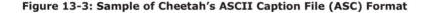

Figure 13-3: Sample of Cheetah's ASCII Caption File (ASC) Format

Importing from other captioning systems is an equally important capability. Although early caption formats were zealously guarded by their developers, some were documented and distributed, and developed into de facto standards. Cheetah Systems (now Cheetah International), provided both a proprietary native (binary) file format and a human-readable format which was fully documented in the user guide. Many systems have the ability to import and export that format, shown in figure 13-3, which is a file generated by the CAPtivator Offline system.

Any lines in a Cheetah ASCII caption file (called an ASC file, since they typically have a file extension of .asc, as opposed to the native binary .cap files) that begin with two asterisks, such as the "Caption Number" lines in figure 13-3, are comments, and are not necessary to file interpreters. The export function provides them only as a reference. The start of a new caption is indicated by a timecode.

It's a good idea to start each file with comment lines explaining what it is, when it was created, and what captioning software it was created by.

Lines in an ASC file that begin with one asterisk, like the first two lines in the sample file, are commands. The most common commands in this file format are shown in table 13-1.

Lines that begin with anything other than an asterisk are caption text.

Text in an ASC file may have embedded attributes, which are enclosed in backslashes and start with the letter A. Attributes include italic and underline (\AI\ and \AU\, respectively), and specifications for the seven allowable colors in line 21.

Position codes, alignments, field numbers, and channel numbers all apply until changed, so each caption requires only the information that's different from the previous one.

Table 13-1: Common Commands in Cheetah's ASCII Caption File (ASC) Format

Command	Description
*DropFrame *NoDropFrame	Sets the SMPTE timing standard for the file. These are explained in Chapter 15 (Caption Timing).
*Width	Sets the caption width in columns.
*PopOn *PaintOn *RollUp	Sets the style of all captions following the command.
*T hh:mm:ss:ff	Sets the display time ("in time") for the caption, in hours, minutes, seconds, and frames.
*E hh:mm:ss:ff	Sets the erase time ("out time") for the caption. Specifying erase times is optional. If omitted, this caption will be erased when the next one is displayed.
(position code)	These set the position for all captions until another position code is specified. Position codes begin with L, R, W, C, Q, or S to set the alignment (explained in table 13-2), followed by a one-character row number from 1 to f (the top nine rows on the screen are numbered 0-9, and the bottom six are numbered a-f), followed by a two-digit column number. The *Cf16 in figure 13-3 means "centered around column 16 on the bottom line of the screen."
*BottomUp *TopDown	These specify the direction the caption builds from the base row. If the position code says row 4, a 3-line bottom-up caption would occupy rows 2, 3, and 4, while a top-down caption would occupy rows 5, 6, and 7.
*F	Specifies the target field number. Valid options are *F1 and *F2.
*C	Specifies the target data channel. *F1 *C1 is CC1. *F2 *C2 is CC4.

The ASC file format is neither as flexible nor as comprehensive as file formats like SAMI, SMIL, and RealText, but it has all of the requirements for line 21 captioning and is widely understood by captioning software of all kinds.

Table 13-2: Alignment Codes in Cheetah's ASCII Caption File (ASC) Format

Alignment	Description
L (left)	All rows have their first character in the specified column.
R (right)	All rows have their last character in the specified column.
C (centered)	All rows are centered around the specified column.
W (widest right)	The caption rows are left-justified with respect to each other, with the last character of the widest row in the specified column.
Q (centered left)	The caption rows are left-justified with respect to each other, with the middle character of the widest row in the specified column.
S (scattered)	Each row has its own position code.

Reverse engineering file formats is generally not an overly daunting task, and several of the offline systems have extensive menus of competitors' file formats that they can read. When captioning a revision to a video that was originally captioned by someone else, it's a great help to be able to read their caption data files.

Splitting

When typing a script into a word processor, most captioners do not bother dividing it up into captions. That's a process better suited to the captioning program, most of which can automate the process at least partially.

Although there are no codified hard and fast rules for caption division, there are general guidelines for the programs—and the people—to use.

- Always try to split at the end of a sentence. Ideally, one sentence = one caption, but many sentences are longer than will fit in a caption.

- Never split after an article or a preposition. "Go get the/big wrench," is a bad split. It should be "Go get/the big wrench," even though that makes one line longer than the other. Similarly, don't break a caption as "Give it to/Mr. Smith." Instead, break it as "Give it/to Mr. Smith."

- Never put two sentences in the same caption unless they're extremely short. It's okay to have, "Hello? You there?" in one caption.

- Do not separate a title from a name or an adjective from its noun. Don't write a caption as "I think Mr./Smith did it," but as "I think/Mr. Smith did it."

- Try to keep line lengths reasonably consistent.

- Shoot for two lines per caption. One or three is okay when you have to. Four line captions should be avoided.

Some of the systems allow you to train their caption splitting programs, defining more rules so that less of the work must be done manually. For more on this subject, see Chapter 15 (Caption Timing).

Capture with Timecodes

Sometimes a tape needs to be edited and recaptioned, and the original caption file is unavailable. Most captioning systems allow you to connect a data recovery decoder, which is described in Chapter 9 (Decoding Equipment).

The captioning program can then import the captions, complete with timing, positioning, and formatting information, directly off the tape. After the editing is performed, the captions can be adjusted to match the video edits and encoded back onto the new master. This dramatically reduces the amount of time required to recaption a show.

Editing

The core of any offline captioning system is its caption editing. The approaches to editing captions are quite different between vendors, and no one approach is better for all users. Some people are very comfortable with mouse-intensive systems, and some prefer editing from a keyboard. Some like toolbars and some don't. Looking at the various systems, it's clear that some user interfaces focus on the video, while others focus on a caption editing area.

WYSIWYG Displays

As mentioned earlier in the chapter, all of the nonlinear captioning systems and several of the linear systems offer video display on the computer screen. The captions are shown superimposed on the video as a caption decoder will render them in the final video.

The primary objective of a WYSIWYG (what you see is what you get) display is to let you see what parts of the video will be covered by the caption, and whether the positioning is appropriate to indicate speaker identification. This must be absolutely accurate to be useful.

A couple of systems also have the option of displaying a rectangle indicating the boundaries of the safe title area, which is described in detail in Chapter 7 (Line 21 Technical Details). This provides a quick and easy visual check on the boundaries of caption positioning.

There is a difference, too, between having an editing area somewhere on the screen and a separate WYSIWYG display compared to editing directly *in* the WYSIWYG display. This is not a common feature, but it does allow users to focus their attention on one place rather than looking back and forth between the editing area and the WYSIWYG display (which is also sometimes called the preview window).

Caption Positioning

There are a lot of possible ways to position a caption. Early systems relied heavily on typed position codes, but these are rarely used today. Instead, formats are defined that specify position and alignment for the caption (e.g., left justified starting on row 2 at column 4). Toolbar buttons for changing alignment and position are common features on the editing screens of offline captioning systems.

Once a caption has been placed, there are different approaches to moving it or tweaking the position. The most intuitive is drag and drop. Users of modern graphical user interface (GUI) systems have grown accustomed to moving objects around on the screen by selecting them and dragging them using the mouse, and captions are no different. They must, of course, snap to the allowable positioning grid when dragged.

Another approach is to tweak positioning using keys that move the caption up, down, left, or right by one position. People who like to edit using the keyboard rather than the mouse can be quite efficient with keys like this.

Back Up and Play

When testing caption timing, or transcribing directly into the captioning system, users frequently find themselves backing the video up a second or two before starting it playing again. To ease this process, several systems offer a single key/button/command that backs up by a preset amount and starts playing.

Block Cut and Paste

Every captioning system allows you to select text and copy it, and then paste it in a different part of the file—or even in a different application. Cut & paste across programs is a powerful tool, and being able to select a block of text in Microsoft Word and paste it into your captioning software can come in very handy. The handling of such pasted text varies widely between systems.

It's also important to be able to select a block of captions and cut or copy it. You may, for example, caption the theme song at the beginning of a show, and find it repeated at the end.

Adjusting Caption Breaks

Whether caption breaks were generated automatically by the system during an import process, or the captioner typed the captions that way, tweaking caption breaks takes up a lot of time. All systems allow basic adjustments, like joining two captions together or splitting a caption in two at a designated point.

Each system has a different approach to tweaking caption breaks, however. Figure 13-4 shows the caption edit area of a CPC CaptionMaker system. Note the editing icons near the middle of the picture.

#	Start	H	V	J	Display	U	D	C	E	A	Caption/Subtitle
1	01:00:00:00	C	B	L	Pop-On	▲	▼	I◀I	II▶	⟳	
2	01:00:01:14	L	B	L	Pop-On	▲	▼	I◀I	II▶	⟳	¿Puedes creerlo, Rose?
3	01:00:03:03	L	B	L	Pop-On	▲	▼	I◀I	II▶	⟳	En verdad vamos a ver el programa
4	01:00:04:24	L	B	L	Pop-On	▲	▼	I◀I	II▶	⟳	"Charlas de Comestibles" en vivo.
5	01:00:06:23	L	B	L	Pop-On	▲	▼	I◀I	II▶	⟳	¡No puedo creer que hayas conseguido entradas!
6	01:00:09:07	R	B	L	Pop-On	▲	▼	I◀I	II▶	⟳	Es que me hijo está saliendo conla asistente
7	01:00:11:01	R	B	L	Pop-On	▲	▼	I◀I	II▶	⟳	del productor.
8	01:00:12:07	L	B	L	Pop-On	▲	▼	I◀I	II▶	⟳	¿Conoce él a mary?
9	01:00:13:24	R	B	L	Pop-On	▲	▼	I◀I	II▶	⟳	Pues claro.
10	01:00:17:00	C	B	L	Pop-On	▲	▼	I◀I	II▶	⟳	

Figure 13-4: Caption Editing in a CPC CaptionMaker System

The triangle icons under the U and D headings push the first word of the caption up to the previous caption, or push the last word down to the next caption, respectively. For anyone editing with a mouse, this is quicker than selecting and dragging, cutting and pasting, or splitting and joining. For those more comfortable editing with the keyboard, other systems may be more convenient.

Similarly, the icon under the C heading squares up a caption that has uneven line lengths, moving words between rows according to predefined rules.

Validation

Once the captions have been created, they must be checked. There are automated tools for a variety of validation methods, but many captioning firms still believe in the final check of just watching the captioned video to see how it feels.

There are two significantly different approaches to validation. Some systems make it a separate step, performed after captioning is complete (or any time you wish). Others let validation run all the time as a background process, flagging captions with errors. A few give you the option of doing it either way.

Spelling Checkers

Almost every application you can type text into has a spelling checker these days. Offline captioning systems are no exception. Ideally, a spelling checker in a captioning system should allow for multiple user dictionaries. This way, all of the special words pertaining to a particular show or series can be saved together and given to another captioner working on a different episode.

With the growing trend toward internationalization, spellcheck dictionaries should be available in languages other than just U.S. English. Shows distributed to other English-speaking countries may have the captions rechecked for British spellings, and captioning in Spanish and French is growing more common.

Timing Validation

Timing validation is typically done on the fly, with each caption showing an error flag if the timing is out of spec.

The most common timing error is insufficient build-up time. Captioning systems must be constantly aware of what overhead will be generated when the caption is converted to line 21 format. A dense three-line caption may have to start transmitting a couple of seconds before its scheduled display time, which isn't possible if there's another caption being built and displayed at that time.

Although shot change detection is becoming more sophisticated, systems don't yet check for synchronization of captions to shot changes during the validation process. This is something that needs to be checked manually.

Reading Rate Validation

Reading rates, which are discussed in Chapters 3 (Captioning Styles and Conventions) and 15 (Caption Timing), are handled very differently by different captioning companies.

Whether captions are presented verbatim or edited, there are still ways to adjust reading rates by splitting, combining, and retiming captions. Most offline systems have a way of showing reading rates (see figures 15-2 and 15-3 for examples) and alerting captioners to out-of-spec timing.

Style Validation

Caption style is highly subjective and hard for a computer to verify. There are rules that can be checked, such as basic punctuation rules and multiple adjacent spaces (considered illegal in line 21 captions).

Sometimes, positioning problems can be classified as errors. When a caption is scattered (as opposed to having all of the rows together), there shouldn't be a portion of one row covering a portion of another. Similarly, a paint-on caption shouldn't cover any of the caption that was on the screen right before it—although there are exceptions to this rule.

Some systems analyze caption shapes and alert captioners to problems with skewed captions, which are disallowed by many companies.[1] See figure 13-5 for an example of a skewed caption.

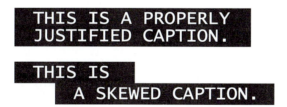

Figure 13-5: Skewed vs. Properly Justified Captions

Other validation ideas have included checking for "jumpy" captions (where positioning constantly moves around the screen), bad caption breaks (splitting a proper name between two captions, for example), and inconsistent capitalization.

---

[1]   According to "Captioning Key: Guidelines and Preferred Techniques," by the Captioned Media Program, the only time a caption should be skewed is when the two lines are identical.

14   Caption Placement Strategies

Placement Objectives

In James Craig's book, *Designing with Type*, he explains an old maxim thus, "The type should be 'invisible,' that is, it should not intrude itself between the reader and the thought expressed on the printed page. This applies especially to sustained reading, such as books, magazines, and newspapers. People are very conservative in their reading habits, regardless of how radical they may be in other areas of their lives. . . ."

This applies equally to closed captioning. After watching a well-captioned show, most people should not be able to tell you how the captions were positioned. If it was done right, the positioning presented the desired subconscious cues without intruding upon the viewer by requiring conscious attention.

Although movement of the captions about the screen is often required due to other factors we'll discuss later in this chapter, such movements should be as minimal and subtle as possible.

Subtitling in the movie theater is traditionally found centered at the bottom of the screen. The position never changes, and the viewer does not have to search the screen, however minimally, to find the subtitles. Although this approach is criticized as being unimaginative, it is functional, which is a good thing.

Ralph Waldo Emerson is frequently quoted as calling consistency the "hobgoblin of little minds." Most of those quoting him are unaware of the full context of that statement: "A *foolish* consistency is the hobgoblin of little minds, adored by little statesmen and philosophers and divines. With consistency a great soul has simply nothing to do"[1] (emphasis mine).

Consistent placement of captions is not a foolish consistency, but a practical one. However much captioners may feel like artists—and captioning has oft been declared more akin to an art than a science—their role is that of interpreter. The director of the video has poured heart and soul into artistic rendering of a story or an idea. The captioner is there to convey that rendering to people unable to hear it.

Relegating captions to a single position such as the standard bottom-of-screen-center used in subtitling causes problems as well as solving them, however, and there are reasons for alternate positioning.

Speaker Identification

There are two primary methods for indicating who is doing the speaking in a captioned TV show. The speaker's name may be inserted into the caption text directly (e.g., "Bob: Hi, Mary"), or the caption positioning may be used as a cue. Examples of both are presented in Chapter 3 (Captioning Styles and Conventions), in figures 3-1 and 3-2.

Theater subtitles usually don't use either method, as they take advantage of an audible cue: subtitle viewers are assumed to be hearing people who just don't happen to understand the language being spoken. It is assumed that they can tell someone different is speaking by the sound of the voice. Since closed captioning is an accessibility tool for deaf and hard-of-hearing people, that cue isn't available.

In roll-up captioning, speaker identification using screen positioning isn't feasible. There is frequently text on-screen from multiple speakers, and the continual reformatting and repositioning of the screen would be so distracting as to render the captioning virtually useless.

It is pop-on, then, where positional speaker identification can be used. The extra unspoken text (the name of the person speaking) can be omitted, and the captions used to present only the dialog.

In keeping with the spirit of consistency and minimal change, captions are generally not positioned directly on or under the person speaking, but rather in a screen position that corresponds to the person's relative on-screen location. In other words, if two people are shown, both of whom are on the right-hand side of the screen, the captions for the leftmost of the two would be shown on the left side of the screen (not under either person) and the other's captions would appear on the right side, under both of them.

---

[1]   From Emerson's essay on self-reliance.

When a third on-screen speaker is added, the three positions become left, right, and center. Some captioners will raise or lower the captions in the center by one row to add one more subtle differentiation, but this is uncommon.

With four or more people speaking, identifying speakers by caption position becomes untenable. Rather than add positions around the middle or top of the screen, most captioners will opt for adding speaker names when identification is important, and identify classes or groups of speakers when it is not (e.g., Bob and Mary on the left, Tom in the center, and Sue and Amy on the right).

The majority of position change from caption to caption is horizontal. Captioning is still generally placed at or near the bottom of the screen whenever possible, with one exception. Off-screen narrators are captioned at the top of the screen and centered. A common, though hardly universal, custom is to italicize captions for off-screen speakers. An italicized, centered, top of screen caption provides the dual visual cues that the speaker is the narrator and that he or she is not visible.

Covering Other Screen Information

Distressingly few camera operators and creative directors are aware of captioning, and those that are give it very little thought when they frame their shots. As a result, captioning must often cover interesting or even critical portions of the image. If captions are consistently presented at the bottom of the screen, they will often cover a football or soccer ball during a game. If they are consistently at the top, we may not see whether the basketball makes it into the basket.

During live events like sports, then, captioners need to select a caption location that will interfere the least, and try to stick with it throughout the entire event. Current sports and news directors make this a challenging proposition. Crawls, statistics, and player names appear frequently at the bottom of the screen, along with "bugs" that are no longer semitransparent logos, but graphic elements in their own right which change size, move, and even make noises.

Placing the captions at the top of the screen keeps them away from the chaos at the bottom, but at the expense of the ubiquitous score boxes that are de rigueur in most sports. This relegates captions to a couple of lines at the top of the screen, pushed left or right to make room for the score box. Unfortunately, even that position isn't always available, as some broadcasters have taken to moving the score box from corner to corner as an indication of which team has possession of the ball.

Realtime captioners, then, are left with the unenviable position of having to make sure the captions do not cover anything, while not bouncing them all over the screen like a modern-day pong game. They are often saved the agony of dealing with this thorny question due to mandates from the broadcaster or the captioning company. Typically, an uneasy truce is reached between consistency and leaving key information unobscured, where the captions are moved every few minutes as the score box appears, disappears, or changes positions, and left in place at all other times, even if something is covered.

With pop-on captioning, the challenge is not so intense—except perhaps in commercials. Typically, only a slight vertical shift of the captions is required to push them clear of screen images that they might obscure, and a jump of one or two row positions isn't egregious.

Indicating Repeated Text

When a character repeats a line exactly, the caption can't simply be repeated. Even if there is a discernable flicker between one caption and the next,[2] it simply isn't obvious that the words have been uttered again.

One common solution is to repeat the caption, but move it slightly—typically up or down one row. The movement of the caption draws the eye back to it, and viewers will naturally read it again as a new caption. Another alternative is to place the text twice in one caption, offsetting the second line slightly to make it clear that it's an intentional repeat, as shown in figure 14-1.

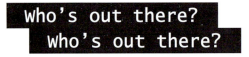

Figure 14-1: Captioning a Repeated Phrase

When there is a change in tone between the two lines (e.g., the character shouts the second time), one can be italicized for emphasis as well, further clarifying that the line was repeated.

Dealing with Air-Time Graphics and Crawls

Imagine a show that has been carefully and precisely captioned. All captions have been painstakingly arranged on the screen for maximum effectiveness. The show is broadcast on election night, and in the middle of it, the TV station drops a crawl on the screen announcing the availability of election results after the show.

Crawls are typically placed at the bottom of the screen. As we've just discussed, captions are as well. Which covers which?

---

[2]   Generally, such a flicker is not visible, although captioners can opt to include codes that cause a one-frame flicker if they wish to add an additional visual cue that a caption has changed. This process is described in Chapter 7 (Line 21 Technical Details).

By the time a video signal is broadcast, a crawl is just part of the picture. It cannot be removed, shy of writing something else over the top of it. The captions, on the other hand, are still closed. Hidden in line 21 in the VBI, they await a decoder to make them visible. When displayed, they will cover everything underneath them, including the crawl.

Even if the crawl contains information that is of no interest to a particular viewer, it will be distracting, as it moves by under the captions, revealed in small bits and pieces. The captions were added to the program long before air time, so moving them is a problem.

Several encoder manufacturers have stepped forth with solutions to this problem. These "bridges," described in Chapter 8 (Encoding Equipment), are capable of keeping video editing equipment from destroying preexisting captions, and also of relocating captions to keep them clear of air-time crawls.

Pushing the captions up out of the way of the crawl may cause them to cover something else on the screen, but the relocation capabilities of caption bridges make them required tools for any broadcaster that adds information to the picture at air time.

Historical Considerations

The display area of a line 21 caption decoder is 15 rows high and 32 columns wide, as shown in figure 7-2. Captions can be placed anywhere within that grid, as long as they line up perfectly on row/column boundaries. It hasn't always been this way.

In the days of the original TeleCaption I decoder, memory was frightfully expensive, and the manufacturer was loath to spend money on anything beyond the bare minimum required. Thus, it was decided that captions could be placed anywhere on the top four and bottom four rows of the screen only. The middle 7 rows became an uninhabitable caption wasteland, where no text could be placed.

When the FCC implemented decoder standards following implementation of the Television Decoder Circuitry Act, this restriction was lifted. For years afterward, caption software had to have compatibility modes that could make captions appear in a desired mid-screen position on a modern decoder, but still remain legible and be placed logically on a TeleCaption I or II.

As clever and creative as the compatibility methods were, they are no longer necessary. As of 2002, support for these older encoders is no longer required and captioners are free to place captions anywhere they desire on the screen.

For those with a historical interest in the operation of the compatibility mode, it centered upon a core decoder design criterion: when the decoder receives data it does not recognize or cannot process, that data should be ignored. Thus, if a caption was intended to appear on row 5, the captioning software would first send a preamble address code (PAC) instructing the decoder to place it on row 4. Both old and new decoders would recognize the command and position the cursor accordingly. Then, the captioning software would send a PAC moving the caption to row 5. New decoders would obey, placing the caption where it belonged. Old decoders wouldn't recognize row 5 as a component of a valid PAC and would leave the cursor where it was.

For a two-line caption on rows 6 and 7, the first line would receive PACs for rows 3 and 6, and the second line for rows 4 and 7. This system, though it dealt with most situations, could not handle a multiline caption that spanned the border between the no-man's-land in the middle of the screen and the old valid locations at top and bottom.

To see why, picture a caption to be placed on rows 4 (valid in all decoders) and 5 (valid only in new decoders). If the double-PAC approach is used, transmitting the "old" row followed by the "new" row, the first line would have PACs for rows 3 and 4, and the second would have PACs for rows 4 and 5. The problem is that the second PAC would be rejected for line 2, but accepted for line 1, placing both caption lines on row 4.

Nonbroadcast Options

Caption positioning is a different issue when captioning streaming media on the Internet. Since the captions don't overlay the video—see figures 19-2 and 19-11—captioners need not be concerned about covering anything. This provides better control and consistency when captions are placed beneath the video. Conventions of positioning to indicate speaker identification can still be followed.

Placing captions above the video for an off-screen narrator, however, is a difficult task; an impossible one in some cases.

Despite this loss of flexibility, captioners of streaming media are offered many new options. One is the speaker ID window pane shown in figure 19-2. Even though the illustrations don't show this structure in the RealOne player, it can be duplicated there as well. This provides a constant reminder of who the current speaker is, and requires no video real estate, nor does it impede available bandwidth.

Line 21 captioners are severely limited in their use of color. There are seven foreground colors available: white, cyan, magenta, yellow, red, blue, and green. The NTSC color-encoding system tends to smear areas of high-saturation red, especially on older televisions. This can lead to streaky, hard-to-read captions, so use of red is strongly discouraged. The blue used by most decoders is quite dark, and even people with good vision often have trouble reading blue captions on a black background. This problem is exacerbated on projection televisions.

This leaves line 21 captioners with five usable colors, all rendered in the same typeface at the same size. The only further differentiation available is italics. Captioners of streaming media, on the other hand, have the whole world of computerized typography at their fingertips. People viewing streaming media on their computers typically have their systems set for at least 16-bit color (65,536 different colors), if not higher. Different speakers can be set apart not only by position, but by type color, background color, typeface, font size, and many other factors.

This is not necessarily a good thing.

At the dawn of the desktop publishing revolution, the original Macintosh computer introduced a program called MacWrite, which allowed personal computer users to change typefaces and sizes within a document. A basic collection of fonts was shipped with the Mac, and hundreds more were soon available, growing to thousands over the following years. Excitable desktop publishers produced newsletters containing a dozen or more fonts all on the same page, just because they could. Soon, this trend settled down as more people learned the basic rules of design: stick to a small handful of compatible fonts and use them consistently.

Someone producing captioned streaming media should stick to a single font family (or at most, one for speaker identification and one for the captions), and use other attributes to convey speaker identification. If you are striving for accessibility, remember the danger inherent in using color as a differentiator: a color-blind viewer will be left with no clue whatsoever as to who is speaking.

Use color, then, as an additional cue, not as the only one. Combine it with positioning, a speaker ID area, and simple typeface changes like italics to represent off-screen speakers.

We return once again to the invisibility of good caption placement. If the captioner does a good job, the viewer won't notice.

15 CAPTION TIMING

Timing Objectives

Captions need to appear on the screen as closely as possible to when the words being captioned are spoken. With realtime captioning, there is an inherent delay, since the stenocaptioner or voice writer is hearing the words as they are broadcast. Live captioning from a script, known as "live display" captioning, is also typically displayed in roll-up mode, and leads the spoken words slightly, so that caption viewers are reading the words at the same time as they are spoken.

In offline captioning, however, timing is a much more complex issue. Offline captioners spend a great deal of time worrying about precise details of caption timing.

One issue is reading speed, which is addressed further in Chapter 3 (Captioning Styles and Conventions). Editing the text of the captions is not the only way to deal with reading speed issues, however. If a burst of speech is very fast, but is followed by a pause, then the words can be presented verbatim, but allowed to remain on the screen longer.

Theoretically, line 21 captioning can present 60 characters each second, equivalent to a reading rate of 600 words per minute. In reality, however, the overhead associated with the caption broadcast reduces that maximum significantly. Captioners attempt to time captions exactly with when words are spoken, but this can be impossible. Transmitting a one-row pop-on caption requires at least 5 frames (1/6 of a second) of control code overhead. Even if there is only one word in the caption, it should be left on screen for a minimum of a second for readability. This can push the appearance of the next caption (its "in time") back significantly.

When a short caption is immediately followed by another short caption, it's often easier—and more readable—to put them both on the screen at the same time, as shown in figure 15-1.

Figure 15-1: Two Captions on the Screen Together

When this is done, the two captions are on separate rows and positioned to indicate who is speaking.

Scene Changes

Research has shown that if a caption remains on the screen when the scene changes behind it, viewers will automatically start reading the caption over again, assuming that the caption changed with the scene. Additionally, when the caption changes shortly before or after the scene (or camera angle) changes, it adds an additional distraction.

For these reasons, offline captioning is timed to change when the scenes change. This puts more restraints on the timing, and makes it more difficult to enforce reading-rate restrictions, but creates much smoother and easier-to-read captions.

Music

Background or theme music is an exception to the caption timing rules. Typically, specific words in the dialog are not synchronized with any particular visual event. This allows captioners to time the lyrics for a consistent reading rate rather than trying to match them to the video. The scene change rules still apply, but the job of timing background music lyrics is much easier than timing dialog.

Many offline captioning programs have the ability to automatically time a series of captions to create a consistent reading rate. After setting the in-time (appearance time) of the first caption and the out-time (erase time) of the last, all of the times in between are generated by the system. The captioner can then tweak individual captions to match up to scene changes.

Timecodes

Captioning of analog materials requires timecode on the tapes to synchronize with. In the United States, this typically means timecodes using one of the two Society of Motion Picture and Television Engineers (SMPTE) standards: vertical interval time code (VITC) or longitudinal time code (LTC). When dealing with PAL video for most European and South American countries, EBU timecodes are used instead.

VITC places the timecodes in the VBI. Unlike captions, they are not required to be on a specific line,[1] although they are commonly placed in line 14 of an NTSC signal (using both fields means that they will also be present in line 277). VITC readers will lock on to the first VITC signal they find, and it's not uncommon to stripe VITC into multiple lines when a tape is made.

Having the timecodes in the VBI has its advantages. They can be read whether the tape is moving forward or backward, and can be read at very slow tape speeds, including still frame. Since the VBI is part of the video signal, no special effort need be made to preserve VITC on tape dubs.

The disadvantage is that you can't rerecord ("restripe") VITC on an existing tape without making a new dub and losing a generation.

LTC, on the other hand, is placed on a separate track from the video.[2] Some tape formats reserve a track for LTC, and with others, it is placed in an audio track. Dubs for captioners often have the program audio on the left channel and LTC on the right (or vice versa) in a stereo format.

Because the LTC is separate from the video, it's easy to restripe a tape without generational loss. It can also be read at high shuttle speeds in both directions. Unfortunately, LTC cannot be read at slow speeds or still frame.

Dropframe Timecoding

Timecodes are assigned to NTSC video assuming a rate of 30 frames per second. Unfortunately, the actual frame rate is closer to 29.97 fps. To compensate for this, SMPTE offers dropframe timecoding.

The term is a bit misleading, as it's not frames that are being dropped—it's frame *numbers*. One hour of video at 30 fps has 108 more frames than one hour at 29.97 fps. Dropping the first two

---

[1]   See SMPTE standard RP 164-1996 (Location of Vertical Interval Time Code).
[2]   See SMPTE standard RP 159-1995 (Vertical Interval Time Code and Longitudinal Time Code Relationship).

frame numbers of each minute gives us 120 fewer frame numbers, which is too big a compensation, so no frames are dropped from frame numbers where the minutes value ends in zero (minutes 0, 10, 20, 30, 40, and 50). This adds 12 frames back in, giving us the 108 that we need.

As an example, table 15-1 shows the progression of timecodes in dropframe and non-dropframe systems.

Table 15-1: Dropframe vs. Non-Dropframe Counting

Non-Dropframe	Dropframe
01:31:59:28	01:31:59:28
01:31:59:29	01:31:59:29
01:32:00:00	01:32:00:02
01:32:00:01	01:32:00:03
01:32:00:02	01:32:00:04

There is a flag in both VITC and LTC that indicates whether timecodes are dropframe or not, so the software knows instantly what it's dealing with.

Timecode Readers

There are many ways to read timecodes from a tape into a computer.

Timecode reader cards are inserted in the computer and either the timecode track (for LTC) or the video (for VITC) is plugged into them. The cards tend to cost a few hundred dollars, and at least one vendor (Adrienne Electronics) offers a combined data recovery decoder card ("caption grabber") with LTC and/or VITC reader.

External timecode readers are available as well, in the form of a box that connects to the VTR and then to the computer's serial (RS-232 or RS-422) or universal serial bus (USB) ports. These tend to be slightly more expensive, but can be quickly and easily moved around between computers, including both notebook and desktop systems.

Many higher-end VTRs have timecode readers built in and can communicate the timecodes to the computer on the same interface used for the machine control.

One company (Image Logic) even offers software that can read LTC using the sound card in a computer, so the only hardware purchase required for timecoding is a cable to connect the LTC output from the VTR to the microphone input on the computer.

Offsets and Simulated Timecodes

Digital video has no VBI, hence no place to store VITC. The base MPEG standard has no provision for timecodes either. Some nonlinear captioning systems have added their own extensions for putting timecodes in the digitized video. Most, however, use an offset system where they store the first timecode in the file and then count frames to determine the timecode of any given frame in the file.

The danger in frame counting is that the digitizing process can sometimes drop frames. It only takes dropping a frame a minute to throw the captions off by two minutes in a one-hour video. To ensure that you don't have this problem, it's a good idea to digitize video with a burned-in timecode (BITC) in the corner. This way, you can compare the timecode shown on your captioning system with the timecode in the BITC and make sure there are no discrepancies. If there are, the different systems have various ways of correcting for them.

Simulated timecodes also have an application in live encoding and rebroadcast applications. If, for example, the captions are saved from a live broadcast of a show with timecodes embedded (either "real" SMPTE timecodes or time-of-day stamps), then the system can be set to output that caption file again when the show is rebroadcast in another time zone. The first caption is synched manually, and the rest are synched automatically using the computer's time-of-day clock.

Concerns at the Start

TV commercials are a potential problem area for captioners in a number of ways. When a commercial is being set up to air, the cue can potentially be off by several frames or more, chopping out the very beginning of the commercial. The producer probably won't quibble over the loss of a quarter-second or less, especially if no dialog is affected. For the captioner who is struggling to get that first caption on the screen in time, it can be quite a headache.

Almost all commercials use pop-on captions. As explained in Chapter 7 (Line 21 Technical Details), the text of the caption is sent to the invisible (nondisplayed) memory, and then an "end of caption" command is sent to make the caption visible. The process of building a caption in the decoder's nondisplayed memory can easily take over a second, so when the commercial has a lot of dialog, the captioner wants to start as close to the beginning of the commercial as possible.

If the captioner has carefully timed the first caption so that its transmission begins in the first frame of the commercial, and then the cue to air is three frames late, the control commands that provide the caption style and screen location will be lost. Depending on what was going on immediately before the commercial break, that first caption could end up building on the end of some other caption, displaying in the wrong place on the screen, or being lost entirely.

To deal with this problem, commercials should begin with at least one "erase displayed memory" command that will clear any existing captions of the screen. Placing one on the first or second frame, followed by another on the fifth or sixth frame, should cover all but the worst cueing problems. Start the actual buildup of the first caption around the eighth frame if you can.

When there's no dialog in the first few seconds or more of a commercial, some broadcasters like to display a caption anyway, just to show deaf viewers that there will be captioning. If there's background music, then a music note on the screen is enough, or perhaps a description of the music (e.g., "upbeat music" or "solemn orchestral music"). If there is no music, sounds can be described (e.g., "crickets chirping" or "engine sounds") or onomatopoeia provided (e.g., "woof" or "crackle"). In a commercial that starts out completely silent, that can be stated in the caption as well (e.g., "silence" or "no audio").

This same timing issue can arise coming out of a commercial break. A precaptioned show should treat the first second or two after each commercial break as a potential problem.

Of course, none of this preparation will help with the viewer who changes channels right in the middle of a caption. That's why every single caption should begin by setting the mode and (if appropriate) clearing memories, so that at most one caption will be mangled during the channel switch.

Assigning Timecodes to Captions

Different captioners have their own ways of creating and timing caption files. Some like to build final captions as they go. Each caption is typed in, aligned, positioned, and timed before moving on to the next one. Others like to go through the file in passes. In the first pass, they enter all of the text. In the second, they format it and fine tune the caption breaks and positioning. In the third, they set the timing, and so on.

Your captioning software should be able to adapt to the way you work. Here are a few timing features common in offline and nonlinear software.

One-Pass Rough Timing

The quickest way to set rough display times for the captions is to play the video, and press a key when each caption should appear. This is the method used for hand-timing live display files in an online system. The expectations for caption timing are higher in an offline environment, however, so the times assigned by this process are usually just a starting point.

Auto-Time Intervals

Often, there are stretches of captions that do not correlate to specific events in the video. This could be a long commentary by an off-screen narrator, the words to a theme song, or a background conversation. Instead of timing these to match up with the spoken (or sung) words, which a deaf person cannot hear, it is better to spread them evenly over the time interval, providing a smooth and consistent reading rate.

To do this, the display time for the first caption and the erase time of the last caption are locked down, and the computer is told to calculate display times for the rest of the captions. The system will calculate the total number of words in each caption and spread them evenly through the time interval. Typically, other rules affect the actual timing as well. For example, systems can be told that no caption in an auto-timed interval should ever be on the screen less than a certain period of time—2 seconds, for example.[3] Even if a particular caption only has one or two words in it, the auto-time function will ensure that it spends the appropriate minimum time on the screen.

Sometimes, there are captions in the middle of a segment which need to be displayed or erased at a specific time. Captioning systems with auto-timing capabilities usually allow timecodes to be designated as "hard" timecodes (or, as they're called by some vendors, "anchor" timecodes), which are not changed by the auto-timing process.

As an example of how this process might be used, imagine a two-minute segment with three "cuts" (shot changes) in the video. The audio consists of a theme song playing. A captioner would enter the text of the theme song and break it into captions as appropriate. The first and last caption in the segment would be assigned hard timecodes, and the system told to auto-time the segment.

Then, the captioner would go to each cut and find the nearest caption change. That caption would be retimed to happen right on the cut, and the time locked down (converted to a hard timecode). Once this process was complete, the captioner would select the entire segment and auto-time it again, spreading the captions out evenly between each of the cuts and maintaining a relatively smooth and consistent reading rate throughout.

Erase ("out") Times

There can be two timecodes associated with a caption. One indicates when it appears on the screen. Editing systems call this an "in time" and captioning systems tend to call it a "display time" (terminology varies between vendors). The other shows when the caption is removed from the screen and is called an "out time" or "erase time."

---

[3]   This is the recommended minimum time on-screen for a caption according to the guidelines published by the Captioned Media Program in "Captioning Key: Guidelines and Preferred Techniques," revised October 2001.

For most captions, the erase time is implied by the display time of the following caption. Since the disappearance of one caption and the appearance of the next take place within the span of a single frame of video, they appear to happen simultaneously, although most captioning systems can be set to have a one-frame "flicker."[4] Some people prefer this, as it makes it more obvious that the caption has changed. Others find it distracting.

Timecode Tweaks

Often, after rough timecodes have been assigned, minor adjustments need to be made to the timing. Rather than forcing captioners to calculate a change and type a timecode, or adjust the video to a specific spot and reassign the timecode, most systems have command keys or buttons that can "tweak" a timecode forward or backward by one frame or a few frames. In systems that supply reading rate indicators, captioners can smooth out reading rates by tweaking a caption's display time and watching the changes in the reading rates.

Figure 15-2 shows a screen from the VNLcc program that I developed for VITAC in 1998 with the video window disabled. At the top of each caption is a frame count showing how long the caption is on the screen and a reading rate in wpm. Caption 3 is highlighted, indicating that the reading rate is too high. To correct this, we could go to caption 4 and use the tweak command to push the display time forward. As the display time on caption 4 increases, its reading rate will increase and the reading rate of caption 3 will decrease.

---

[4]   Chapter 7 (Line 21 Technical Details) describes the process of inserting an optional EDM command before the EOC at the end of a pop-on caption, which causes the flicker.

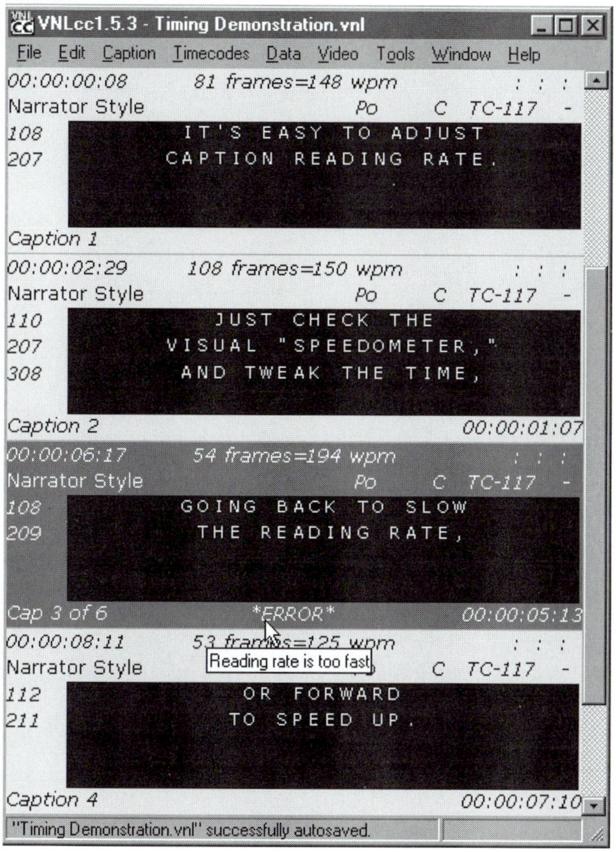

Figure 15-2: Tweaking Display Times to Adjust Reading Rates

VNLcc uses different colors to indicate timing errors. Other systems indicate reading rates with various graphical cues like bar charts, as shown in the Image Logic AutoCaption software in figure 15-3, but the principle is the same.

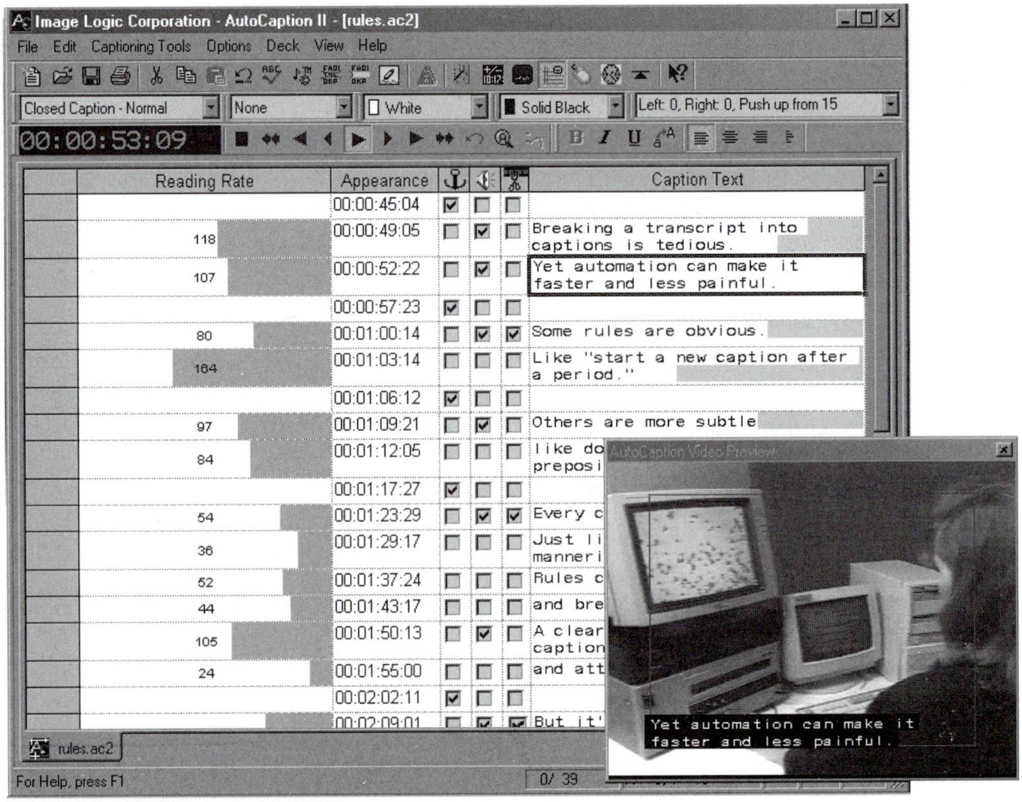

Figure 15-3: Graphic Depiction of Reading Rates in AutoCaption

Timecode Transformations

Sometimes the timing of an entire block of captions must be adjusted. One common example is with theme songs. Even when the same theme song is used for a show with every episode, it may start a little earlier or a little later each time. Similarly, if something is copied from one part of a show and pasted into another, the timecodes will be wrong.

All offline systems allow you to select a block of captions and adjust the timecodes. The way that they do it varies from vendor to vendor.

In some systems, you enter an offset (e.g., add 00:05:12:21 to each caption) and the software makes the adjustment. This can be complicated if you can't do timecode math in your head—which is quite a trick with dropframe timecodes. That's why other systems allow you to enter a new timecode for the first caption in the block. The system then calculates how much needs to be added or subtracted to that caption's timecode, and applies the same offset to the rest of the block.

This may also need to be applied to an entire file if, for example, the timecode track is restriped and all of the captions slip. Similarly, if the captions were generated by capturing realtime captioning from a broadcast, you may want to adjust them all back a couple of seconds to compensate for the inherent delay of stenocaptioning or voice-based captioning.

Expand/Compress Times

Another timecode transformation that's frequently required is compression or expansion. If a video is captioned, and then run through a compression system that drops or interpolates frames to change the length of the program, the line 21 data will be mangled *and* the caption file will require a lot of work to retime. On a system that allows compression/expansion adjustments, you just enter a new start and end time for the video, and the system will readjust all of the captions accordingly.

Video compression is not perfectly linear, as more frames are removed during quiet times with little changing in the picture and fewer frames are removed during action-intensive times. The compression/expansion adjustment will get things close enough, however, that very little tweaking will be required.

Standards Conversions

A similar process is needed during standards conversions. If a (nominally) 30 fps NTSC video from the U.S. is converted to 25 fps PAL for export to Europe, roughly 1/6 of the frames in the video must be removed. Caption timing must be adjusted to compensate for this, and doing a straight transformation based on timecodes isn't enough. NTSC video allows for a bandwidth of 60 characters per second (cps), while PAL only allows for 50 cps. A caption that has plenty of build-up time at 60 cps may need to be displayed several frames late at 50 cps. A video converted from NTSC to PAL must be carefully checked[5] to make sure that adjustments haven't taken captions out-of-sync with shot changes or created significant timing errors.

Shot Change Detection

A significant amount of a captioner's time is spent tweaking captions to make sure that they appear exactly synchronized with shot changes (a.k.a. edits or cuts). This can be a painstaking process of stepping the video back and forth until you find the exact frame of the shot change.

The use of a virtual frame store (VFS) helps this quite a bit. The captioner can see the current frame, plus several frames before and after, which makes it easy to spot the shot change and grab the timecode.

---

[5] A video converted the other direction (PAL to NTSC) will end up with 20% *more* bandwidth in line 21, so these timing problems don't occur.

Some systems take this a step farther, attempting to locate shot changes automatically and mark them for the captioner. Figure 15-4 shows how the Swift system from Softel accomplishes this.

The VFS is displayed along the top of the screen, and the current frame marked with a red dot (the rightmost frame in figure 15-4). Automatically detected shot changes are listed down the left side of the screen and indicated in the VFS by a yellow dot (the highlighted frame just left of center).

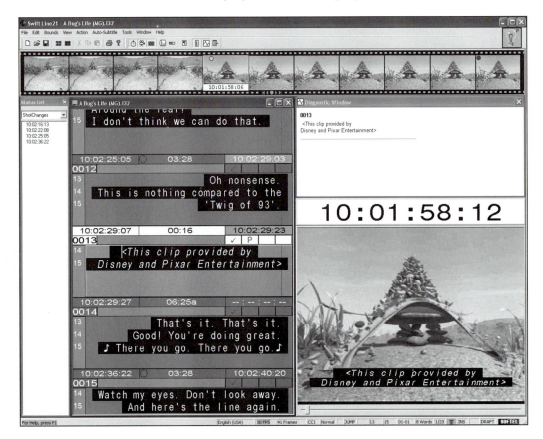

Figure 15-4: Finding Shot Changes in the Swift Software

There are a variety of methods for detecting shot changes, and most vendors are reluctant to give out details of their process for competitive reasons. In a nutshell, they are all based on analyzing differences between frames and scoring them. Tracking pixels is a difficult proposition, because panning and zooming will be detected as a shot change (every pixel changes). A more reliable method assigns scores to each frame based on the overall total luminance and chroma, and looks for significant changes in score between adjacent frames. With fast-moving action like explosions or lights being turned on and off, shot changes can still be falsely detected, but this won't happen often in most productions.

The other problem comes with slow effects like fades, which may not be detected as a shot change at all, or shutter transitions, which may be detected as a series of changes.

There are more sophisticated tricks that can be added, such as looking for similarities in large blocks of solid or near-solid color and shape recognition/mapping, but all of the systems I looked at with shot change detectors do a pretty good job of it.

Synchronizing to Speech

When there are no shot changes, captions are synchronized to the person speaking. Several of the software companies have put a great deal of effort into detecting the onset and cessation of speech in a soundtrack to make the synchronization as easy as possible to accomplish.

Image Logic uses a combination of Fourier analysis and vector cross-product analysis to pick out human speech from background noise. Their algorithm is proprietary, but is based on analyzing resonance in the sound levels. The process is basically invisible to the user, but allows captioners to "snap" a caption to the nearest start of speech.

Softel uses a more visual approach in their Swift system, as shown in figure 15-5. They display a time chart with audio levels. The light gray zones in the figure show where captions are being displayed. The background chart indicates sound levels, color-coded to indicate the probability that any given frame contains voice data. They call their system Voice Auto-Detect (VAD).

Figure 15-5: Voice Auto-Detect in the Swift Software

Letting the cursor hover over a caption indicator on the VAD will display the text of the caption. To adjust a caption's display and erase times to coincide with speech, the captioner can drag the caption directly on the VAD display.

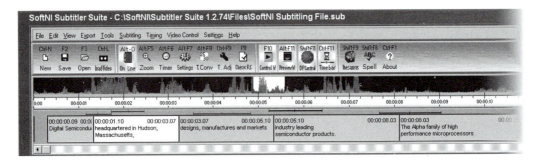

Figure 15-6: Using the AudioBar in SoftNI Subtitler Suite

SoftNI, in their Subtitler Suite, displays an "AudioBar," similar to the VAD display in Swift. The captions are shown in the "BoxTitles" area under the AudioBar (see figure 15-6), with bars showing their duration. Captioners can select segments to play and adjust caption timing from this display.

Timing Multiple Caption Streams

When providing two caption streams for a program (e.g., two languages, or providing both standard and "easy-reader" captions), it is best to keep the streams in two different fields. You'll see that in shows like *60 Minutes*, which has English captions in CC1 (which is in field 1) and Spanish captions in CC3 (which is in field 2). With the limited bandwidth of line 21 captioning (roughly 60 characters per second in each field), it is possible to place two languages in a single field, but very difficult and problematic.

Since 60 characters per second is roughly equivalent to 600 words per minute[6] (wpm), it would seem that there wouldn't be a problem using CC1 and CC2, both of which are in field 1. Each would have available bandwidth of about 300 wpm, which is faster than almost all speech. It doesn't work out that way in reality, for several reasons:

- **Overhead**. Each caption must contain various command codes setting decoder modes, caption placement, and text attributes. With short captions, the overhead can eat up half of the bandwidth, although typically it's closer to 20 or 25%. When using two streams, the percentage of bandwidth lost to overhead goes up, as you lose extra frames switching back and forth between the streams.

- **Bursting Behavior**. While the *average* speaking rate may be under 200 wpm, speech tends to be "bursty," meaning that there may be a couple of seconds at a 20 wpm rate,

---

[6]   Using the standard definition of a word as five letters and a space, 60 characters = 10 words, and 10 words per second equals 600 words per minute.

followed by a couple of seconds at 400 wpm. The bursts will tend to appear in both languages at the same time, making readable caption timing nearly impossible.

- **Synchronization**. Even if the speech follows a nice, steady pace with no bursts, you always want the captions to synch up with certain events in the audio or video, such as a scene change or when someone on-screen begins to speak. These events are the same for both languages. To make CC1 and CC2 both synch to a shot change, you must transmit both captions to their respective nondisplayed memories, and then issue the CC1 EOC (end-of-caption) command and the CC2 EOC command in successive frames. This can be done, but it requires a lot of juggling and you'll still be a frame off with one of them.

Field 1 and field 2 data are totally independent of each other. That means that you can produce CC1 captions as if CC3 didn't exist, and vice versa. None of the problems listed above applies.

Asynchronous Data

When inserting invisible or asynchronous information[7] like text, ITV Links, and most XDS packets, there is one overriding rule to remember: caption data takes priority. It is acceptable for the program guide in TEXT1 or the XDS network name packet in field 2 to slip by two seconds. It is not acceptable for caption data to slip.

---

[7] These data types may not be fully asynchronous, but they can slip back and forth by quite a few frames with no deleterious effects.

16 DTV CAPTIONING

Digital television (DTV) does not have a vertical blanking interval (VBI), and so cannot embed the equivalent of line 21 captioning there. When the Electronic Industries Alliance (EIA) set forth to define standards for DTV closed captioning (DTVCC), they started from scratch, taking the venerable line 21 captioning system, designed in the 1970s, into the 21st century. As we'll see later in this chapter, care was taken to preserve legacy line 21 captioning as well.

This chapter is not intended to be a replacement for the 100-page CEA-708-B specification for DTVCC, but rather an overview of how everything works, perhaps explained for a slightly less technical audience. Engineers designing equipment or writing code for DTVCC should have a copy of CEA-708 at hand.

A full implementation of CEA-708 is complex, and the specification marks many of the features as optional, defining allowable minimum subsets for each class of feature. In general, degradation is smooth, but those sourcing DTVCC should be fully cognizant of the minimum implementations when getting "tricky" with advanced features.

Although screen aspect ratios other than 4:3 (standard NTSC) and 16:9 ("wide-screen") are allowed, and CEA-708 allows for them, these two aspect ratios represent the vast majority of television sets being manufactured, and this chapter will not discuss any others.

Bandwidth

Bandwidth is a constant problem for those trying to insert multiple languages into line 21 caption signals. The two fields cannot share bandwidth, and have a combined maximum throughput just shy of 120 bytes per second,[1] or 960 bits per second (bps). This limitation was imposed because of the difficulty of inserting robust digital data into an analog signal.

DTV, on the other hand, is a high-bandwidth digital signal, of which 9,600 bps is allocated for a logical data channel for DTVCC.

A straight count of bit-per-second transmission rates doesn't tell the whole story, though. Line 21 caption data is 7-bit with parity, which limits the basic character and command set to 127 codes plus a null. This means that many extended characters and virtually all commands have to be two bytes long. DTVCC data is 8-bit, which doubles the available number of character and command codes and allows far more characters and commands to be one-byte.

Also, line 21 commands (control codes) are usually sent twice—the redundancy is designed for a more robust signal, tolerant of dropped frames—while this is not required in DTVCC.

The structure and increased complexity of DTVCC do call for more overhead than line 21 captioning, but the effective available bandwidth is better than ten times what's offered in NTSC analog TV.

DTVCC Caption Windows

The design of line 21 captioning began with the assumptions that the aspect ratio and resolution of the screen were fixed. Character sizes and the placement grid were chosen to allow maximum readability for average viewers seated at an average distance from the screen.

In the DTV world, however, these things are not constants. Screen resolutions vary from 480×704 through 1080×1920. Aspect ratios may be NTSC's 4:3 or the wide-screen 16:9. A fixed character grid is no longer the most appropriate way to present caption data.

DTVCC is based around a caption "window," a concept familiar to any user of a modern computer operating system. The caption window overlays the video, and text is arranged within it.

A grid, or coordinate system, is still required as a way to tell the display equipment where to place the windows. The safe title area of the DTV screen (the area in which captions can be placed) is defined as 75 units high. On a 16:9 screen the placement grid is 210 units wide, and on a 4:3 screen it is 160 units wide. Figure 16-1 shows the grid on a 16:9 screen. The coordinate system is used for placing caption *windows* on the screen, not for caption *text*.

---

[1]   If NTSC video were a full 30 fps, the bandwidth would be precisely 60 bytes per second per field.

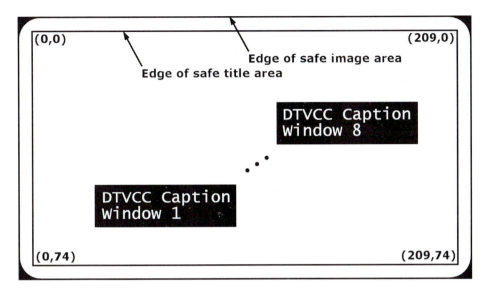

Figure 16-1: DTVCC Caption Window on a 16:9 Screen

Each caption service may have up to eight active windows at a time.

The position of a DTVCC caption window is designated by a single point, known as the "anchor point," which is specified in the coordinate system shown in figure 16-1. The anchor point represents the point of the window that is locked to the screen.

There are nine possible locations for the anchor point: the four corners of the window, the middles of the four sides, and the center of the window. These nine anchor point locations are assigned index numbers from 0 to 8.

In DTVCC, viewers can change the size of the text through a mechanism called the "caption volume control." A viewer who has trouble reading the captions can make them larger, and a viewer who finds them intrusive, but still wants them there, can make them smaller.

Figure 16-2 shows the three different text sizes and how they relate when using each of the anchor points.

Figure 16-2: Using Anchor Points with Various Text Sizes

If the viewer selects smaller text, the window will shrink toward the anchor point. If the viewer selects larger text, the window will grow away from the anchor point.

The size of a window is not expressed in screen coordinates, but in rows and columns, so the size of a window changes as the size of the text within it changes. The maximum window size is the same as in line 21: 15 rows by 32 columns.

Since DTVCC allows for multiple fonts, including proportionally spaced fonts, specifying window size in columns may seem ambiguous. For window sizing purposes, one column width is defined as the width of the widest character in the selected font (often the capital W) at the selected size.

Unlocking Rows and Columns for Word Wrapping

In the examples in figure 16-2, the shape of the caption remains the same as it shrinks and grows. That's because the number of rows and columns is "locked" and doesn't change as the viewer uses the caption volume control to change text size.

In roll-up captioning, that may not be the desired behavior. By unlocking rows and/or columns, the viewer can be shown more text when the size is reduced, or less text when the size is increased.

For example, if there is 3-line roll-up captioning at the bottom of the screen, and the captioner has specified that the number of rows is locked, then it will remain 3-line when the text size is reduced (taking up less of the screen), and when the text size is increased (taking up more of the screen).

If, on the other hand, the captioner has unlocked the number of rows, then the window's physical size will remain the same. If the viewer reduces the text size with 3-line roll-up captioning, the same amount of screen space will be occupied, but the viewer will see four rows of roll-up captions. If the viewer increases the text size, there will only be room for two rows.

If the number of columns is unlocked and the text size changed, then the physical width of the window will remain the same, and the captions will be word wrapped to fit the appropriate larger or smaller number of characters per line.

Justification vs. Anchor Points

Justification determines how the rows of text in a caption are placed horizontally within the window. It is quite different from the anchor point.

For example, let's look at a center-justified caption whose longest row is the full width of a window with columns locked (e.g., the window is 28 columns wide and there are 28 characters on the first row). If that caption is in a window with a top left anchor point and the viewer shrinks the text size, all of the rows will pull up and to the left as they shrink, but they will remain centered with respect to each other and the new (smaller) window dimensions.

If caption positioning is being used for speaker identification, then the left-hand speaker's captions might be in a window with a bottom-left anchor point, placed at coordinate (0, 74) of a 16:9 screen. The right-hand speaker's captions could then be in a window with a bottom-right anchor point at coordinate (209, 74). The captions for *both* speakers could be left justified. There is no need to right justify the captions when the anchor point is on the right side of the window.

The specification also allows for caption text to be specified as fully justified, like the paragraphs in this book, with spacing added between characters to make both the left and right margins even. This is an optional feature which carries a lot of ambiguity, and decoder manufacturers are free to display fully justified text as left justified.

Text Print Direction and Scroll Direction

English text is printed from left to right. Other languages run right→left (e.g., Hebrew) or top→bottom (e.g., Japanese). DTVCC allows the text print direction to be any of the four cardinal directions, no matter what alphabet is being used. If you wish to specify English text reading top to bottom l

i

k

e

t

h

i

s, you are free to do so.

Line 21 roll-up captions scroll from bottom to top: new rows are added at the bottom, and old lines scroll upward. DTVCC allows the scrolling direction to be specified, but it must be orthogonal to the print direction. In other words, if the print direction is horizontal (left→right or right→left), then the scroll direction must be vertical (bottom→top or top→bottom), and vice versa.

This allows for some fascinating—although mostly useless—special effects. One, however, could be useful in several circumstances: the crawl.

To create a crawl across the bottom of the screen, you could specify a window one row high by 32 columns wide (the minimum height and maximum width), with a bottom-center anchor point centered at the bottom of the screen. Make the scroll direction right→left (so new text appears on the right side of the window), and the print direction top→bottom (or bottom→top, since it's only a one-row caption).

The end result (depending upon the character formatting, of course) could be made to look just like a crawl from a CG at the station, except that it would be turned off when the captions were turned off.

There are plenty of variations on this theme, from vertical crawls running up the side of the screen to multiline stock tickers.

Pop-On, Roll-Up, and New Effects

To simulate line 21 roll-up captions in DTVCC, simply define the window with a print direction of left→right and a scroll direction of bottom→top, make it visible, and start writing text to it.

"Paint-on" captioning works the same way—just don't write more than one line of text per window and don't allow it to scroll.

Pop-on captions require two windows. One serves the function of the "displayed memory" in line 21, and the other is the "nondisplayed memory." To build pop-on captions, start with two blank windows, both invisible and both empty. Fill one with caption text and make it visible. Then fill the other window (the invisible one). To swap them, hide the visible caption and show the invisible one.

DTVCC windows have an attribute called "Display Effect." This is set to "snap" to create a pop-on effect, where captions are displayed instantly. It can also be set to make the caption window fade on or off the screen or to wipe in a specified direction (orthogonally only—no diagonal wipes).

Window Borders and Backgrounds

In line 21 captioning, the text always appears on a plain black background. In DTVCC, as you might expect, there are many more options.

The background is specified through a combination of color and opacity. There are 64 different colors, and each one can be transparent (completely invisible), translucent (a colored background that the video still partially shows through), or opaque (solid color). There is also an option for a flashing background (alternating transparent/opaque), which will hopefully be used sparingly, if at all.

Windows can be borderless, have plain borders, or use one of four effects: raised, lowered, left drop-shadowed, or right drop-shadowed. The raised and lowered effects are similar to what you see in an operating system with a graphical user interface (GUI). Buttons have raised borders and data entry fields have lowered borders.

DTVCC Colors

When colors are specified in window backgrounds or caption text, DTVCC allows for 64 different possibilities. The color is expressed as an RGB (red, green, blue) triplet, with each value ranging from 0 to 3. Table 16-1 provides some examples.

There is no inherent protection in the system against creating completely illegible captions. A captioner is free to create yellow captions on a bright white background (or even yellow-on-yellow), and the receiver is not required to detect and fix the problem. It would be a good idea for captioning software engineers to build some readability checks into their products.

Table 16-1: DTVCC Color Specification Examples

RGB Value	Color
(0,0,0)	black
(1,1,1)	dark gray
(2,2,2)	light gray
(3,3,3)	bright white
(3,0,0)	red
(0,3,0)	green
(0,0,3)	blue
(3,3,0)	yellow
(0,3,3)	cyan
(3,0,3)	magenta

In fact, decoders are not required to supply more than the basic eight colors (those shown in table 16-1, less the two grays). In this case, the red, green, and blue values are each reduced to either on or off rather than four possible shades. Any specified RGB value of 1 or 0 becomes "off" and a value of 2 or 3 becomes "on." Thus, dark gray becomes black and light gray becomes bright white.

Captioners (or validation routines in captioning software) should make sure that text and background are far enough apart in the color space that they will still have adequate contrast even after being reduced to this potential minimum color set.

Character Formatting in DTVCC

All of the attributes of text characters in DTVCC are contained in the caption "pen." This is a metaphorical holder for the attributes that will be given to the next character drawn.

As mentioned in the discussion of caption windows, the text size in DTVCC can vary. There are three possible sizes (small, standard, and large). The captioner may choose a size, but the viewer at home can override that choice.

Colors and Text Backgrounds

The color of the text is specified using the same system as the color of the window background. Like the window, the text characters themselves can have variable opacity. This allows for effects like transparent letters on a solid background. As with the color, the system does not protect caption service providers against themselves, and it is possible to specify combinations like transparent text on a transparent background, which is completely invisible.

In addition to the window background, the text itself has a background, which can have its own color specification. Each character's background is a rectangle as tall as the defined font height and wide enough to touch the background rectangles of the characters to its left and right. Figure 16-3 illustrates the difference between the two backgrounds.

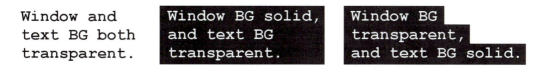

Figure 16-3: Window Backgrounds vs. Text Backgrounds

When the window background is solid, the captions will be displayed in a rectangle large enough to enclose the whole caption. When the text background is solid, each individual row will have its own bounding rectangle, providing the legacy look of line 21 captions.

In a situation where both the window background and the text background are transparent, the text characters themselves will be shown directly on the video. Since video color is rarely uniform across the entire area being covered by the captions, some characters in the text may show up against the video backdrop, and others blend in.

To solve this problem, text characters may be assigned borders ("edges"), just as windows can. A plain ("uniform") edge outlines each character in a contrasting color. This way, if the character blends in with the background, the edges will stand out, and vice versa. Plain edging is common in movie subtitles, as is drop-shadowing, which is another DTVCC edge option. In addition, the same raised and lowered effects described for window borders can be used, or edging can be turned off entirely.

As if this didn't supply enough options, text edges may also be assigned an opacity value.

Fonts and Styles

The two forms of font emphasis provided in line 21 captions, italics and underlining, are provided in DTVCC as well, along with superscripts and subscripts (characters raised and lowered, respectively, with respect to the baseline).

DTVCC captions may also utilize eight different typefaces. The specification defines only the general style of the typeface, and equipment manufacturers are free to choose the specific typefaces implemented. Support for multiple typefaces is optional for equipment manufacturers, and if a particular option isn't supported, a similar typeface should be substituted. The available options are shown in table 16-2. The examples are just that, provided as samples of various typeface families.

Table 16-2: DTVCC Typeface Options

Font #	Description	Examples
0	Default	manufacturer's choice
1	Monospaced serif	Courier
2	Proportional serif	Times New Roman, Garamond
3	Monospaced sans-serif	Helvetica Monospaced
4	Proportional sans-serif	Arial, Verdana, Swiss, Helvetica
5	Casual	Dom, Impress
6	Cursive	Coronet, Marigold, Bradley Hand
7	Small capitals	Engraver's Gothic

A "serif" is the decoration at the end of a stroke in writing a character, as shown in figure 16-4. Monospaced fonts take the same amount of horizontal space for each character, while proportional fonts allow each character to have its own individual spacing. Figure 16-5 shows examples of fonts 1-4 from table 16-2.

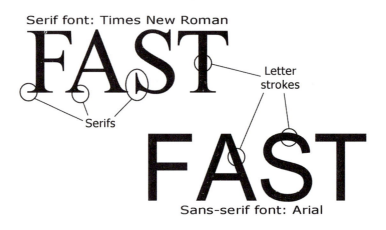

Figure 16-4: Serif vs. Sans-Serif Fonts

Type 1:   Monospaced serif   (Courier New)

Type 2:   Proportional serif   (Times New Roman)

Type 3:   Monospaced sans-serif (Lucida Console)

Type 4:   Proportional sans-serif   (Verdana)

Figure 16-5: Font Samples for DTVCC

Line 21 captioning is always done in a monospaced sans-serif font. In a DTVCC environment, with its higher resolutions and greater processing power, you have a lot of flexibility to introduce different fonts and different looks for the captions.

Remember, however, that the captions need to be legible to people across the room. A decorative script font is hard to read, especially at small sizes. Although serif fonts are traditionally used in print media because of their classic look and high legibility, sans-serif fonts are often easier to read at smaller sizes, as you can see in figure 16-6, which uses Times New Roman and Verdana as its font examples. This is especially true on video screens.

Serif 16 point   Sans-serif 16 point

Serif 14 point   Sans-serif 14 point

Serif 12 point   Sans-serif 12 point

Serif 10 point   Sans-serif 10 point

Serif 8 point   Sans-serif 8 point

Serif 7 point   Sans-serif 7 point

Serif 6 point   Sans-serif 6 point

Serif 5 point   Sans-serif 5 point

Serif 4 point   Sans-serif 4 point

Figure 16-6: Font Legibility at Small Sizes

Character Set

The code space in DTVCC is eight bits deep, providing 256 possible commands and character codes. It is divided up into two command spaces, each containing 32 commands, and two character set spaces, each containing 96 displayable characters. There are also extended sets available.

The basic character set ("G0") is based on the ANSI X3.4 ASCII printable character set, with the addition of the music note character, and is shown in table 16-3.

The second character set ("G1") is the ISO 8859-1 Latin-1 character (a.k.a. "Windows/ANSI") character set, which contains all of the characters required for the majority of Latin-based languages, including the majority of the languages discussed in Chapter 24 (Language Issues in Line 21). This character set is shown in table 16-4.

The first extended character set ("G2") contains a collection of miscellaneous characters not present in the other sets. It is shown in table 16-5.

The second extended character set ("G3") is reserved for future expansion. It contains only one character, the CC (closed captioning) icon, which is in character position A0.

Table 16-3: The DTVCC G0 (ASCII) Character Set

Code	Symbol	Description	Code	Symbol	Description
20		space	50	P	uppercase P
21	!	exclamation mark	51	Q	uppercase Q
22	"	quotation mark	52	R	uppercase R
23	#	number (pound) sign	53	S	uppercase S
24	$	dollar sign	54	T	uppercase T
25	%	percent sign	55	U	uppercase U
26	&	ampersand	56	V	uppercase V
27	'	apostrophe	57	W	uppercase W
28	(	open parenthesis	58	X	uppercase X
29	)	close parenthesis	59	Y	uppercase Y
2A	*	asterisk	5A	Z	uppercase Z
2B	+	plus sign	5B	[	open square bracket
2C	,	comma	5C	\	backslash
2D	-	hyphen (minus sign)	5D	]	close square bracket
2E	.	period	5E	^	caret
2F	/	slash	5F	_	underscore
30	0	zero	60	`	backtick
31	1	one	61	a	lowercase a
32	2	two	62	b	lowercase b
33	3	three	63	c	lowercase c
34	4	four	64	d	lowercase d
35	5	five	65	e	lowercase e
36	6	six	66	f	lowercase f
37	7	seven	67	g	lowercase g
38	8	eight	68	h	lowercase h
39	9	nine	69	i	lowercase i
3A	:	colon	6A	j	lowercase j
3B	;	semicolon	6B	k	lowercase k
3C	<	less-than sign	6C	l	lowercase l
3D	=	equal sign	6D	m	lowercase m
3E	>	greater-than sign	6E	n	lowercase n
3F	?	question mark	6F	o	lowercase o
40	@	at sign	70	p	lowercase p
41	A	uppercase A	71	q	lowercase q
42	B	uppercase B	72	r	lowercase r
43	C	uppercase C	73	s	lowercase s
44	D	uppercase D	74	t	lowercase t
45	E	uppercase E	75	u	lowercase u
46	F	uppercase F	76	v	lowercase v
47	G	uppercase G	77	w	lowercase w
48	H	uppercase H	78	x	lowercase x
49	I	uppercase I	79	y	lowercase y
4A	J	uppercase J	7A	z	lowercase z
4B	K	uppercase K	7B	{	left curly brace
4C	L	uppercase L	7C			vertical bar
4D	M	uppercase M	7D	}	right curly brace
4E	N	uppercase N	7E	~	tilde
4F	O	uppercase O	7F	♪	music note

Table 16-4: The DTVCC G1 (Latin-1) Character Set

Code	Symbol	Description	Code	Symbol	Description
A0	NBS	nonbreaking space	D0	Ð	uppercase eth
A1	¡	inverted (open) exclamation	D1	Ñ	uppercase N, tilde
A2	¢	cents symbol	D2	Ò	uppercase O, grave accent
A3	£	pounds Sterling	D3	Ó	uppercase O, acute accent
A4	¤	currency symbol	D4	Ô	uppercase O, circumflex
A5	¥	yen	D5	Õ	uppercase O, tilde
A6	¦	pipe (broken bar)	D6	Ö	uppercase O, umlaut
A7	§	section mark	D7	×	multiplication sign
A8	¨	umlaut (diaeresis)	D8	Ø	uppercase O, slash
A9	©	copyright	D9	Ù	uppercase U, grave accent
AA	ª	feminine ordinal	DA	Ú	uppercase U, acute accent
AB	«	open guillemets (quotes)	DB	Û	uppercase U, circumflex
AC	¬	logical not	DC	Ü	uppercase U, umlaut
AD	-	soft hyphen	DD	Ý	uppercase Y, acute accent
AE	®	registered trademark	DE	Þ	uppercase thorn
AF	‾	macron	DF	ß	esszett (sharp S)
B0	°	degree sign	E0	à	lowercase a, grave accent
B1	±	plus or minus	E1	á	lowercase a, acute accent
B2	²	superscript 2 (squared)	E2	â	lowercase a, circumflex
B3	³	superscript 3 (cubed)	E3	ã	lowercase a, tilde
B4	´	acute accent	E4	ä	lowercase a, umlaut
B5	µ	"micro" (Greek letter mu)	E5	å	lowercase a, ring
B6	¶	paragraph sign	E6	æ	lowercase ae ligature
B7	·	middle dot	E7	ç	lowercase c, cedilla
B8	¸	cedilla	E8	è	lowercase e, grave accent
B9	¹	superscript 1	E9	é	lowercase e, acute accent
BA	º	masculine ordinal	EA	ê	lowercase e, circumflex
BB	»	closing guillemets	EB	ë	lowercase e, umlaut
BC	¼	one quarter	EC	ì	lowercase i, grave accent
BD	½	one half	ED	í	lowercase i, acute accent
BE	¾	three quarters	EE	î	lowercase i, circumflex
BF	¿	inverted (open) question mark	EF	ï	lowercase i, umlaut
C0	À	uppercase A, grave accent	F0	ð	lowercase eth
C1	Á	uppercase A, acute accent	F1	ñ	lowercase n, tilde
C2	Â	uppercase A, circumflex	F2	ò	lowercase o, grave accent
C3	Ã	uppercase A, tilde	F3	ó	lowercase o, acute accent
C4	Ä	uppercase A, umlaut	F4	ô	lowercase o, circumflex
C5	Å	uppercase A, ring	F5	õ	lowercase o, tilde
C6	Æ	uppercase AE ligature	F6	ö	lowercase o, umlaut
C7	Ç	uppercase C, cedilla	F7	÷	division symbol
C8	È	uppercase E, grave accent	F8	ø	lowercase o, slash
C9	É	uppercase E, acute accent	F9	ù	lowercase u, grave accent
CA	Ê	uppercase E, circumflex	FA	ú	lowercase u, acute accent
CB	Ë	uppercase E, umlaut	FB	û	lowercase u, circumflex
CC	Ì	uppercase I, grave accent	FC	ü	lowercase u, umlaut
CD	Í	uppercase I, acute accent	FD	ý	lowercase y, acute accent
CE	Î	uppercase I, circumflex	FE	þ	lowercase thorn
CF	Ï	uppercase I, umlaut	FF	ÿ	lowercase y, tilde

Table 16-5: The DTVCC G2 (Miscellaneous) Character Set

Code	Symbol	Description	Code	Symbol	Description
20	TSP	transparent space	3C	œ	lowercase OE ligature
21	NBTSP	nonbreaking transparent space	3D		servicemark
25	…	ellipsis	3F	Ÿ	uppercase Y, umlaut
2A	Š	uppercase S, caron	76	⅛	one eighth
2C	Œœ	uppercase OE ligature	77	⅜	three eighths
30	∎	solid block	78	⅝	five eighths
31	`	open single quote	79	⅞	seven eighths
32	'	close single quote	7A	|	vertical bar
33	"	open double quote	7B	┐	upper right corner[2]
34	"	close double quote	7C	└	lower left corner
35	•	bullet	7D	–	horizontal bar
39	™	trademark	7E	┘	lower right corner
4F	š	lowercase S, caron	7F	┌	upper left corner

DTVCC Layering Model

If you've worked in computer networking, you're familiar with the seven-layer Open Systems Interconnect (OSI) network reference model. DTVCC has been hierarchically structured in layers as well, to take advantage of the separation of functionality this approach offers. The DTVCC model doesn't use the lower three levels of the OSI networking model (physical, link, and transport). Its five layers are mapped onto the upper four levels of the OSI model as shown in table 16-6.

Table 16-6: DTVCC Hierarchy Mapped onto OSI Reference Model

DTVCC Layer	OSI Layer
Interpretation	7. Application
Coding	6. Presentation
Service	5. Session
Packet	-
Transport	4. Transport
-	3. Network
-	2. Data Link
-	1. Physical

As we prepare DTV captioning data for transmission, it must pass through each of these layers on its journey from the captioning system to the consumer's television set.

---

[2]   The four corner characters all extend to the edges of their character cells so that they can be used with the horizontal and vertical bar characters to draw boxes.

Interpretation Layer

At the top, we have the interpretation layer, which contains the captions themselves and the formatting commands that determine how they'll look. At this level, we're dealing with five components that define the captions:

- The caption text itself

- Caption "pens," which define the appearance (e.g., colors and other attributes) of the caption text

- Caption windows, which contain individual caption text. Note that there can be more than one caption window at a time.

- The Caption screen, which contains all of the caption windows and overlays the video screen

- Caption synchronization, which controls the timing of all of the various components.

At this level, much of the captioning data is conceptual. Individual captioning systems may have dramatically different representations of data at the interpretation level, but it will all be standardized as we move down the protocol stack.

Coding Layer

At the coding layer, commands and text characters are assigned their numerical codes. Information at this layer is a collection of standardized data bytes.

Service Layer

At this layer, the codes are sorted into services (e.g., languages) and collected into blocks. The service layer may be receiving codes from several different sources, such as multiple captioning systems, each providing captions destined for a different service.

In line 21 captioning, we're limited to four "languages," called CC1 through CC4. In DTVCC, there may be up to 63 services, which may include different languages, "easy-reader" captions, or meta-data. There is no "field" concept in DTVCC. All of the services will end up sharing the same bandwidth.

Each block of information at the service layer is called a caption channel service block. DTV receivers examine each channel service block's headers to determine which service it belongs to, and route it appropriately.

Packet Layer

At this layer, DTVCC channel service blocks are gathered together into packets and assigned rolling sequence numbers to aid the receivers in detecting lost data.

Transport Layer

The transport layer is the point at which captions are integrated into the DTV data stream. Figure 16-7 shows the structure of the data coming into this point.

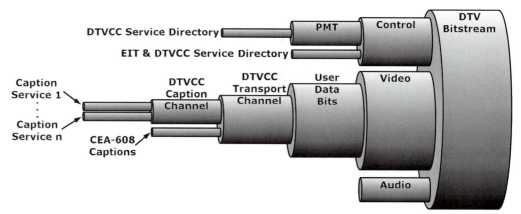

Figure 16-7: How DTVCC Fits in the Overall DTV Data Stream

At the far left side of the figure, in the service layer, caption channel service blocks are being assembled from their various sources, and the services are being defined.

At the next level in, the service blocks are being gathered into packets in the packet layer, and all of the services are turning into a single bit stream.

From there, we reach the transport layer. The DTVCC packets are given error correction and merged in with legacy line 21 captions in CEA-608 format. Quite a bit more takes place from here.

The three major components of the DTV bit stream are audio, video, and control data. They are not transmitted as coordinated frames, as NTSC video is, but as independent streams. DTVCC was assigned a fixed amount of bandwidth (9,600 bps) in the picture portion of the stream. This bandwidth is always reserved, even when there is no caption data present, to ensure that (a) there is room in the stream for downstream insertion of caption data, and (b) latency (temporal separation of captions from their associated frames) is kept to a minimum.

Into that reserved 9,600 bps go the DTVCC data and the CEA-608 captions. As we discussed in Chapter 7 (Line 21 Technical Details), line 21 captions require 960 bps of bandwidth, which comes out of the 9,600 bps that is reserved, leaving 8,640 bps for DTVCC data. In a 60 fps interleaved signal, that's 2 bytes of line 21 data and 18 bytes of DTVCC data per frame.

Although the caption data itself is all encoded into the user data bits in the MPEG-2 video stream, there is other caption-related information in the DTV bit stream.

The Program Mapping Table (PMT), shown at the top of figure 16-7, is given a caption service directory, showing what caption services are available. When an Event Information Table (EIT) is broadcast, it will also receive a caption service directory.

This entire process is reversed at the receiving end, peeling out the data and routing it appropriately. As with networking that follows the OSI model, each layer is independent of the others. When caption channel service blocks are being gathered into packets at the packet layer, for example, no attempt is made to interpret the data from the interpretation or coding layers.

Legacy Captioning

During the phase-over period from analog to digital television, much programming is sourced in analog, upconverted to DTV, transmitted, and then downconverted in the home to be watched on an analog TV set. Rather than forcing two-way conversion of the caption data, line 21 is simply extracted intact and all of its data inserted into the DTV signal.

Some of the information in line 21 is redundant in DTV. Data like program content advisories (V-Chip) have been separated from the DTVCC data flow (and bandwidth). This data can be left intact in line 21, however. The DTV receiver will pass it through to analog equipment or ignore it on digital equipment.

Conversion from CEA-608 (line 21) captioning to CEA-708 (DTVCC) is relatively simple and straightforward. The look and feel of the captioning can be maintained, and transcoding equipment such as those described in Chapter 8 (Encoding Equipment) automate the process nicely.

Conversion in the other direction (CEA-708 to CEA-608) can be nearly impossible. CEA-708 allows far more options for text, fonts, and placement. Much more data can be transmitted in DTVCC than will fit in line 21. DTVCC has concepts that simply don't exist in line 21 captions.

By including a mechanism for transmitting legacy captioning along with the DTVCC data, receiving equipment is spared the task of attempting to downconvert caption data for consumers that have DTV receivers along with analog TVs or monitors.

17 CAPTIONING AND SUBTITLING ON DVDS

DVDs are like CDs, only more so. When originally conceived, the DVD was intended to be to the video world what the CD is to the audio world, hence the original acronym, Digital Video Disc. As the technical experts met and worked on defining and refining the specifications for DVD, it became clear that it could be a lot more. The DVD Forum suggested that DVD should instead stand for Digital Versatile Disc, to show how it could be used as a video medium replacing the laser disc, an audio storage medium capable of holding far more than a CD, and a removable medium for a computer that could store 4.4 to 16 gigabytes of information.

Unable to agree on what it stood for, most people were happy to let it just be DVD.

When used as a computer disk, a DVD can store any kind of digital data, including all of the media formats described in Chapter 19 (Captions in Internet Streaming and Computer Media). In this chapter, however, we're going to focus on DVD-Video, which is what you pop into the DVD player hooked up to your TV at home.

When the DVD format was being defined, its originators wanted a way to store movies with subtitles. More than that, they wanted viewers to be able to turn those subtitles on and off. And they wanted more than one subtitle language on each feature. In other words, they wanted closed captioning (or at least closed subtitling).

The method used for subtitling on DVDs is quite versatile, supporting up to 32 different sets of subtitles. Each one could be a different language, a different text size, or a different reading level. Through a mechanism discussed later in the chapter, subtitles can be rendered in any font, and any character set, even with embedded pictures and logos.

Despite this versatility, DVD subtitling isn't a perfect substitute for captioning. If you have a device attached to your TV set that looks for information in line 21 such as ITV links, there won't be any, as these subtitles don't make use of line 21 at all. Additionally, devices that capture caption text won't be able to read the subtitles. Again, they're not in line 21.

At the last minute, support was thrown into the DVD specifications for embedded line 21 captioning, which is discussed later in the chapter. Thus, DVDs today can have both subtitles *and* captions. Unfortunately, not all commercial players support the line 21 captioning capability, and consumers are left wrestling with compatibility issues.

Whenever possible, both subtitles and captions should be included on a DVD, allowing viewers the maximum flexibility in viewing.

DVD Subtitles

DVDs store video in a slightly modified version of the MPEG-2 digital video format. Subtitling on a DVD is accomplished through a feature known as subpictures.

Each individual subtitle is rendered into a bitmap (picture) file and compressed. Scheduling information is written to the DVD along with the bitmaps for each subtitle. As the DVD is playing, each subpicture bitmap is called up at the appropriate time and displayed over top of the video picture.

The DVD specification allows for up to 32 different sets of subtitles on a single disc. Each set of subtitles is marked with a two-letter language code using the ISO639 language standard—the same standard used for specifying languages in SAMI files. In addition, the subtitles can be assigned a "language extension," further identifying what they are. Table 17-1 provides a list of defined language extensions.

Table 17-1: DVD Subtitle Language Extensions

Code	Extension Type
0	Not specified (default)
1	Normal subtitles
2	Large subtitles
3	Subtitles for children
5	Normal closed captions
6	Large closed captions
7	Closed captions for children
9	Forced subtitles
13	Director comments
14	Large director comments
15	Director comments for children

The terminology in table 17-1 is somewhat confusing. Codes 5-7 are referred to as "closed captions." This does not mean that it refers to line 21 captioning. They are still presented using the subpicture system on the DVD, but the *information* contained in them is caption-style rather than subtitle-style. For example, the "code 1" subpictures (normal subtitles) would not contain sound effects, but the "code 5" subpictures (normal closed captions) would.

As of this writing, few production companies are going to the expense of producing more than one set of subtitles per language. Additionally, with the large amount of video and extra features included on DVDs, there remains little room for extra subtitling.

Each subpicture can be a different size, and can be positioned independently on the screen with a high degree of accuracy. Even though the bitmaps are quite large compared to the sparse, low-bandwidth approach of line 21 captioning, the overall DVD data stream is so fast that it is capable of displaying a new subpicture with every frame, allowing for 30 fps animation-like effects.

At this time, there are dozens of different DVD authoring systems, all with different formats for storing subtitle data. Those writing captioning software are forced to deal with similar but different interfaces, in some cases even involving different file formats for authoring systems from the same vendor.

In most cases, the system can import the data as a collection of subpicture files in a standard file format (typically TIFF), along with a "navigation file," which lists information about each of the subtitles, as shown in figure 17-1.

```
directory c:\capdemo\comedy
ccom0001.tif 00:00:00.10 00:00:01.69 400 105 160 345
ccom0002.tif 00:00:01.70 00:00:03.09 400 105 160 345
ccom0003.tif 00:00:03.10 00:00:06.29 400 105 160 345
ccom0004.tif 00:00:06.30 00:00:22.29 400 105 160 345
ccom0005.tif 00:00:22.30 00:00:31.49 400 105 160 345
ccom0006.tif 00:00:31.50 00:00:37:19 400 105 160 345
```

Figure 17-1: Sample DVD Subtitle Navigation File

Each line begins with the name of the TIFF file for the subpicture, followed by its display and erase times. The next two numbers are the subtitle size, and the last two are the subtitle position.

The DVD screen is 720 pixels wide by 480 pixels high for widescreen (16:9) pictures, and 540×480 for standard (4:3).[1] Subpictures always use the widescreen positioning coordinates. In the example in figure 17-1, all of the subpictures are the same size (400 wide by 105 high) and are shown at the same position (160 pixels from the left and 345 pixels from the top).

Special effects can be coded into DVD subtitles, such as wiping, fading, or scrolling; and many more effects can be built by building an animation out of multiple subpictures shown in successive frames.

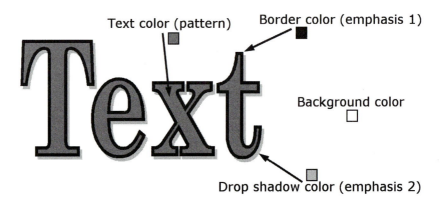

Figure 17-2: Edged and Drop-Shadowed Text in a DVD Subpicture

The format for the subpicture files allows for only four colors, known as background, pattern, emphasis 1, and emphasis 2. The background color is typically transparent, allowing edged and drop-shadowed letters to be displayed as shown in figure 17-2.

---

[1]   These are the dimensions for NTSC. PAL is 720×576.

With only four colors to work with (three if you don't count the transparent background), anti-aliasing isn't possible, but the jaggies aren't likely to be noticed.

It is possible, of course, to emulate the look of line 21 captions in DVD subtitles, but this isn't what viewers are used to seeing, and wouldn't be well received.

In addition to the four colors, there are also four contrast levels, which can be used to produce special effects, like lightening the video under the background of the subpicture.

Even with only four bits of data per pixel (two for the color and two for the contrast), subtitles for a feature-length movie could take up quite a bit of space—easily ten megabytes—and the space available on a DVD is finite. To keep storage requirements under control, the subpictures are stored using a run length encoded (RLE) data format.

RLE is quite straightforward. Each pixel in the subpicture can have one of four color values: 0 (background), 1 (pattern), 2 (emphasis 1), or 3 (emphasis 4). Each horizontal row of pixels, therefore, is a row of numbers between 0 and 3. In a text environment, there will likely be a lot of zeros (background area), divided by blocks of the other values. If the subpicture is 200 pixels wide, then each row would have 200 numbers.

With RLE, however, the system stores a repeat count for each number. Figure 17-3 gives an example of RLE, by showing three lines before and after encoding:

Without RLE:
```
00000000001110000001110000000000222211122220000000000111000000
0000000011111110011111110000002222111111122220000000001110000
0000001110000011100000111000222211100011122200000000000011100
```

With RLE:
0_{10} 1_3 0_6 1_3 0_{10} 2_4 1_3 2_4 0_{10} 1_3 0_6

0_8 1_7 0_2 1_7 0_6 2_4 1_7 2_4 0_{10} 1_3 0_4

0_6 1_3 0_5 1_4 0_5 1_3 0_3 2_4 1_3 0_3 1_3 2_4 0_{11} 1_3 0_2

Figure 17-3: Run Length Encoding (RLE)

Looking at the first line in the example, it begins with ten zeros, represented by 0000000000 without RLE, or 0_{10} with RLE. That's followed by three ones (111 or 1_3) and six more zeros (000000 or 0_6).

When using RLE, the amount of compression depends on the number of *transitions* in each horizontal line of the picture, not on the total amount of data. A repeating pattern of 200 pixels alternating zero and one (01010101...) could not be compressed at all, as the repeat count would always be one. You'd have to include all 200 numbers. But if the line was 100 zeros (all at the beginning) followed by 100 ones (all at the end), you could represent the whole line with two numbers and their repeat counts (0_{100} 1_{100}).

By encoding all of the subpictures using RLE, all of the subtitles on a DVD rarely take more than about half of one percent of the total allocated storage.

Line 21 on a DVD

In addition to using subtitles, line 21 can be encoded on a DVD in its entirety, and DVD players that understand it (an increasing number) can recreate it. In this case, the TV set will be receiving a captioned signal just as if it was coming from a videotape.

If present on the DVD, line 21 data is always passed through to the video output. The DVD player makes no attempt to interpret, decode, or display it. It is passed through whether subtitling is on or off, which can lead to some confusion if the TV has caption decoding enabled and the DVD player has subtitles turned on. In this case, the DVD player will show the subtitles and the TV will show captions, probably right over the top of the subtitles.

Ripping and Fansubs

An entire subculture has sprung up around subtitling on DVDs. It began with American fans of Japanese animation and artwork, like manga and anime. They found that there were a lot of anime DVDs released in Japan that were released in the U.S., but didn't have English subtitles. Programs called DVD rippers allow computer users to copy a DVD onto their hard disk (assuming they have a large enough disk), and then "burn" a new DVD copy of it.

It takes a lot of editing and specialized equipment to subtitle or caption a videotape. Once you've ripped a DVD, the subtitling is a reasonably straightforward process, which can be done with no special equipment. The fan subtitlers ("fansubs") could rip a DVD, translate the dialog, and burn a new copy with English subtitles. Despite the obvious questions of legality, fansub Web sites sprang up all over, distributing the translated subtitles in file formats for various DVD burners.

This, in turn, led to development of more sophisticated subtitling capability in ripping and burning software for home users. Some of these programs take their input as SAMI files or in proprietary formats that look vaguely like XML or HTML, not requiring users to do their own rendering and TIFF file generation.

The popularity of anime in the U.S. has led to most new Japanese releases being subtitled and/or dubbed in English for North American release, so the fansubs have been fading of late, but their legacy lives on in the form of cheap (sometimes free) software tools for home DVD makers.

18

ITV Links

In 1997, a company called WebTV (now owned by Microsoft) had a set-top box that allowed people to access the Web using their TVs. The unit that was available at the time had little interconnection between the Web and what was being broadcast on TV, but they had an idea they called TV Crossover Links, or TCLs.

The concept was that Internet addresses, in the form of Uniform Resource Locators (URLs), could be embedded somewhere in the TV signal, and the WebTV unit would recognize them. An icon would be displayed over the TV picture, and the viewer could press a button to bring up the referenced Web page. They took the idea to a leading caption service provider (VITAC), and the two businesses developed a system for transmitting TCLs. Cheetah Systems (now Cheetah International) then worked with WebTV to add the capability into their offline captioning software, CAPtivator Offline. This system was later introduced to the EIA, at which time the name was changed from TV Crossover Links to Interactive Television Links (ITV links), where it was accepted as a standard (originally EIA-746, but now incorporated as a part of CEA-608-B).

WebTV planned to make these links carry more information relevant to the program or commercial being watched. When a program mentioned a certain artifact being in one of the museums at the Smithsonian, the (i) icon might pop up with a link to `www.si.edu/museums/`. When a commercial mentioned the latest product from your favorite auto manufacturer, the (i) icon would link to that car's Web site.

ITV links are placed in TEXT2. They consist of a URL in angle brackets, an optional string of attributes in square brackets, and a checksum, also in square brackets.

Because TEXT2 is lower priority than CC1 or CC2, and because ITV links can be long, transmission of an ITV link can be interrupted by caption data. If this happens, the Resume Text Display command tells the decoder to continue building the ITV link. The Text Restart command, on the other hand, tells the decoder to discard any ITV links currently in process.

Character Set

ITV links use US-ASCII (ISO-8859-1) characters rather than the standard line 21 character set used for captions. Because of the constraints of line 21 (seven-bit characters with control codes in the 00 to 20 hex range), characters are limited to those between 20 and 7F, inclusive.

If a URL or attribute uses characters that aren't otherwise allowed (such as an accented letter or a square bracket in an attribute), then it should use the standard mechanism of replacing the character with a percent sign followed by the character's 2-digit hex value in the ISO-8859-1 character set (e.g., the character "©" would be replaced by %A9).

URLs

The URL field is not limited only to Web addresses, so the protocol portion of the link is required. For example, http, mailto, news, and ftp are all valid URL protocols for an ITV link. For specific examples, see the end of this section. A device that receives a URL of a type it can't process (a set-top box, for example, that receives a "news:" link but can't access Usenet) should ignore it.

CEA-608-B recommends that the URLs be kept as short as possible to avoid using up undue amounts of bandwidth. If possible, move pages or directories to the root, eliminate redundant specifications of default pages (e.g., use `www.captioncentral.com` instead of `www.captioncentral.com/index.html`), and consider building pages with short URLs that redirect to pages with long URLs.

When building ITV links into a show, remember that the show may be rebroadcast at a later date, and don't use temporary URLs. Wherever possible, establish a permanent location for the page.

Attributes

There are four standard attributes at this time, although more may be created. All receiving devices should ignore attributes they don't understand. Each of them has a full name and an abbreviation (the first letter of its name) that should be used to conserve bandwidth. The attributes are:

- **NAME:** For systems that associate a name with the link (to be displayed when the cursor hovers over the icon, for example), any text name can be displayed. For example, [Name:Our Sponsor] or [n:Sponsor].

- **EXPIRES:** If the URL is only valid until a certain date or time, an expiration date may be specified. This is of the form *YYYYMMDD*, for example [Expires:20040501] for expiration on May 1, 2004. If a time is specified, follow the date with the letter T, and then the time in *HHMMSS* or *HHMM* format, as in [e:20040501T1200] to expire at noon on May 1, 2004). Times are UTC (also known as GMT, or Greenwich Meridian Time).

- **SCRIPT:** This attribute can contain a snippet of JavaScript or JScript, which is run in the Web browser as soon as page referenced by the URL is displayed.

- **TYPE:** This defines the scope of the link. There are five defined types which, like the attributes, can be abbreviated to one letter. Note that "Sponsor" is abbreviated as A (for advertiser) rather than S. The original specification allowed the word "type" or its abbreviation to be omitted, allowing [sponsor] instead of [type:sponsor]. As of the latest standard, this is no longer permitted. Types are case insensitive, so P, p, Program, program, and PrOgRaM all mean the same thing. If a type is abbreviated, it must be abbreviated all the way. In other words, S and STATION are both valid, while STAT is not. Table 18-1 shows the meanings of each Type attribute.

Table 18-1: ITV Link Types

Full Attribute	Abbreviation	Meaning
[Type:Program]	[t:p]	Applies to the current program
[Type:Network]	[t:n]	Applies to this broadcast network
[Type:Station]	[t:s]	Applies to the local station
[Type:Operator]	[t:o]	Applies to the service operator, e.g., cable or satellite company
[Type:Sponsor]	[t:a]	Applies to advertisers within the current program

Checksums

All ITV links must contain a checksum to verify data integrity. Receiving devices should verify the checksum, and if it doesn't match, discard the entire ITV link.

The checksums are computed using the algorithm described in Internet RFC 1071. All of the bytes in the string, starting with the left angle bracket in front of the URL and ending with the right square bracket after the last attribute (if there are any attributes), are paired off to form 16-bit numbers. If there is an odd number of bytes, a null (zero) byte is paired up with the last byte of the string. The 16-bit numbers are added together using ones-complement math, and the ones complement of the result is expressed as a four-digit hexadecimal number in angle brackets.

```
Private Function CalculateChecksum(code as String) as String
' Input should be an ITV link including everything from the
' open < of the URL to the closing ] of the last attribute
' (or > of the URL if there are no attributes). Do not
' include previously calculated checksums.

    Dim i As Integer
    Dim CS As Long
    Dim c As String

    i = 1
    CS = 0

    ' Build the checksum using long-integer arithmetic
    Do While i <= Len(code)
        If i + 1 <= Len(code) Then
            CS = CS + Asc(Mid(code, i + 1, 1))
        End If
        CS = CS + (256 * Asc(Mid(code, i, 1)))
        i = i + 2
    Loop

    ' Convert to ones-complement
    CS = (CS Mod 65536) + ((CS And &HFFFF0000) / 65536)

    ' Invert
    CS = 65535 - CS

    ' Convert to hexadecimal and add leading zeros as required
    c = Hex(CS)
    While Len(c) < 4
        c = "0" & c
    Wend

    ' Return checksum as bracketed string
    CalculateChecksum = "[" & c & "]"
End Function
```

Figure 18-1: VB Function to Calculate ITV Link Checksums

The Visual Basic routine in figure 18-1 provides an example of the checksum algorithm.

Sample ITV Links

`<http://www.robson.org/gary/>[t:p][n:Gary Robson][BD55]`

This is a standard Web page ITV link with no expiration date. The [t:p] attribute ties the link to the current program. If the receiving set-top box or computer is equipped to place a name on the link, the [n:Gary Robson] attribute instructs it to show "Gary Robson."

`<mailto:gary@robson.org>[t:p][n:Contact the Author][FFC0]`

This is an email link, which will only be processed by systems equipped to send email. Like the previous example, it has both type and name attributes.

`<news:comp.compression>[Name:See Discussion][F129]`

This link pulls up the Usenet newsgroup comp.compression (discussion of data compression methods and algorithms). There is no type attribute specified.

`<http://www.faqs.org/rfcs/rfc1071.html>[n:RFC][e:20101231T235959][9D24]`

Here is an example of an ITV link with an expiration. If a receiving device gets this link after 1 second to midnight on December 31, 2010, it should be ignored.

XDS Data

Line 21 extended data services (XDS) consist of a set of data packets that convey information about the current program, upcoming programs, the station, and general status (such as the current time of day).

All XDS packets are carried in field 2 so that they won't interfere with CC1 bandwidth. XDS packets should be the last data added to field 2, filling in the unused space between other types of data. Many encoding products are available that handle this process automatically, as described in Chapter 8 (Encoding Equipment). These XDS encoders are given the appropriate packet information, along with a desired repeat frequency for each, and they handle all packet generation and insertion.

Due to their low priority, XDS packets can be interrupted by other types of information, such as CC3/4 and TEXT3/4 streams, or even other XDS packets.

Structure of an XDS Packet

Each packet begins with a two-character code, known as a control code, both characters of which must reside in the same frame. The first character is a **control character**, which specifies the class of the packet according to table 18-2, and indicates whether this control code is starting a new XDS packet or continuing one that was interrupted. Control characters are always in the range of 01 to 0F hex. The second character is a **type character** that identifies the information contained in the packet. Type characters, like control characters, are between 01 and 0F hex.

Unlike captioning control codes, XDS codes are not doubled (repeated). If there is bad data, indicated by an invalid control code or a failed checksum calculation, the packet is simply discarded.

Table 18-2: XDS Control Characters

Packet Class	Start Code	Continue Code	Description
Current	01	02	Information about this program
Future	03	04	Info about programs to be aired later
Channel	05	06	Non-program-specific channel information
Miscellaneous	07	08	Various other data
Public service	09	0A	Weather warnings, etc.
Reserved	0B	0C	Set aside for future use
Private data	0D	0E	May be used in closed-loop systems
End	0F	0F	Indicates end-of-packet

Following the control code may be 2 to 32 **informational characters**. There must be an even number of informational characters so that frames are filled completely. If necessary, add a NUL (00 hex) character to the end to make the number even.

If packet transmission is interrupted by caption data, then the control code must be re-sent to return to XDS mode, substituting the "continue" code for the "start" code in the control character. For example, if a Network Name packet is being transmitted, it would begin with 05 01 (channel class, type 1). If it was interrupted during transmission of the informational characters, it would be resumed by sending 06 01. If a control code is received containing the start code of an interrupted packet that is currently being built, the current packet is discarded and a new one started.

After all informational characters have been sent, an end-of-packet code is sent, with the end code (0F) as its first character and a **checksum character** as the second. *XDS checksums are not the same as the ITV link checksums described earlier in this chapter.* Figure 18-2 shows a Visual Basic function that calculates checksums for XDS packets.

```
Private Function XDSChecksum(packet As String) As Byte
' Packet should include Start, Type, and End bytes, along
' with all informational characters, but not include any
' continue codes or previously calculated checksums

    Dim i As Integer     ' counter
    Dim cs As Integer    ' checksum

    cs = 0

    ' Sum up the characters, keeping 7 bits only
    For i = 1 To Len(packet)
        cs = cs + Asc(Mid(packet, i, 1))
        cs = cs And &H7F
    Next i

    ' Convert to 2's complement & discard high-order bit
    cs = (128 - cs) And &H7F

    ' Return result
    XDSChecksum = cs
End Function
```

Figure 18-2: VB Function to Calculate XDS Checksums

Representing Times in XDS Packets

A number of different XDS packets show times of day, with formats varying only slightly between packet types. Table 18-3 shows a typical time-of-day format.

Table 18-3: Time-of-Day in an XDS Packet

Character	b6	b5	b4	b3	b2	b1	b0
Second	1	S_5	S_4	S_3	S_2	S_1	S_0
Minute	1	M_5	M_4	M_3	M_2	M_1	M_0
Hour	1	D	H_4	H_3	H_2	H_1	H_0

Seconds and minutes, when specified, are a 6-bit number from 0 to 59.

Hours are a 5-bit number from 0 to 23. The D bit is 1 for Daylight Savings Time, and 0 otherwise.

All times are specified in Universal Coordinated Time (UTC), which used to be known as Greenwich Meridian Time (GMT).

Bit 6 of all time characters is always set to 1.

Representing Dates in XDS Packets

A number of different XDS packets show dates, and they all use the same format. A full date is represented as three characters—one each for year, month, date (day of month), and day of week. Many packets, such as the Schedule Start Time packet, omit the year, as they are never transmitted that far in advance, and only the Time of Day packet uses day of the week. The standard representation of a date is shown in table 18-4.

Table 18-4: Dates in an XDS Packet

Character	b6	b5	b4	b3	b2	b1	b0
Date	1	L	D_4	D_3	D_2	D_1	D_0
Day of Week	1	-	-	-	W_2	W_1	W_0
Month	1	Z	T	M_3	M_2	M_1	M_0
Year	1	Y_5	Y_4	Y_3	Y_2	Y_1	Y_0

Dates (days of the month) are represented in four bits, and have legal values between 1 and 31. When the L bit is used, it handles leap year situations. Since times are represented in UTC, the time transmitted in XDS will pass midnight before the local time. If applying the offset puts the current day into the previous month, it's an easy calculation, except on March 1. In this case, if the L bit is 0, then the previous day is February 28, and if L is 1, the previous day is February 29.

Days of the week are represented in three bits and have legal values from 1 (Sunday) to 7 (Saturday).

Months are represented in four bits and have legal values from 1 (January) to 12 (December). When the T bit is used (set to 1), it indicates that the current program is tape-delayed for western time zones. The Z bit is used only by the Time of Day packet, and is described there. It should be zero in all other packets.

Years, when present, are specified as a 6-bit number between 0 and 63, which is added to 1990 to produce a year. As an example, the year 2007 would be represented as 17.

Bit 6 of all date characters is always set to 1.

Current and Future Packets

01 – Program Identification Number (Start Time)

This packet uses four informational characters: minutes, hours, date, and month (see table 18-3 for the first two and table 18-4 for the second two). The D, L, and Z bits should be set to 0 and will be ignored by the decoder if used.

When a decoder receives a Program Identification Number packet in the Current class (a 01 01 packet) that is different than the previous one, it should interpret it as the beginning of a new program, and discard all stored information about the current program.

02 – Program Length/Time-in-Show

This packet may contain two, four, or six informational characters. The first two indicate the length of the program, using standard minute and hour characters (see table 18-3). The next two, if present, show the elapsed time since the beginning of the program, also using standard minute and hour characters. The final two, if present, are a seconds count for the elapsed time and a NUL character. The D bit in the hours is not used in either the second or fourth informational character and should be set to zero.

03 – Program Name

This is a variable-length packet, containing anywhere from 2 to 32 informational characters (as always, padded out with a NUL at the end if the name contains an odd number of letters). It may use any single-byte character for the program name, but none of the two-byte characters shown in table 7-2 or table 24-1.

When a decoder receives a Program Name packet in the Current class (a 01 03 packet) that is different than the previous one, it should interpret it as the beginning of a new program, and discard all stored information about the current program.

04 – Program Type

This packet identifies the type of program using keywords encoded as single characters. It may use from 2 to 32 information characters. The first character should identify a basic type using one of the first 7 characters in table 18-5. If keywords 20-25 do not apply, specify keyword 26, "Other." The remaining characters may include additional basic types (keywords 20-26) as well as detail types (keywords 27-7F). Always specify all of the applicable basic types before listing any detail types. The full list of types is shown in table 18-5.

Sending multiple program types helps to specify the content better. A show about pending Federal legislation affecting subsidies for farms producing health foods might have basic types 20 (Education) and 23 (News), and detail types Farm, Food, Government, and Politics.

At least one basic type is required in a Program Type packet, but detail types may be omitted if none of them fits the program content.

Table 18-5: XDS Program Types

Hex Code	Description	Hex Code	Description	Hex Code	Description
20	Education	40	Fantasy	60	Music
21	Entertainment	41	Farm	61	Mystery
22	Movie	42	Fashion	62	National
23	News	43	Fiction	63	Nature
24	Religious	44	Food	64	Police
25	Sports	45	Football	65	Politics
26	OTHER	46	Foreign	66	Premiere
27	Action	47	Fund Raiser	67	Prerecorded
28	Advertisement	48	Game/Quiz	68	Product
29	Animated	49	Garden	69	Professional
2A	Anthology	4A	Golf	6A	Public
2B	Automobile	4B	Government	6B	Racing
2C	Awards	4C	Health	6C	Reading
2D	Baseball	4D	High School	6D	Repair
2E	Basketball	4E	History	6E	Repeat
2F	Bulletin	4F	Hobby	6F	Review
30	Business	50	Hockey	70	Romance
31	Classical	51	Home	71	Science
32	College	52	Horror	72	Series
33	Combat	53	Information	73	Service
34	Comedy	54	Instruction	74	Shopping
35	Commentary	55	International	75	Soap Opera
36	Concert	56	Interview	76	Special
37	Consumer	57	Language	77	Suspense
38	Contemporary	58	Legal	78	Talk
39	Crime	59	Live	79	Technical
3A	Dance	5A	Local	7A	Tennis
3B	Documentary	5B	Math	7B	Travel
3C	Drama	5C	Medical	7C	Variety
3D	Elementary	5D	Meeting	7D	Video
3E	Erotica	5E	Military	7E	Weather
3F	Exercise	5F	Miniseries	7F	Western

05 – Content Advisory

These are described later in this chapter under "V-Chip."

06 – Audio Services

The Audio Services packet describes both the language and the presentation of the audio track(s) in the program. It consists of two informational characters. The first is for the main audio program, and next is for the Second Audio Program (SAP). Table 18-6 shows the overall packet structure, and tables 18-7 and 18-8 define the meanings of the language and type bits.

Table 18-6: XDS Audio Services Packet

Character	b6	b5	b4	b3	b2	b1	b0
Main Audio	1	L_2	L_1	L_0	T_2	T_1	T_0
SAP	1	L_2	L_1	L_0	T_2	T_1	T_0

Table 18-7: XDS Language Definitions

L_2	L_1	L_0	Language
0	0	0	Unknown
0	0	1	English
0	1	0	Spanish
0	1	1	French
1	0	0	German
1	0	1	Italian
1	1	0	Other
1	1	1	None

Table 18-8: XDS Audio Types

T_2	T_1	T_0	Type (Main)	Type (SAP)
0	0	0	Unknown	Unknown
0	0	1	Mono	Mono
0	1	0	Simulated Stereo	Audio Description
0	1	1	True Stereo	Non-program Audio
1	0	0	Stereo Surround	Special Effects
1	0	1	Data Service	Data Service
1	1	0	Other	Other
1	1	1	None	None

07 – Caption Services

This packet may have from two to eight informational characters, each defining an available type of captioning in the program. One character is required for each available service, and they all follow the format shown in table 18-9. The meanings of the language bits (L_2-L_0) are shown in table 18-7 (language definitions are the same as in Audio Services packets). The F bit shows the field, the C bit means caption data, and the T bit means text data, as shown in table 18-10.

Table 18-9: XDS Caption Services Informational Character

b6	b5	b4	b3	b2	b1	b0
1	L_2	L_1	L_0	F	C	T

Table 18-10: Caption Services

F	C	T	Service
0	0	0	CC1
0	0	1	TEXT1
0	1	0	CC2
0	1	1	TEXT2
1	0	0	CC3
1	0	1	TEXT3
1	1	0	CC4
1	1	1	TEXT4

08 – Copy Generation Management System (CGMS)

Only one informational character is required for the CGMS Analog (CGMS-A) copy protection definitions, so it must be followed by a NUL. Table 18-11 shows the format of the CGMS-A character. ASB is the analog source bit. The meanings of the CGMS bits and the APS bits are shown in table 18-12 and 18-13, respectively.

The APS bits should both be zero unless both CGMS bits are one.

Table 18-11: Copy Generation Management System Informational Character

b6	b5	b4	b3	b2	b1	b0
1	0	$CGMS_1$	$CGMS_0$	APS_1	APS_0	ASB

Table 18-12: CGMS-A Bits

$CGMS_1$	$CGMS_0$	Definition
0	0	Copying permitted without restriction
0	1	-Invalid-
1	0	One generation of copies allowed
1	1	No copying allowed

Table 18-13: Analog Protection Service (APS) Bits

CGMS$_1$	CGMS$_0$	Definition
0	0	No APS
0	1	pseudo-sync pulse on, split burst off
1	0	pseudo-sync pulse on, 2-line split burst
1	1	pseudo-sync pulse on, 4-line split burst

09 – Program Aspect Ratio

This packet defines the vertical height of the picture, which in turn defines its aspect ratio. It typically consists of two informational characters, which are both zero for a standard NTSC 4:3 picture (the 4:3 aspect ratio should also be considered the default if this packet is not detected).

Table 18-14 shows the structure of the Program Aspect Ratio packet. If the third character is used, then it must be followed by a NUL to fill out the frame.

Table 18-14: XDS Program Aspect Ratio Packet

Character	b6	b5	b4	b3	b2	b1	b0
Start Line	1	S_5	S_4	S_3	S_2	S_1	S_0
End Line	1	E_5	E_4	E_3	E_2	E_1	E_0
Squeeze (optional)	1	-	-	-	-	-	Q

The actual starting line of the video is calculated by extracting the 6-bit number represented by S_5-S_0 and adding 22. This allows for a possible range of 22 (normal) to 85.

The actual ending line of the video is calculated by extracting the 6-bit number represented by E_5-E_0 and subtracting it from 262. This allows for a possible range of 199 to 262 (normal).

The active picture height is the actual ending line minus the actual starting line.

The aspect ratio is 320 divided by the active picture height. In the default condition, the starting line is 262, the ending line is 22, their difference is 240, so the aspect ratio is 320/240, or 4/3.

Squeezed video (a 16:9 picture compressed horizontally to 4:3 without cropping pixels at the sides) is indicated by the Q bit being set to one. If the third informational character is omitted or Q is zero, then video is not squeezed.

0C – Composite Packet 1

This packet was designed to conserve bandwidth by combining the information from several packets into one. The definitions of the characters in each field are the same as they are in their individual packets, except that the lengths are limited. No more than five types may be specified, and the program name may not exceed 22 characters—although it is legal to send a Composite Packet 1 with a zero-character name, and then use a Program Name packet to transmit a longer name. The order of the fields must be exactly as shown in table 18-15, and the first three fields must be exactly the length shown, no longer or shorter.

Table 18-15: XDS Composite Packet 1 Structure

Field	Characters
Program Type	5
Content Advisory	1
Length + Time-in-Show	4
Program Title	0-22

0D – Composite Packet 2

This packet, like the Composite Packet 1, was designed to conserve bandwidth by combining the information from several packets into one, although the Composite Packet 2 mixes in Channel Class packet data.. The definitions of the characters in each field are the same as they are in their individual packets, except that the lengths are limited. The network name may not exceed 18 characters (although it is legal to send a Composite Packet 2 with a zero-character network name, and then use a Network Name packet to transmit a longer name. The order of the fields must be exactly as shown in table 18-16, and the first five fields must be exactly the length shown, no longer or shorter.

Table 18-16: XDS Composite Packet 2 Structure

Field	Characters
Program ID# (start time)	4
Audio Services	2
Caption Services	2
Call Letters	4
Native Channel	2
Network Name	0-18

10-17 – Program Description, Rows 1-8

Each of these eight packets contains 0 to 32 informational characters of detailed description about the program. Unused rows should be cleared with empty packets to avoid carrying leftover information through from old descriptions (although the description should be cleared when a new

Program Identification packet is received). Some decoders may not be able to handle more than four rows of description, so the most critical information should be in the first four rows, and they should stand alone, still making sense if rows 5-8 are omitted.

Channel Packets

01 – Network Name

The network name packet uses 2 to 32 informational characters to transmit the network identification. The name should use only single-byte characters in the line 21 character set (see table 7-1).

02 – Call Letters and Native Channel

This packet may contain either four or six informational characters. The first four represent the call letters of the local broadcast station, using the standard line 21 character set. If the station has a three-letter call sign, the fourth character should be a space (character 20 hex) rather than a NUL.

If the native channel is present, it is the two-digit channel number assigned to the station by the FCC for terrestrial broadcasts. Single-digit numbers may be preceded by either a zero character or a NUL, so channel 7 could be sent as 30 37 or as 00 37.

A full packet for KCC Channel 23 would be sent as 05 02 4B 43 43 20 32 33 0F 14.

03 – Tape Delay

When the Program Identification packet has the T bit set, it indicates that the station tape-delays programs from the network. The Tape Delay packet defines the length of the delay time, using standard minute and hour characters (see table 18-3) with the D bit set to zero. Tape Delay packets always have exactly two informational characters.

04 – Transmission Signal Identifier (TSID)

Broadcast licensees are assigned a unique 16-bit Transmission Signal Identifier (TSID) number in the range of 0 to 65535. This packet uses four information characters to transmit the TSID, encoded as shown in table 18-17.

Table 18-17: XDS Transmission Signal Identifier Packet

Character	b6	b5	b4	b3	b2	b1	b0
TSID 1	1	0	0	T_3	T_2	T_1	T_0
TSID 2	1	0	0	T_7	T_6	T_5	T_4
TSID 3	1	0	0	T_{11}	T_{10}	T_9	T_8
TSID 4	1	0	0	T_{15}	T_{14}	T_{13}	T_{12}

Miscellaneous Packets

01 – Time of Day

This packet can be used by decoding equipment such as VCRs to set the current time and date. It contains six informational characters containing (in this order) minutes, hours, date, month, day of the week, and year. The format of each of these characters is explained in tables 18-3 and 18-4. The first four characters of this code are the same as the Program Identification Number packet.

If the Z bit (bit 5 of the Month character) is set to one, then the seconds counter should be reset to zero. If the Z bit is zero, the seconds bit should not be changed.

A Time of Day packet with the Z bit set should take precedence over all other XDS data packets, to allow the clock synchronization to be as accurate as possible.

02 – Impulse Capture ID

The Impulse Capture packet was designed to work with VCRs and DVRs to allow single-button recording of an entire show. The packet contains six informational characters. The first four are the same as a Program Identification Number packet, and the last two are the same as the "length" portion of a Program Length packet.

Devices that respond to this packet can display an on-screen message allowing viewers to press a button on the remote that activates recording of the program.

03 – Supplemental Data Location

This packet directs decoding devices to a different line of the VBI to find information. Table 18-18 shows the format of each informational character in the packet. Up to 32 different lines may be specified in a single Supplemental Data Location packet.

Table 18-18: XDS Supplemental Data Location Character Format

Character	b6	b5	b4	b3	b2	b1	b0
Line Location	1	F	N_4	N_3	N_2	N_1	N_0

The F bit is 0 for field 1, or 1 for field 2. Bits N_4-N_0 represent a five-bit number with a valid range of 7 to 31, which indicates the line within the VBI.

04 – Local Time Zone

This packet requires only one informational character (followed by a NUL to fill out the frame), in the "hours" character format shown in table 18-3. Bits H_4-H_0 contain a five-bit number that represents the local time zone, which is defined as the number of time zones west of Greenwich, England (zone 0 in UTC). Eastern Standard Time (EST) is zone 5. If the D bit is set, then the local area observes Daylight Savings Time.

This packet is not permitted on any signal that can be received in more than one time zone.

40 to 43 – Out-of-Band Channel Number and Map

These four packet types define channel maps for receivers that support out-of-band information. Their format and use is defined in CEA-608-B.

Public Service Packets

01 – National Weather Service Code

These National Weather Service (NWS) warnings are in line 21 displayable characters (as opposed to binary codes). The format is compatible with NWS's Weather Radio Specific Area Message Encoder (WRSAME) system. Packets begin with a three-letter NWS category code from table 18-19, followed by the six-digit Federal Information Processing System (FIPS) number for the affected state and county, and then a two-digit number showing how long the message is valid (in 15-minute segments).

Table 18-19: National Weather Service Category Codes

Code	Event	Code	Event
TOA	Tornado Watch	WSA	Winter Storm Watch
TOR	Tornado Warning	WSW	Winter Storm Warning
SVA	Severe Thunderstorm Watch	BZW	Blizzard Warning
SVR	Severe Thunderstorm Warning	HWA	High Wind Watch
SVS	Severe Weather Statement	HWW	High Wind Warning
SPS	Special Weather Statement	HUA	Hurricane Watch
FFA	Flash Flood Watch	HUW	Hurricane Warning
FFW	Flash Flood Warning	HLS	Hurricane Statement
FFS	Flash Flood Statement	LFP	Service Area Forecast
FLA	Flood Watch	BRT	Composite Broadcast Statement
FLW	Flood Warning	CEM	Civil Emergency Message
FLS	Flood Statement	DMO	Practice/Demo Warning
		ADR	Administrative Message

02 – National Weather Service Message

This packet contains the actual text of a message from the National Weather Service. Packets may contain up to 32 characters. If the NWS message is longer, it should be split into packets, and the decoding device can reassemble them in the order received.

V-Chip

Program content advisories, or V-Chip ratings, are also transmitted as XDS packets. When the system is enabled on a receiving device such as a TV or cable set-top box, the viewer sets a maximum rating. The receiving device compares this rating with the content advisory XDS packets, and if the program is not allowed, the screen is blanked or blurred and the audio muted.

The information portion of a V-Chip packet is two bytes long, as shown in table 18-20.

Table 18-20: V-Chip Packet Structure

Character	b6	b5	b4	b3	b2	b1	b0
C1 (MPAA)	1	A_2 (D)	A_1	A_0	R_2	R_1	R_0
C2 (TV)	1	V/FV	S	A_3 (L)	G_2	G_1	G_0

There are four rating systems defined for V-Chip data and two more reserved for future use, shown in table 18-21. The meanings of Character 1, bit 5 and Character 2, bit 3 change depending upon the rating system.

Table 18-21: V-Chip Rating Systems

A$_3$	A$_2$	A$_1$	A$_0$	Rating System
-	-	0	0	MPAA
L	D	0	1	U.S. TV Parental Guidelines
-	-	1	0	MPAA (for backward compatibility)
0	0	1	1	Canadian English
0	1	1	1	Canadian French
1	0	1	1	Reserved (system 5)
1	1	1	1	Reserved (system 6)

Unused bits should be set to zero. This means that in MPAA packets, A$_2$, A$_3$, and G$_0$-G$_2$ should be zero. In all other packets, R$_0$-R$_2$ should be zero.

The rating systems are mutually exclusive: Only one system may be used at a time. The rating may not be changed during the course of the program. In other words, a program may not be rated TV-G, and then change to TV-14V during a violent scene. It must be consistent throughout.

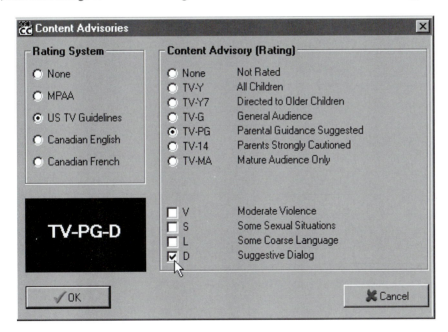

Figure 18-3: Sample Content Advisory Dialog

Captioning software can provide a single dialog box that changes dynamically to set the rating system and specific content advisory, as shown by the example in figure 18-3. In this dialog box, taken from the VNLcc program I wrote for VITAC in 1999, setting the rating system on the left changes the "Content Advisory" frame on the right. Selecting a rating displays the appropriate additional checkboxes at the bottom of the frame.

USTV Ratings

The United States TV parental guideline system was designed to cover all television programming in the U.S., although unedited theatrical releases may retain their MPAA ratings rather than being rerated under this system.

In USTV packets, the ratings themselves are carried in bits G_2 through G_0, with additional information in the V/FV (violence or fantasy violence), S (sexual content), L (adult language), and D (sexually suggestive dialog) bits. Table 18-22 shows which of these extra bits may be used with each of the ratings. If a checkmark does not appear in the table, then that bit may not be used with that rating. For example, TV-Y-D is not a valid combination.

Table 18-22: U.S. TV Parental Guideline System

G_2	G_1	G_0	Rating	FV	V	S	L	D
0	0	0	none					
0	0	1	TV-Y					
0	1	0	TV-Y7	✓				
0	1	1	TV-G					
1	0	0	TV-PG		✓	✓	✓	✓
1	0	1	TV-14		✓	✓	✓	✓
1	1	0	TV-MA		✓	✓	✓	
1	1	1	none					

The packet identifying a show as TV-14-VS, therefore, would be C8 75 (11001000 01110101 in binary) after applying the appropriate odd parity.

Receiving devices, by default, should not apply any filtering to programs with USTV packets specified as "none" (G_2-G_0 = 000 or 111). Programming such as emergency bulletins, news, political programs, public service announcements (PSAs), religious programs, sports, and weather do not have to be rated.

The following descriptions, provided by the TV Parental Guidelines Monitoring Board, explain the individual USTV ratings:

TV-Y: All Children

This program is designed to be appropriate for all children. Whether animated or live-action, the themes and elements in this program are specifically

designed for a very young audience, including children from ages 2–6. This program is not expected to frighten younger children.

TV-Y7: Directed to Older Children

This program is designed for children age 7 and above. It may be more appropriate for children who have acquired the developmental skills needed to distinguish between make-believe and reality. Themes and elements in this program may include mild fantasy violence or comedic violence, or may frighten children under the age of 7. Therefore, parents may wish to consider the suitability of this program for their very young children.

TV-Y7-FV: Directed to Older Children - Fantasy Violence

For those programs where fantasy violence may be more intense or more combative than other programs in this category, such programs will be designated TV-Y7-FV. The S, L, and D designations are never used with TV-Y7.

TV-G: General Audience

Most parents would find this program suitable for all ages. Although this rating does not signify a program designed specifically for children, most parents may let younger children watch this program unattended. It contains little or no violence, no strong language, and little or no sexual dialog or situations.

TV-PG: Parental Guidance Suggested

This program contains material that parents may find unsuitable for younger children. Many parents may want to watch it with their younger children. The theme itself may call for parental guidance and/or the program contains one or more of the following: moderate violence (V), some sexual situations (S), infrequent coarse language (L), or some suggestive dialog (D).

TV-14: Parents Strongly Cautioned

This program contains some material that many parents would find unsuitable for children under 14 years of age. Parents are strongly urged to exercise greater care in monitoring this program and are cautioned against letting children under the age of 14 watch unattended. This program contains one or more of the following: intense violence (V), intense sexual situations (S), strong coarse language (L), or intensely suggestive dialog (D).

TV-MA: Mature Audience Only

This program is specifically designed to be viewed by adults and therefore may be unsuitable for children under 17. This program contains one or more of the following: graphic violence (V), explicit sexual activity (S), or crude indecent language (L).

MPAA Ratings

This is the rating system used by the Motion Picture Association of America (MPAA) for theatrical releases. Broadcasters that show these movies in their entirety, such as Home Box Office and Showtime, may choose to keep the original MPAA rating rather than rerating the movie under the USTV system.

Table 18-23 shows the values of R_2-R_0 for the MPAA system. The "X" rating is no longer used, and is present in this system for compatibility with movies rated before September of 1990, when X was changed to NC-17.

N/A (all three bits zero) means that the MPAA rating system is not applicable to this program. "Not Rated" (all three bits one) means that the program has not been rated (perhaps because it hasn't yet been submitted to MPAA for rating).

Table 18-23: MPAA Rating System

R_2	R_1	R_0	Rating
0	0	0	N/A
0	0	1	G
0	1	0	PG
0	1	1	PG-13
1	0	0	R
1	0	1	NC-17
1	1	0	X
1	1	1	Not rated

Canadian English Ratings

This is the rating system used in the English-speaking portions of Canada. Note that there are differences other than language between this system and the Canadian French system. Table 18-24 shows the values of R_2-R_0 for this system.

Table 18-24: Canadian English Rating System

R_2	R_1	R_0	Rating
0	0	0	E-Exempt
0	0	1	C
0	1	0	C8+
0	1	1	G
1	0	0	PG
1	0	1	14+
1	1	0	18+
1	1	1	invalid

A rating of "Exempt" (bits R_2-R_0 = 000) means that the program does not have to be rated. This applies to content like news, sports, documentaries and other information programming; talk shows, music videos, and variety programming.

The "invalid" rating (bits R_2-R_0 = 111) is not a legal packet and should be ignored by all receiving devices.

The following descriptions, provided by Canada's Action Group on Violence on Television (AGVOT), explain the individual Canadian English ratings:

C: Children

Programming intended for children with this designation must adhere to the provisions of the Children's section of the Canadian Association of Broadcasters (CAB) Voluntary Code on Violence in Television Programming.

As this programming is intended for younger children under the age of 8 years, it will pay careful attention to themes which could threaten their sense of security and well-being. As programming for children requires particular caution in the depiction of violence, there will be no realistic scenes of violence. Depictions of aggressive behavior will be infrequent and limited to portrayals that are clearly imaginary and unrealistic in nature.

Programming rated C might contain occasional comedic, unrealistic depictions of violence. There will be no offensive language, sex, or nudity.

C8+: Children Over 8 Years

This classification is applied to children's programming that is generally considered acceptable for youngsters 8 years and over to view on their own. It is suggested that a parent/guardian co-view programming assigned this classification with children under the age of 8.

Programming with this designation adheres to the provisions of the Children's Section of the CAB Voluntary Code on Violence. These include not portraying violence as the preferred, acceptable, or only way to resolve conflict; or encouraging children to imitate dangerous acts which they may see on the screen.

Programming within this classification might deal with themes that could be unsuitable for younger children. References to any such controversial themes shall be discreet and sensitive to the 8 to 12-year age range of this viewing group.

Any realistic depictions of violence will be infrequent, discreet, of low intensity, and shall portray the consequences of violence. Violence portrayed must be within the context of the storyline or character development. This might include mild physical violence, comedic violence, comic horror, special effects; fantasy, supernatural, or animated violence.

There will be no profanity, but programs rated C8+ might have infrequent use of language that may be considered by some to be socially offensive or discriminatory, and then only if employed within the context of storyline or character development. There will be no sex or nudity.

G: General

Considered acceptable for all age groups. Appropriate viewing for the entire family.

This is programming intended for a broad, general audience. While not designed specifically for children, it is understood that younger viewers may be part of the audience. Therefore programming within this classification shall contain very little violence, either physical, verbal, or emotional.

It will be sensitive to themes which could threaten a younger child's sense of security and will depict no realistic scenes of violence which minimize or gloss over the effects of violent acts. Programs rated G may have minimal, infrequent violence; may contain comedic, unrealistic depictions; and will contain no frightening special effects not required by the storyline.

There may be some inoffensive slang, but no profanity, sex, or nudity.

PG: Parental Guidance

This programming, while intended for a general audience, may not be suitable for younger children (under the age of 8). Parents/guardians should be aware that there might be content elements which some could consider inappropriate for unsupervised viewing by children in the 8-13 age range.

Programming within this classification might address controversial themes or issues. Cognizant that preteens and early teens could be part of this viewing group, particular care must be taken not to encourage imitational behavior, and consequences of violent actions shall not be minimized.

Any depiction of conflict and/or aggression will be limited and moderate; it might include physical, fantasy, or supernatural violence. Any such depictions should not be pervasive, and must be justified within the context of theme, storyline, or character development.

There may be infrequent and mild profanity and mildly suggestive language. Programs rated PG could possibly contain brief scenes of nudity, and might have limited and discreet sexual references or content when appropriate to the storyline or theme.

14+: Over 14 Years

Programming with this classification contains themes or content elements which might not be suitable for viewers under the age of 14. Parents are strongly cautioned to exercise discretion in permitting viewing by preteens and early teens without parent/guardian supervision, as programming with this classification could deal with mature themes and societal issues in a realistic fashion.

While violence could be one of the dominant elements of the storyline, it must be integral to the development of plot or character. Programs rated 14+ might contain intense scenes of violence. They might also possibly include strong or frequent use of profanity, and scenes of nudity and/or sexual activity within the context of narrative or theme.

18+: Adults

Intended for viewers 18 years and older.

This classification applies to programming which could contain any or all of the following content elements which would make the program unsuitable for viewers under the age of 18.

Programs rated 18+ might contain depictions of violence, which while integral to the development of plot, character or themes, are intended for adult viewing, and thus are not suitable for audiences under 18 years of age. They might also contain graphic language and explicit portrayals of sex and/or nudity.

Canadian French Ratings

This is the rating system used in the French-speaking portions of Canada. Note that there are differences other than language between this system and the Canadian English system. Table 18-25 shows the values of R_2-R_0 for this system.

Table 18-25: Canadian French Rating System

R_2	R_1	R_0	Rating
0	0	0	E-Exempt
0	0	1	G
0	1	0	8 ans +
0	1	1	13 ans +
1	0	0	16 ans +
1	0	1	18 ans +
1	1	0	invalid
1	1	1	invalid

A rating of "Exempt" (bits R_2-R_0 = 000) means that the program does not have to be rated. This applies to content like news, sports, documentaries, and other information programming; talk shows, music videos, and variety programming.

The "invalid" rating (bits R_2-R_0 = 110 or 111) is not a legal packet and should be ignored by all receiving devices.

The following descriptions, provided by the Canadian Radio-television and Telecommunications Commission (CRTC), explain the Canadian French ratings:

G: General

Programming intended for audiences of all ages. Contains no violence, or the violence it contains is minimal or is depicted appropriately with humor or caricature or in an unrealistic manner.

8 Ans+

Not recommended for young children. Programming intended for a broad audience but contains light or occasional violence that could disturb young children. Viewing with an adult is therefore recommended for young children (under the age of 8) who cannot differentiate between real and imaginary portrayals.

13 Ans+

Programming may not be suitable for children under the age of 13. Contains either a few violent scenes or one or more sufficiently violent scenes to affect them. Viewing with an adult is therefore strongly recommended for children under 13.

16 Ans+

Programming is not suitable for children under the age of 16. Contains frequent scenes of violence or intense violence.

18 Ans+

Programming restricted to adults. Contains constant violence or scenes of extreme violence.

Content Filters

The V-Chip is a go/no-go system. Either the entire program is allowed, or the entire program is blocked. At least two companies have set forth to create parental control filtering systems that block only portions of a show.

Principle Solutions, Inc., of Rogers, AR (www.tvguardian.com), brings us the TVGuardian, and CaptionTV Inc., of Calgary, Alberta, Canada (www.captiontv.com), calls theirs ProtecTV. ProtecTV is now owned by IPCO, Inc., of Chattanooga, Tennessee.

Both devices read the captions and scan them against a built-in obscenity dictionary. Both have the ability to block obscene words from the captions and selectively mute the audio. Their methods vary significantly.

TVGuardian, invented and patented[1] by Rick Bray, attempts to turn R-rated shows into PG-rated shows. When it finds an obscenity, it substitutes a less-objectionable word or phrase, so "Oh, s---" turns into "Oh, crud," and "You son of a b----" turns into "You jerk" in the captions. It has a normal and a strict setting. In my tests, the word substitutions sometimes distorted the sentences so badly that they made no sense (like when "sex" turned into "hugs"), and it muted out very large chunks of audio, especially in sentences with more than one profanity. The system works only with pop-on captions, so no filtering is performed on live shows like news and sports.

Diane LaPierre's ProtecTV, patented[2] the same year as Bray's, replaces each obscene word with X's rather than attempting to reword the sentence. It, also, takes the "too much is better than too little" approach to muting the audio.

LaPierre and Bray both found that muting the audio based on caption data requires guesswork. There is an art to caption timing, and synchronization to the spoken audio isn't perfect. Even in cases where the caption is displayed precisely when the speech begins in the audio track, the decoding device has to estimate the speaking rate to determine when the audio should be muted.

In an attempt to remedy this situation, CaptionTV hired me in 2001 to develop a system for embedding timing cues in line 21 to indicate precisely when audio and video should be blocked to remove objectionable scenes. I, along with James Gee of IPCO, developed a system that they call CC+. As of this writing, the system has not yet been brought before the CEA for consideration as an industry standard, but has been shared with equipment manufacturers.

The CC+ system of filter codes was developed to be compatible with ITV link insertion (described earlier in this chapter). They are placed in TEXT2, and use a similar structure.

There are three types of filter codes, based on the material being filtered and the methodology to be used for filtering it.

All of the filter codes share a common syntax, although some of the elements are not present in all code types. The general form is (lowercase words and letters are included as shown, and UPPERCASE italic words describe the element to be inserted):

```
<filter:TYPE>[w:WORD][c:CHANNEL][i:INTENSITY][d:DURATION][a:AREA]
             [m][CHECKSUM][s]
```

---

[1]   U.S. Patent #6,166,780 granted December 26, 2000.
[2]   U.S. Patent #6,075,550 granted June 13, 2000.

The start of the filter code is enclosed in angle brackets, and uses the keyword "filter" to distinguish it from a URL, which will typically begin with http.

The "type" portion of the code will consist of the letter A, S, or V, for audio, sex, and violence.

A-Codes (Audio)

A, or Audio, codes mark the beginning and ending timing of a word that will potentially be removed. As described below, each A-code consists of a preamble containing the word being marked, so that end users (consumers) can program their set-top boxes to accept or filter on a word-by-word basis.

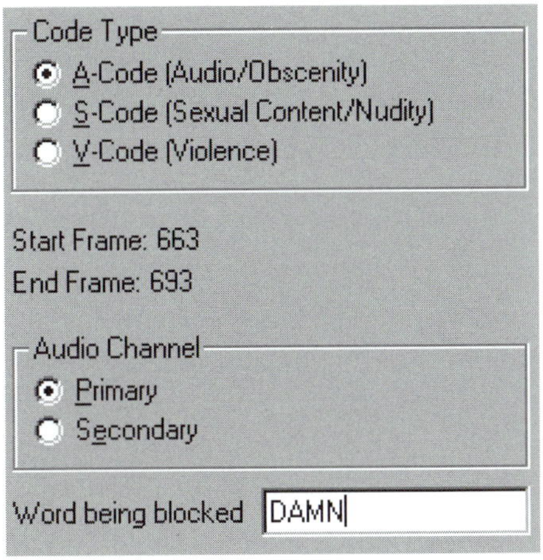

Figure 18-4: Sample A-Code Insertion Dialog

A-codes require the Word, Channel, and Duration attributes, as shown in figure 18-4. If Intensity or Area is included, it will be ignored.

V-Codes (Video)

V, or Violence, codes show where and when portions of the video contain violence. End users can set their equipment to either use or ignore these codes. V-codes have no affect on the audio or the captions—only on the video image.

V-codes require the Area, Intensity, and Duration attributes, as shown in figure 18-5. The "Mute" attribute is optional, and if present, indicates that the audio should be muted along with the video filtering. If Word or Channel is included, it will be ignored.

Figure 18-5: Sample V-Code Insertion Dialog

Code Type
- ○ A-Code (Audio/Obscenity)
- ○ S-Code (Sexual Content/Nudity)
- ⦿ V-Code (Violence)

Start Frame: 1393
End Frame: 1457

Intensity
- ⦿ Mild or fantasy violence
- ○ Graphic violence
- ○ Extreme violence or rape

☑ Also mute audio

Area: (46,15) to (95,95)

Code Type
- ○ A-Code (Audio/Obscenity)
- ⦿ S-Code (Sexual Content/Nudity)
- ○ V-Code (Violence)

Start Frame: 663
End Frame: 693

Intensity
- ○ Mild nudity (topless, see-through)
- ⦿ Full nudity/highly sexual behavior
- ○ Graphic sex or strong sexual content

☑ Also mute audio

Area: (23,8) to (72,88)

Figure 18-6: Sample S-Code Insertion Dialog

S-Codes (Sexual Content)

S, or Sexual content, codes show where and when portions of the video contain nudity or explicit sexual content. Their function is identical to V-codes. They are differentiated only to allow end users to filter these independently of V-codes.

S-codes use all of the same attributes as V-codes, although the intensity factor has a somewhat different meaning. Figure 18-6 shows a sample program dialog for inserting S-codes.

Filter Code Attributes

[w:WORD] Attribute

Used for A-codes only, this is the actual word being marked for potential filtering, rendered in all uppercase. Since many televisions and decoders allow viewers to see TEXT2 data, the word being filtered should not appear in plaintext. Therefore, we apply a simple ROT-13 code, as used in most Usenet news reader programs. Each alphabetic character is replaced by the character that follows 13 positions later, wrapping around if necessary. A becomes N, B becomes O, and so forth. Non-alphabetic characters are left alone. The word being marked may not include a right square bracket character (]), but may contain other nonalphabetic characters such as numbers, apostrophes, and other punctuation marks.

```
Private Function Rot13(InText As String) As String
    Dim i As Integer
    Dim OutText As String
    Dim ThisChar As Integer

    InText = UCase(InText)          ' Change to all uppercase
    OutText = ""
    For i = 1 To Len(InText)        ' Loop through input text
        ThisChar = Asc(Mid(InText, i, 1))
        If (ThisChar >= Asc("A")) And (ThisChar <= Asc("Z")) Then
            ' It's an alphabetic character - rotate it
            If ThisChar < Asc("N") Then
                OutText = OutText & Chr(ThisChar + 13)
            Else
                OutText = OutText & Chr(ThisChar - 13)
            End If
        Else
            ' It's non-alphabetic - include as-is
            OutText = OutText & Chr(ThisChar)
        End If
    Next i

    Rot13 = OutText
End Function
```

Figure 18-7: VB Function to Perform ROT-13 Encoding

ROT-13 coding for this application was chosen because it is self-reversing (applying ROT-13 again brings back the original plaintext), easy to code, fast executing, and adequately obscures the text.

The Visual Basic routine shown in figure 18-7 provides an example of ROT-13 coding.

[c:CHANNEL] Attribute

NTSC television as used in North America allows for a primary audio program and SAP (second audio program), which can be another language or a descriptive audio channel for blind viewers. For primary audio, specify [c:P] or omit the attribute entirely, and for SAP, specify [c:S].

This attribute is meaningful only for A-codes.

[i:INTENSITY] Attribute

The intensity attribute is applied to V-codes and S-codes only, and represents the level of violence or sexual content in the scene. The attribute value is specified as a single digit (e.g., [i:2] for level 2 violence). The intensity factors for V-codes are:

> 1 – Mild or fantasy violence
> 2 – Graphic violence
> 3 – Extreme violence or rape

The intensity factors for S-codes are:

> 1 – Mild nudity (topless, see-through clothing)
> 2 – Full nudity or highly suggestive sexual behavior
> 3 – Graphic sex or strong sexual content

The valid range of intensities is 1-3. Level 0 is not used, as it is equivalent to omitting the filter code entirely.

If a set-top box receives a filter code with an intensity attribute greater than 3, it should treat the filter code as a level 3 intensity. If it receives an intensity attribute that is not a valid positive integer, it should ignore the filter code entirely.

[d:DURATION] Attribute

The duration attribute, which is required for all codes, specifies for how many frames (thirtieths of a second) the filter will be present. In the case of A-codes, it specifies how long the audio will be blanked, and for V-codes and S-codes, it specifies how long a portion of the screen will be blocked.

The valid range of durations is 1-300 frames (1/30 second to 10 seconds). If audio blanking for more than 10 seconds is required, a second filter code must be used. This puts a maximum limit on the amount of program audio that will be removed by an erroneous or poorly coded filter code.

If a set-top box receives a filter code with a duration greater than 300 frames, it should treat the filter code as having a 300-frame duration. If it receives a duration attribute that is not a valid positive integer, it should ignore the filter code entirely.

[a:AREA] Attribute

This attribute is used in V-codes and S-codes only and specifies the screen coordinates of the area to be filtered. The format used is [a:x1,y1-x2,y2]. As an example, to block from coordinates (10,20) to (40,60), the attribute would read [a:10,20-40,60].

The upper left corner of the screen is coordinate 0,0 and the lower right is 100,100. The area should always be expressed so that x1<x2 and y1<y2. *These coordinates are relative to the full video picture, not just the safe image area or safe title area.* Because of the way televisions are designed and manufactured, the edges of the picture are not visible on all sets. All calculations or the area attribute should measure from the actual edges of the transmitted video.

Different set-top boxes will use different methods for generating the blocking rectangle. Some may use the caption decoding chip to generate a background, some may use an on-screen display (OSD) chip, and others may have custom circuitry. This means that set-top boxes will be constrained to different coordinate systems depending on how the blocking rectangle is generated.

This also means that the safe image area and safe title area will vary between set-top boxes. An OSD, for example, may be able to generate on-screen graphics considerably closer to the edge of the picture than a caption decoder chip.

If the set-top box receives an area attribute that goes outside of the area it can cover, then it is possible that objectionable material may be visible around the outside edge of the picture. If the set-top box has the ability to generate a complete blue screen, it should do that instead of generating an obscuring rectangle whenever this situation arises, blocking the video signal in its entirety. This ensures that everything that's supposed to be blocked, is blocked.

A blue screen is preferable to generating a total black screen. If the screen goes black, viewers may think they've lost their signal or that there's something wrong with the equipment. If it goes to blue (or some other color), they'll know the equipment is still working, especially if a message is displayed, such as "video temporarily blocked." Each set-top box will generate the smallest blocking rectangle that completely covers the area to be filtered. This means that when converting from the filter code coordinate system to the set-top box coordinate system, x1 and y1 should always be rounded *down*, and x2 and y2 should always be rounded *up*. A colored rectangle obscuring the filtered area is preferred to blurring or pixelating, as it guarantees total obfuscation of the specified area.

If any of the four numbers (x1, y1, x2, or y2) are outside of the range 0-100, or if x1≥x2, or if y1≥y2, or if the attribute is syntactically invalid, then the partially completed filter code should be discarded, and all incoming characters ignored until the next < character is received.

[m] Attribute (Mute)

At times, when using a V-code or S-code to block a portion of the video, you will want to also mute the audio. As an example, a violent scene may have a dying person's scream. Including the optional [m] attribute causes the audio to be muted at the same time that the video is blocked without having to add an additional A-code.

If an [m] attribute is included with an A-code, it is ignored.

[s] Attribute (Start)

All filtering codes require the start attribute. Note that it *follows* the checksum at the end of the filtering code. This allows precise frame-accurate placement of the start attribute after the set-top box has had time to process the entire code.

Filtering will begin in the frame containing the closing bracket of the start attribute and will continue for the number of frames specified in the duration attribute. There can be a delay of up to ten seconds between a the checksum and the start attribute, which allows the encoding system maximum flexibility in fitting the data from CC1, CC2, and Text1 around the code in Text2.

If more than ten seconds elapses between the closing square bracket ( ]) on a filter code and the start attribute, then the code is cleared from the decoder and start attributes are ignored until another filter code is received.

General Notes on Parsing Filter Codes

When there is no partially completed filter code pending, all characters in Text2 should be ignored by the set-top box until a left angle bracket (<) is detected.

If the seven characters immediately following the left angle bracket are anything other than "filter:", then the partial code should be discarded and the set-top box should return to ignoring anything other than < characters.

If the two characters after "<filter:" are anything other than "a>", "s>", or "v>", then the partial code will be discarded.

If a filter code is missing a required attribute (such as the duration), the code should be ignored.

The attributes of a filter code are not required to be in any particular order, except that the checksum always comes last (right before the [s] start code). These two filter codes are equivalent:

```
<filter:a>[w:QNZA][c:P][d:10][0755][s]
<filter:a>[d:10][c:P][w:QNZA][D982][s]
```

Checksums

The checksum is computed using all data in the code from the opening < character to the closing] character of the last attribute *not including the checksum itself or the start code*. The calculation is performed according to same algorithm used for ITV links, described earlier in this chapter.

19 Captions in Internet Streaming and Computer Media

A Historical Perspective

The first efforts to stream realtime text to the Internet or other online venues happened when streaming video was still experimental. Text generated by a stenocaptioner was sent to chat rooms in CompuServe for private seminars in the early 1990s, with no associated audio or video broadcast.

In 1994, two events really got the ball rolling. RealTime Reporters, a company that was providing realtime text of meetings for Sun Microsystems, first streamed their text to the Internet Multicast Backbone (MBone), and I organized the online "captioning" of a speech by then-Vice President Al Gore onto CompuServe.

Once the ground had been broken, streaming realtime quickly spread into other areas online. In 1995, Discovery Communications sent live realtime transcription of their show *Live! with Derek McGinty* onto America Online and later the Internet, using technology I developed for Cheetah Broadcasting. Other companies began developing systems for sending and receiving the text stream, and soon there were a number of ways to do it.

The easiest way then was to use a well-documented chat protocol, such as Internet Relay Chat (IRC) on the server end, and build a dedicated client in Java that could display the text inside of a Web browser window. Figure 19-1 shows a Java program from one of Cheetah Broadcasting's early live events. Note the buttons that turn audio on and off and bring up a full-page transcript. In programs like that one, the text was the important stream and audio was optional. In today's media players—as we'll see later in this chapter—it's the audio that's always on and the text that's optional.

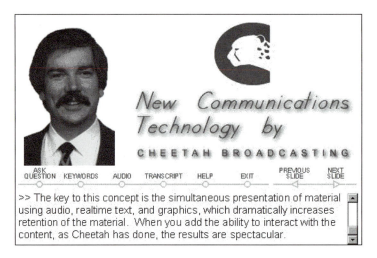

Figure 19-1: A Program Client Receiving Live Realtime Text

Since this was used before reliable streaming video was available, it was a mix of audio, slides, live text, and a static picture of the person speaking. This technology was used mostly for training purposes—sales training, distance learning, and educational seminars. It was also used for live broadcasts from several trade shows, including the National Court Reporters Association (NCRA) annual convention in 1995, Comdex in 1996, and the National Religious Broadcasters (NRB) Public Policy Conference in 1996.

The first use of this technology by television broadcasters was in the 1996 elections, where both Presidential and Vice Presidential debates were cybercast with live realtime captioning.

The difficulty with this system, if you weren't operating in a live environment, was in synchronizing the text to the audio or video stream. Figure 19-1 shows that Cheetah Broadcasting's system was designed more for interactive live events (note the "Ask Question" button) than broadcast or archived video. One very useful feature in live broadcasting, however, is the "Keywords" button, which allows the viewer to enter keywords and receive an alert when that keyword is mentioned. This ability is present in several video capture cards sold today, as described under "Caption Monitoring and Alarms" in Chapter 5 (Consumer Captioning Equipment).

Captions in Today's Media Players

Today, closed captioning capability is built into Microsoft's Windows Media Player and RealNetworks' RealOne player. Since video formats like MPEG do not allow for embedded synchronized text, the caption data is carried in a separate file (more on this later in the chapter).

Apple's QuickTime uses a different approach more akin to open captioning, in which it is the video server or source that controls whether the captioning is visible rather than the player.

With media players, the captioning is usually not displayed over the video, as it is on a TV with line 21 captions, so none of the underlying video is being covered up. There is far more flexibility in terms of fonts and formatting, as you can see in figure 19-2, which shows captioned video in Windows Media Player.

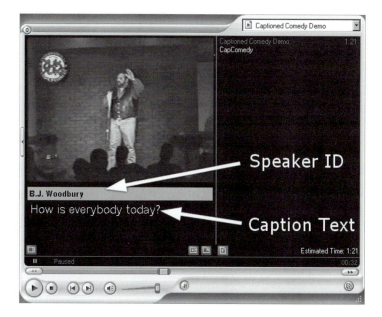

Figure 19-2: Captioned Video in Windows Media Player

Notice in figure 19-2 that the speaker identification can be formatted and positioned independently of the caption text itself.

Enabling Caption Display

Just like with closed captioning on a TV, the closed captions on streaming media are not visible until the viewer turns them on. The procedure for doing this is different in each media player.

To enable captioning in the RealOne player, select "Preferences" from the Tools menu. In the dialog box that appears (shown in figure 19-3), choose "Content" from the list on the left side. In the bottom right, you'll see a box labeled "Accessibility." In this box, you can check "Use supplemental text captioning when available."

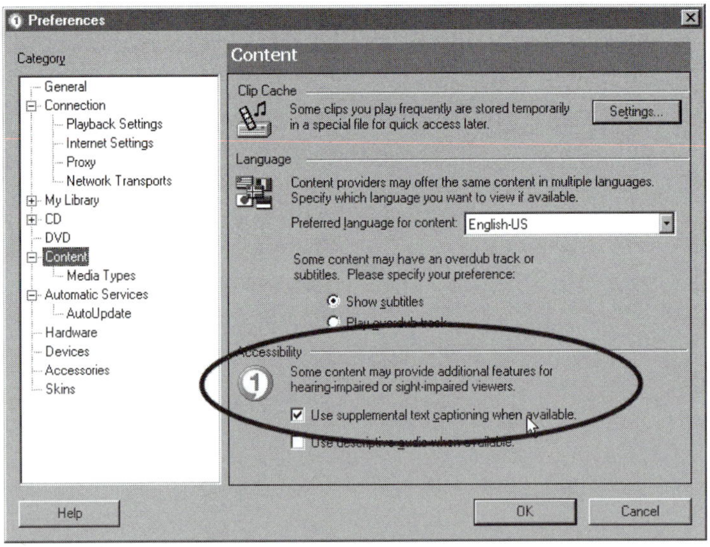

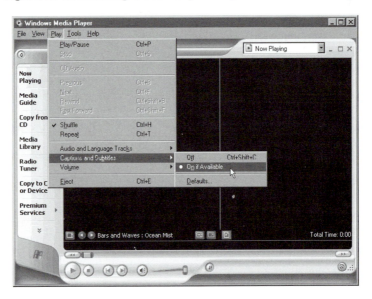

Figure 19-3: Enabling Closed Captioning in the RealOne Player

Figure 19-4: Enabling Closed Captioning in Windows Media Player

In Windows Media Player, you do not have to bring up a dialog box. On the "Play" menu, select "Captions and Subtitles," and you'll see an option for "Off" and one for "On if Available" (see figure 19-4). If you have a multimedia file loaded that contains captioning, then the language name will appear on the list instead, as shown in figure 19-5.

Figure 19-5: Enabling Closed Captioning in Windows Media Player

Standards

Unfortunately, no industry organization stepped forward with a standard for streaming synchronized captions, so each company in the media player market developed their own. Microsoft started the ball rolling with their SAMI format. RealNetworks developed SMIL and RealText. Apple has its own file format (Quicktext) to work with SMIL files.

SAMI

Microsoft's synchronized accessible media interchange (SAMI) is a file format designed for adding captioning to computer video files. SAMI files are human readable, and the format is similar to hypertext markup language (HTML), using tags and style sheets to format and present the text. According to the specification, SAMI files can use either the .smi or .sami extension, although I've experienced difficulties with the Windows Media Player not recognizing .sami in some situations. You're safer always using .smi.

NOTE: SMIL and SAMI both use the .smi file extension. If you are working with both, use subdirectories or different root names to keep them separate!

Figure 19-6 shows a sample SAMI file. As with HTML, spaces are collapsed, so indenting and aligning are purely optional.

```
<SAMI>
<HEAD>
<TITLE>Captioned Comedy Video</TITLE>

<STYLE TYPE="text/css">
<!--
P {
    margin-left: 4pt;           margin-right: 4pt;
    font-family: sans-serif;    font-size: 14pt;
    font-weight: normal;        text-align: left;
    color: yellow;              background-color: black;   }
.CC {
    Name: English; lang: en-US;
}
#Source {
    margin-bottom: -12pt;       padding: 2pt;
    margin-left: 0pt;           margin-right: 0pt;
    font-family: sans-serif;    font-size: 10pt;
    font-weight: bold;          text-align: left;
    color: black;               background-color: silver;   }
-->
</STYLE>
</HEAD>

<BODY>
<SYNC Start=100>
<P Class=CC ID=Source>Host
<P Class=CC>He's got a huge list of credits I gotta go through.

<SYNC Start=1700>
<P Class=CC>Let me think here--Okay, what is it?

<SYNC Start=3100>
<P Class=CC>He's from Ottawa... <i>B.J. Woodbury</i>!

<SYNC Start=6300>
<P Class=CC ID=Source>Audience
<P Class=CC>[Clapping and cheering]

<SYNC Start=22300>
<P Class=CC ID=Source>B.J. Woodbury
<P Class=CC>I don't know, eh?

<SYNC Start=31500>
<P Class=CC>How is everybody today?
</BODY>
</SAMI>
```

Figure 19-6: Sample SAMI Caption File

SAMI files must begin with the <SAMI> tag and end with </SAMI>. Within the file, there are two sections, HEAD and BODY, just like an HTML file. Also like HTML, tags are case insensitive. <BODY>, <Body>, <body>, and <bOdY> are all equivalent.

The HEAD section contains metadata about the captions and the file, such as the title of the file, and the style sheet information. The styles use the same format as the standard cascading style sheets (CSS) used on the Web. For everything you ever wanted to know about style sheets, visit the World Wide Web Consortium (W3C) CSS home page at www.w3.org/Style/CSS/.

In the example in figure 19-6, we define a standard paragraph style with large (14pt) yellow text in a sans-serif font. It is indented slightly, as you can see in figure 19-1, which was generated using this sample file.

Next, we specify the caption language in our CC class as American English (en-US). The Windows Media Player allows the viewer to choose between multiple languages, which can be embedded in the same SAMI file. We could define a CCUS class for American English captions and a CCFR class for French captions. Naming of languages and countries follows ISO639 and ISO3166 standards.

You can specify alternate formatting for the various languages at this time as well. For example, the SAMI code fragment in figure 19-7 provides three different caption languages, each in a different color. The three languages shown here are the most common for North American work (U.S. English, Canadian French, and Mexican Spanish).

```
.CCENG {
    Name: English; lang: en-US; color: white
}
.CCFR {
    Name: French; lang: fr-CA; color: yellow
}
.CCMEX {
    Name: Spanish; lang: es-MX; color: cyan
}
```

Figure 19-7: SAMI Code For Multiple Languages and Formats

The various options do not have to be different languages. A single SAMI file can also contain different styles for the same captions (e.g., large print or high contrast) or different captions in the same language (e.g., verbatim or easy reader). The Windows Media Player will display the various options as shown in figure 19-4, using whatever text is specified in the "Name" field of the class.

After we close out the HEAD section, we get to the meat of the file, which is in the BODY section. Here, we have a combination of text (following a <P> tag) and timing cues (in the <SYNC> tag). Neither paragraph tags nor SYNC tags have to be closed—in other words, you don't need </P> or </SYNC> tags in the document. If you omit the </SYNC>, then the end of a SYNC tag is deduced by the presence of the next SYNC tag.

A SYNC tag contains the display time for the following caption, in milliseconds. To display a caption exactly 10 seconds from the start of the video, the tag would read <SYNC Start=10000>.

To erase a caption, put in another caption containing only a nonbreaking space character, as shown in figure 19-8, which will display a greeting in either of three languages, and then erase it four seconds later.

```
<SYNC Start=24700>
<P Class=CCEN>Hello.
<P Class=CCFR>Bonjour.
<P Class=CCES>Hola.

<SYNC Start=28700>
<P Class=CCEN> 
<P Class=CCFR> 
<P Class=CCES> 
```

Figure 19-8: SAMI Code for Erasing a Caption

The text itself can contain embedded HTML. To use special characters or accented letters, follow the HTML standards. To include the text "¿Qué está?" you would write "¿Qué está?" A full list of these special characters is included in the HTML 4.01 specification, which can be found on the World Wide Web Consortium Web site at www.w3.org.

The caption text can also include HTML formatting specifications, such as bold, italics (note where the comedian is introduced in figure 19-6), underlining, font changes, colors, text alignment, and even bullet lists.

To add the captions to a video file requires the use of a metafile with an ASX extension. The ASX file provides information about the video itself, such as title, author, and copyright, and also directs the media player to a SAMI file containing the captions. Figure 19-9 contains a sample of an ASX file.

```
<ASX version = "3.0">
<TITLE>Captioned Comedy Demo</TITLE>

     <ENTRY>
          <TITLE>Captioned Comedy Demo</TITLE>
          <AUTHOR>Gary Robson</AUTHOR>
          <COPYRIGHT>2003</COPYRIGHT>
          <REF href="http://www.robson.org/CapComedy.asf" />
     </ENTRY>

     <ENTRY>
          <REF href="http://www.robson.org/CapComedy.smi" />
     </ENTRY>
</ASX>
```

Figure 19-9: Sample ASX File

SMIL

The Synchronized Multimedia Integration Language (SMIL) was developed to coordinate realtime multimedia presentations. The World Wide Web Consortium (W3C) adopted SMIL (pronounced "smile") in 1998 and has continued to enhance it since then.

SMIL isn't just a way to embed closed captioning. It can link together a wide variety of materials and synchronize them, including slides, Web pages, caption text, audio, and video.

NOTE: SMIL and SAMI both use the .smi file extension. If you are working with both, use subdirectories or different root names to keep them separate!

Unlike SAMI, tags in SMIL are case sensitive and must be written in lowercase. Tags must also be closed. Some use standard closing syntax with a preceding slash (e.g., <head>...</head>), and others combine the opening and closing tag into one by putting a slash at the end of the tag (e.g., <time begin="00:00:06.26"/>).

A SMIL document begins with a <smil> tag and ends with </smil>. Like HTML or SAMI, it contains a HEAD and BODY section within it.

When creating content for RealOne or RealPlayer, the SMIL file performs the same function as the ASX file does for Windows Media Player—defining all of the source information. The captions themselves are contained in a RealText file (with a .rt extension). Figure 19-10 shows a sample SMIL file that specifies both a video clip and a caption file.

```
<smil>
<head>
    <meta name="title" content="Captioned Comedy Demo"/>
    <meta name="author" content="Gary Robson"/>
    <meta name="copyright" content="2003"/>
    <meta name="base" content="http://www.robson.org/"/>
    <layout>
        <root-layout width="320" height="300"
            background-color="black"/>
        <region id="vid" width="320" height="240"/>
        <region id="cc"  width="320" height="60"
            top="240" left="0"/>
    </layout>
</head>
<body>
    <!-- Video stream -->
    <par>
    <video src="CapComedy.avi" region="vid"/>

    <!-- Captions -->
    <switch>
    <textstream src="CapComedyEnglish.rt" region="cc"
        system-language="en" system-captions="on"/>
    <textstream src="CapComedyFrench.rt" region="cc"
        system-language="fr" system-captions="on"/>
    </switch>
    </par>
</body>
</smil>
```

Figure 19-10: Sample SMIL File

The meta "base" tag shows where the files can be found, and the LAYOUT section shows how the windows will be arranged on the screen. In this example, the window is 320 pixels wide by 300 pixels tall, with the video in a 320×240 area and the captions in a 60-pixel-high rectangle underneath.

In the BODY section of the file, we specify the video file to play and what region (screen area) to show it in. Then, the <switch> tag checks the currently selected language and whether captions are turned on, and loads the appropriate RealText caption file. The two <textstream> tags specify the source file and the region, and then list the two parameters for <switch>.

Figure 19-11 shows what this sample file looks like when playing in the RealOne player.

Figure 19-11: Captioned Video Playing in RealOne Player

Figure 19-12 shows the associated file "CapComedyEnglish.rt," which contains the English-language captions. There is no need to specify the language in the RealText file, as the loading is controlled in the SMIL file.

The first line of the RealText file is a `<window>` tag, which provides basic information about the display of the text and the duration of the clip. Note that the width and height specified here can be smaller than the total size of the region if you want to leave borders around the captions.

The `<time begin>` tags in RealText are similar in function to the `<SYNC START>` tags in SAMI, with two key differences. First, the tag must be closed (note the slash before the closing angle bracket in the `<time>` tags in figure 19-12). Second, the time in a RealText file is not specified as a raw number of milliseconds, but in HH:MM:SS.FF format (HH=hours, MM=minutes, SS=seconds, FF=fractional seconds in hundredths).

The `<clear>` tag erases the current contents of the caption window. As with SAMI, formatting can be included, like the italics `<i>` tags used when the host is introduced.

In this example, the speaker identifications are in-line, located in the same window with the caption text itself, rather than being in their own region as we did in the SAMI example. Putting speaker IDs in a separate region is certainly possible with SMIL, but if you're hand-coding files, it's more complex than it is with SAMI.

If you wish control over line breaks in a RealText file, insert the HTML
 (break) tag, as shown in the final caption at the end of the file, before the <time end> tag.

```
<window type="TelePrompter" bgcolor="white" wordwrap="true"
        width="320" height="60" duration="00:05:00.00">

<time begin="00:00:00.10"/><clear/>
Host: He's got a huge list of credits I gotta go through.
<time begin="00:00:01.70"/><clear/>
Let me think here--Okay, what is it?
<time begin="00:00:03.10"/><clear/>
He's from Ottawa... <i>B.J. Woodbury</i>!
<time begin="00:00:06.30"/><clear/>
[Audience Clapping and cheering]
<time begin="00:00:22.30"/><clear/>
B.J. Woodbury: I don't know, eh?
<time begin="00:00:31.50"/><clear/>
How is everybody today?
<time begin="00:05:00.00"/><clear/>
<br>
<time end="00:05:00.00"/><clear/>
```

Figure 19-12: Sample RealText Caption File

There are many other formatting options, most of which follow the XML conventions.

Software Tools

For those who prefer to use software tools instead of hand-coding SMIL or SAMI, there are lots of programs available. Many of the captioning programs designed for line 21 use can also produce SMIL/RealText and SAMI output, and there are several designed specifically for this purpose. The National Center for Accessible Media (NCAM) offers a free program called MAGpie (short for Media Access Generator).

The MAGpie program, shown in figure 19-13, lacks some of the refinements found in commercial captioning software, but includes a lot of features that make a captioner's life easy, such as a spelling checker, timecode transformations, and multiple playback speeds. And, just to drive the point home, it's free.

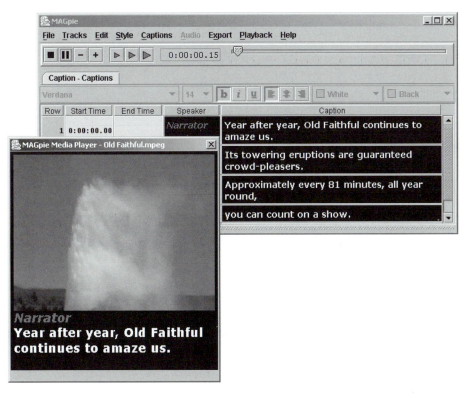

Figure 19-13: Captioning an MPEG Movie Using MAGpie 2.01

To use MAGpie, you must first install Java, and then QuickTime for Java. Once that's done, get the MAGpie installation file from the NCAM Web site, and the process is smooth and straightforward from there. MAGpie runs on both Macintosh and Windows systems, although I experienced problems with it on the Windows 9x series (95, 98, and Me), so if you're using Windows, I'd recommend one of the NT-based operating systems, such as Windows 2000 or Windows XP. If you're using a Macintosh, you'll need OS X.

When you create a new project, you'll be asked to select the media file, and to specify the default caption style for the project, including the size of the display region. You can select any font that is installed on your system, but since fonts are not embedded in SAMI or SMIL files, you should only select fonts that you know will be on the viewer's machine as well.

Formats can be applied to individual words or letters, to allow fancy effects and highlighting.

One particularly nice feature of MAGpie is that you can caption a video once, and then produce captions for all three major media players, as shown in figure 19-14.

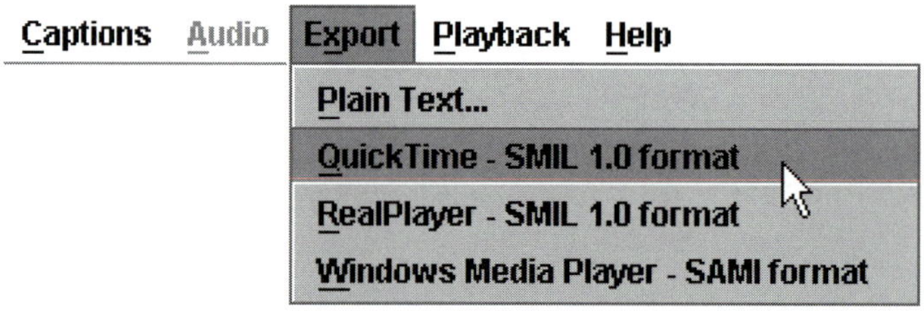

Captions   Audio   **Export**   Playback   Help

Plain Text...

QuickTime - SMIL 1.0 format

RealPlayer - SMIL 1.0 format

Windows Media Player - SAMI format

Figure 19-14: Exporting Captions in Various Formats from MAGpie 2.01

When you do your export, MAGpie takes care of naming the files to avoid conflicts. In this example, the SMIL file for QuickTime was named "Old Faithful.qt.smil" and the one for RealPlayer was named "Old Faithful.real.smil." The RealText caption files also have the language as a part of the filename, so once again you don't have to worry about overwriting one of your other files from the project.

HiSoftware is a company that focuses on accessibility and management tools for Web designers, and they offer a commercial program called Hi-Caption. It offers the same core functionality as MAGpie, but is aimed more at Web developers. They offer style creation and editing and a set of prepared templates as well. This program can also caption Flash presentations, which is discussed in more detail in Chapter 20 (Accessible Web Site Design).

Captioning Live Streaming Video

Tools like Hi-Caption and MAGpie are offline programs, designed for captioning video that has already been produced. For live events, you need either a realtime closed captioning system that offers output formats for online media (such as ProCAT's CaptiVision) or a program that accepts realtime input from a stenocaptioning or voice writing system and builds the output stream on the fly.

CSpeech, shown in figure 19-15, is one such program. It allows anyone capable of producing realtime output from a captioning or court reporting program to have their output redirected and formatted to become part of a live RealOne video presentation.

The approach taken by CSpeech is similar to that used in earlier systems by Cheetah Broadcasting and RealTime Reporting,[1] except that it uses generic standards-compliant media players as the target rather than proprietary playback software.

---

[1]   In fact, CSpeech and the RealTime Reporting tools were developed by the same people.

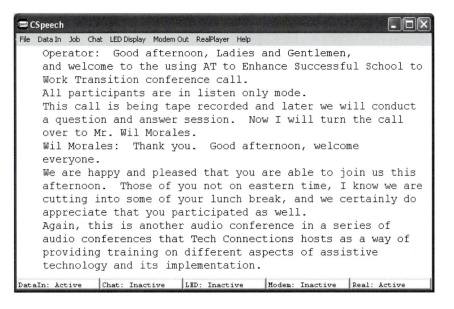

Figure 19-15: CSpeech Taking Live Realtime Input for SMIL/RealText Output

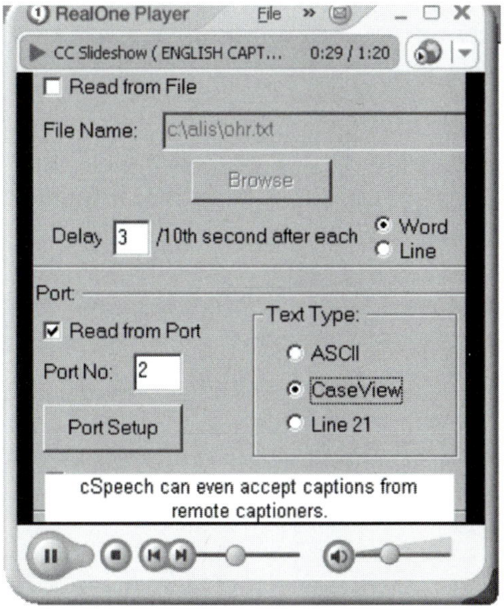

Figure 19-16: CSpeech Slide Show

Because the output is SMIL/RealText, CSpeech can be used for more than just video captioning. It can be used in audio-only environments, or for captioning slide presentations. Figure 19-16 shows a RealOne player running a product demo from CSpeech. The text at the bottom is from the RealText file, and the image is from the slide show.

The CSpeech dialog box used as a slide in figure 19-16 shows the input configuration. The "Text Type" frame in the lower-right corner shows the format of the incoming stream. "CaseView" is a courtroom viewer program from Stenograph, whose realtime input format has become a de facto standard in the court reporting industry. Nearly all court reporting software can output realtime text in CaseView format. "Line 21" is the output format from realtime captioning software—either stenocaptioning or voice writing. "ASCII" is the generic catchall for any unformatted stream.

Proprietary Streaming Systems

Proprietary systems for streaming text online have also multiplied in recent years. Several vendors of computer-aided transcription (CAT) software have built software allowing attorneys and other parties to connect to the realtime transcripts of depositions and court proceedings, and companies like Speche Communications (a subsidiary of Stenograph) have viewers that can be embedded in Web pages, much like the Cheetah Broadcasting applet described at the beginning of this chapter. Figure 19-17 shows the Speche viewer.

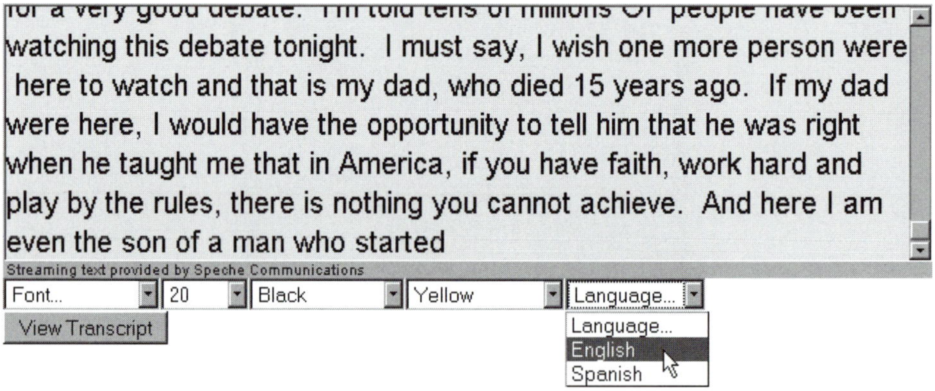

Figure 19-17: The Speche Communications Embedded Streaming Realtime Viewer

20 ACCESSIBLE WEB SITE DESIGN

When it comes to standards, we live in paradoxical times. Organizations like ISO, W3C, ANSI, CEA, SMPTE, and ATSC have standards for virtually anything you can imagine. Companies large and small rush to jump on the standards bandwagon—if for no other reason than to list the buzzwords in their advertising.

At the same time, every Web designer knows how hard it is to come up with standards-compliant code that actually *works* in every available browser. Even if your page uses rock-solid HTML 4.01 and CSS 1.0, it may look significantly different in Internet Explorer and Netscape (Mozilla), and each browser company has their own proprietary extensions to the standards. As we saw in Chapter 19 (Captions in Internet Streaming and Computer Media), the two primary methods for captioning streaming video are thoroughly incompatible, even though both are HTML/XML based.

On the Internet these days, accessibility and compatibility run hand-in-hand. The closer you roam to the bleeding edge of technological advancement, the more likely you are to exclude the very people you are trying to reach with your message, whether it be through traditional media like television or the mighty morphing juggernaut of the Net.

Think of the presentation of your Web site as a door to the content within. Every time your design throws up a barrier, that door is slamming in someone's face—someone who never sees what your site offers. When I see a Web site stating "You must be running Internet Explorer 6.0 or later," or "This site requires MacroMedia Flash," I wonder at the hubris of the designers. Do they really feel that their content is so compelling that people will drop everything to install new software just to see it? In reality, they've just closed the door on a whole class of users, who will instead go and see what their competitors have to offer.

Very few sites have a compelling reason for locking out these people. If you are a Flash designer, perhaps it makes sense for your résumé site to be written entirely in Flash to showcase your talents. On the other hand, if you lose one job or contract opportunity because someone couldn't view your site, was it worth it? You could just as easily create a fully accessible front page with résumé download capability and an index into a gallery of Flash designs.

Of course, if you are using Flash on your site, you can dramatically increase accessibility by providing closed captioning for the Flash content, as we'll see later in this chapter.

Since the Web is primarily a visual medium, and closed captioning is an assistive technology for people with hearing impairments, a chapter on Web accessibility may seem out of place in a captioning book. In fact, captioning and Web accessibility are both about broadening the reach of your content, and the subjects have become further linked with the advent of Section 508 of the Rehabilitation Act, described in Chapter 4 (Captioning Law).

Fundamentals of Accessibility

Accessibility is largely about choice. Each time you are faced with a decision during the design process, ask yourself which choice least limits access to your site, and go that way. Accessibility cynics, applying the principle of *reductio ad absurdum*, argue that this turns all Web sites into bland spreads of text, eliminating all creativity. Not true.

Items added to your site don't have to *increase* the accessibility, they just shouldn't *decrease* it. Go ahead and add that JavaScript menu—as long as there's a plain text menu at the bottom of the page, too. Include the Java program that scrolls the latest news—but include a clearly marked link that presents the news in text format as well. Present your welcome message as an audio file—and caption it.

TIP: If it isn't text, present a textual alternative. It is common practice for graphic or dynamic menus to be repeated in text-only form at the bottom of a Web page. Do the same with the rest of your content.

Adapt to the User

This may seem like just plain common sense, but it's well worth stating. Make sure your Web site adapts to visitors, rather than requiring them to adapt to the site. Stating a requirement on the front page of the site that the site must be viewed at 1024×768 resolution locks people out. Sure, virtually all monitors and video cards on the market today support that resolution, but what about the people with poor eyesight that keep theirs at 640×480 to improve readability? What about people with ten-year-old computers who can't afford the price of a new monitor and video card?

When tables in HTML achieved wide acceptance, they became the layout tool of choice. Designers found that a table was an easy way to put their menu down the left side of the page, split content into columns, arrange images in a grid, and control the overall layout of the page. This technique works well in virtually all browsers, and with thoughtful design, it doesn't interfere with screen readers at all.

Unfortunately, some "pixel-accurate" Web design tools forced the page to a specific width. Users with lower-resolution screens (or those that like to keep the browser in a smaller window) have to scroll horizontally to see the whole page. Users with higher-resolution screens see big bands of empty space that the page doesn't fill, forcing them to scroll vertically. This practice restricts the usability of the site while gaining virtually nothing, yet it gained a huge following among designers.

Tables have their place in Web design: the presentation of tabular data. Using tables for layout was a workaround because there was no better way. Now, there is a better way. Cascading Style Sheets (CSS) can handle almost all of the layout tasks on your Web pages with greater flexibility and faster download times, while making the site more accessible at the same time. Web designers can return to the use of structural elements such as multilevel headers to organize the page, while using CSS to present the information attractively on the screen.

TIP: If you must specify the width of your tables, specify it as a percentage of the screen width rather than a fixed number of pixels. That way, your content can flow gracefully into narrower or wider windows. For example, this code creates a table that fills the entire width of the screen: `<table width="100%" border=0 cellspacing=0>`.

You have no way of predicting why your site's visitors select a particular browser. It makes sense to try to support whatever they're using rather than trying to force them to use *your* favorite browser. Microsoft's Internet Explorer has a huge chunk of market share these days. Even if 90% of your visitors use it, why exclude the other 10%? Netscape is still a thriving product with tens of millions of users, and Opera is the browser of choice for many people with disabilities. If you stick with straight standards-compliant HTML and CSS, your site should work well in all major browsers.

TIP: Test your site on a variety of platforms. If you don't have access to everything, find someone who can check your site on various operating systems (e.g., Windows, Macintosh, and Linux) using various browsers (e.g., Internet Explorer, Mozilla, and Opera).

Enhance Your Links

The concept of documents containing embedded links to other documents was the innovation most responsible for the huge success of the World Wide Web. Keeping a few simple guidelines in mind when you create links can dramatically increase the accessibility and value of your Web site.

TIP: Make sure the link text makes sense out of context. Screen readers and other accessibility tools may collect together all of the links in a page. A link like "You can click here for more information" provides no clue where the link goes, especially after it's extracted and just reads, "click here." On the other hand, "The 1997 Jensema study provides further background" shows exactly what you get when you click on the link, and when extracted, it would read, "1997 Jensema study." You'll find when you build your pages this way, they tend to read more smoothly as well.

When the cursor hovers over an image with ALT text in most browsers, the text of the ALT attribute is displayed over the image. HTML also provides the rarely used ability to assign similar text to links. By using the TITLE attribute, you can provide more information about your links. For example, see the code and screen shot in figure 20-1.

```
This was described in more detail in
<a href="rogner.html" title="Captioned
Videotapes and Word Recognition">Rogner's
Thesis</a> from 1992.
```

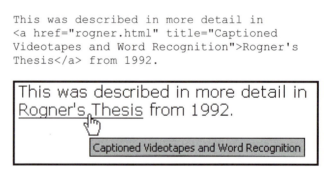

Figure 20-1: Using the TITLE Attribute in a Link

A related feature allows you to define acronyms inline, without having a link, footnote, or parenthetical. Using the ABBR (abbreviation) and ACRONYM tags allows you to attach text to just about anything you wish. By default, the tagged text has a dotted underline in Netscape and looks like normal text in Internet Explorer, although you can change this with style sheets. Figure 20-2 shows how ABBR tags work.

```
This site follows the Web Content Accessibility
Guidelines from the <abbr title="World Wide Web
Consortium">W3C</abbr>.
```

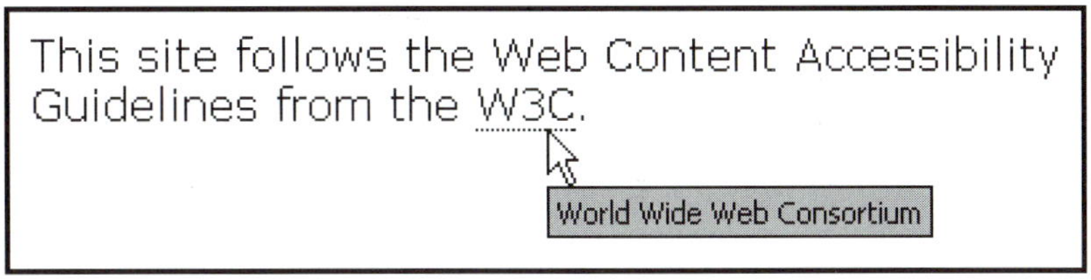

This site follows the Web Content Accessibility Guidelines from the W3C.

World Wide Web Consortium

Figure 20-2: Using the ABBR Tag

TIP: Although the ACRONYM tag seems to be well supported, Internet Explorer 6 has some problems with the ABBR tag. Although they have some difference in meaning, using the ACRONYM tag instead of the ABBR tag provides better support for your Web site.

Images

Rule one in most accessibility references for the Web says to include ALT text for all of your images. That's a very good start (but see the tip below); although there's a lot more to do if you wish to make a Web site with graphics fully accessible.

TIP: When using images as spacers or dividers, including ALT text is more likely to be confusing than helpful. If you omit the ALT text, though, HTML validators are going to complain. The best solution to this is to provide an empty ALT attribute, like this: `<IMG src="spacer.gif" height=4 width=12 alt="">`

ALT text is a good way to provide very brief descriptions. Some browsers (most notably Netscape 7.0) have trouble displaying ALT text that's too long, and when describing an image for someone who can't see it, you often need more than just a few words. There are two accepted ways to add longer descriptions.

With the LONGDESC attribute, you provide a link to a file containing a detailed description of the picture. On some sites, all of these descriptions are gathered into a single file with anchors for each description. Others have a separate HTML file for each image that needs a long description.

In the tag shown below, the GIF file might contain a chart by month showing what percentage of the programs on a network have captioning. The ALT text ("Percentage of programming with captions") tells someone who can't see the image what it's about, but doesn't convey the information. The LONGDESC file "percentcc.html" could contain a summary of the data in the chart.

```
<IMG src="percentcc.gif" alt="Percentage of programming with
captions" longdesc="percentcc.html">
```

Another way to approach this, which works even on browsers that don't support LONGDESC, is the "description link." This is typically a letter D in square brackets next to the image. Viewers can click on the D to see the long description. The previous example, coded with a description link, would look like this:

```
<IMG src="percentcc.gif" alt="Percentage of programming with
captions"><A href="percentcc.html" title="Description of CC
percentage chart">[D]</A>
```

Another advantage to the description link is that it can appear next to an image that acts as a link, letting the image do double duty. The disadvantage, however, is that D links are rather obscure, and many people won't know what to do with them.

The more you can describe what the image is about in the main text of the page, the less users will have to rely on LONGDESC files or D links.

TIP: In many cases, it's more useful to describe what an image *does* instead of—or in addition to—what it looks like. For example, it's common practice to put a logo at the top of each Web page on a site, and make the logo a link to the home page. If the ALT text says "ABC Logo," that doesn't explain what clicking on it does. On the other hand, "Go to ABC Home Page" tells you what it does without saying what it is. Something like "ABC Logo-link to home page" does both.

When creating ALT text, the best way to see how well they'll work is to turn off image loading in your Web browser (Opera has a button on the toolbar for this—you can do it in Explorer and Netscape but it takes a bit of menu navigation). This will show you the page with ALT text instead of images. In some cases, you'll need to clear out your browser caches—both RAM and disk—to get rid of the images if you've been working on the site recently.

Video

First, caption all of the video clips on your Web site, as described in Chapter 19 (Captions in Internet Streaming and Computer Media). For full accessibility, you can also add audio description. Chapter 23 (Audio Description for the Blind) covers the basic concepts.

TIP: Generally speaking, it's better to place well-described links to the video on your Web pages instead of embedding a player. This way, you can support multiple players instead of forcing visitors to download your player of choice. Also, there have been problems reported with captions using embedded media players.

In many cases, video presented on Web sites contains little value beyond the text itself. Even people with no hearing impairments, given the option, may choose an annotated transcript of the video presented in HTML format over a "talking head" presentation.

Once you've transcribed the video presentation anyway to produce the captions, consider making the transcript itself available as a separate file.

Audio

Audio files can be captioned using the same techniques as video. Figure 20-3 shows a captioned MPEG-3 music file playing in Windows Media Player. This example shows a "visualization" (the round pattern of dots fluctuating above the caption), which is under viewer control.

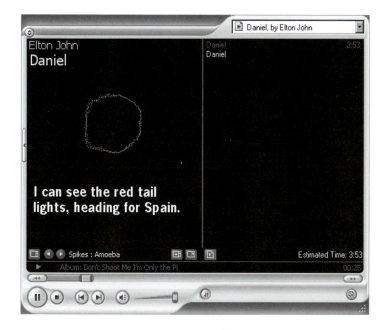

Figure 20-3: Captioned MP3 File Playing in Windows Media Player

Note the captions are in fairly large, bold type. This is all controlled in the STYLE section of the SAMI file. Even hearing viewers appreciate the option to turn on captions and see the lyrics to music!

TIP: Always give the viewer control. If there is audio embedded in a Web page, the controls for turning it on and off and adjusting volume should be clear and obvious.

I've encountered many Web sites that start playing embedded audio files as soon as the home page comes up. In most cases, the audio is simply background music—often a MIDI file. As a general rule, audio should never start playing automatically on a Web page. Always let the viewer turn it on if they desire.

People with hearing impairments may have their volume control turned up high so that they can hear an alert when they receive email or instant messages. Having music or voices suddenly come blasting out of the speakers can be startling and disconcerting. If there are hearing people in the area, it is quite an annoyance.

Macromedia Flash

Flash has always had the capability to embed text in presentations, and much of the Flash content on the Web is fully accessible without audio. The text has always been a permanent fixture of the Flash animation, however, much like subtitling or open captioning in a movie.

Since Flash has extensive built-in scripting capabilities, designers can certainly make display of the text optional, but this is a great deal of work. Manually formatting and placing each block of text and making its visibility optional take far longer than traditional captioning does.

HiSoftware has eased that burden, however, with the Flash closed-captioning capabilities in their Hi-Caption SE product. The downside to HiSoftware's approach is that each viewer will have to download a Flash extension called the "Hi-Caption Viewer" and install it on their system.

When the final product is viewed, it will show a "CC" button on the Flash window. The viewer can click on that button to show or hide the captions. The caption window, which is displayed on the Flash video (as opposed to putting captions outside the video window like the RealOne player does), has extensive formatting options. The window background color, transparency, and border can be set much like CEA-708 allows in DTVCC. The text can be presented in a variety of typefaces, colors, and sizes.

Captioning a Flash movie in Hi-Caption works just like captioning content for the RealOne player or Microsoft Media Player. Caption text is typed in and synchronized, and a SAMI file built as you work. When the captioning process is complete, however, you convert the SAMI file to XML to save along with the Flash presentation. That XML file is stored along with the final Flash presentation, and downloaded as necessary.

The captions can be formatted (e.g., italics and colors) during editing using HTML tags, which are appropriately handled in the conversion to XML.

Like movie content, Flash presentations can be captioned in a variety of languages, and users can choose which language they'd like to read when the presentation is viewed.

Remember that any textual content inside of Flash presentations or programs will not be read by Web search engines like Google or Alta Vista, so you will need to include keywords in your HTML file headers if you want people to be able to find your pages.

Embedded Programming

Accessibility does not imply minimalist design. A Web page loaded with Java applets, JavaScript menus and effects, ActiveX controls, and Flash animations can still be fully accessible.

The primary rule, which was already mentioned earlier in this chapter, is to provide alternate access to the content. This can be in the form of links to static versions of what's presented in animations, text menus at the bottom of the page, and links explaining what Java applets do. Flash animations can be captioned, just like video files.

Making pages accessible in this way doesn't just benefit visually impaired people—it increases the overall availability of your content. With ever-more-sophisticated viruses running rampant, and annoying JavaScript pop-ups becoming harder to get rid of, Web surfers are turning off Java and JavaScript in their browsers. Tens of millions of people can't use ActiveX anyway, because their system and software don't support it. By providing alternatives, you can let all of these people reach the full content of your site.

Is Attractive Layout Incompatible with Accessibility?

Table-driven layouts can wreak havoc with screen readers for blind people. Try turning off table support in your browser (Opera has this option), and seeing just how scrambled many Web sites become.

There is an alternative to tables, however. Cascading Style Sheets (CSS) are widely supported now, in virtually every Web browser. Support for the CSS-1 standard is reasonably solid as of this writing, and some of the features of CSS-2 are prevalent.

With CSS, you can lay out a page so that it looks quite attractive, allows for accessibility features (like changing the text size), and still makes complete sense to screen readers and Web browsers that don't have style sheet capability.

To see how gracefully your design degrades, load a Web browser like Opera and turn off style sheet support. If you are using Microsoft Internet Explorer, you can get the same feeling by bringing up the Internet options, going to the "General" tab, and selecting "Accessibility," as shown in figure 20-4.

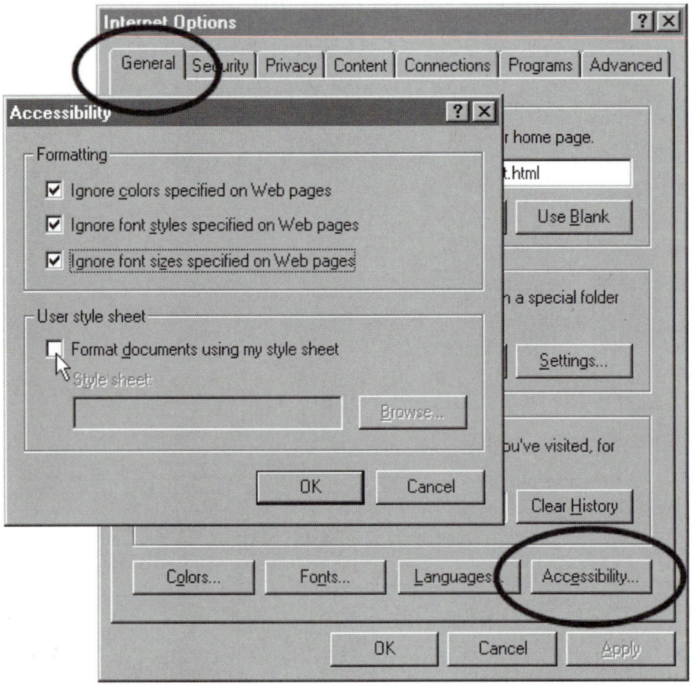

Figure 20-4: Viewing Options in Internet Explorer

By telling the browser to ignore settings coded into the Web pages, you can take over local control of fonts, font sizes, and colors—which many visually impaired people do.

TIP: Color, italics, underlining, font size, and screen positioning may be used as *additional* cues, but never as the only method for communicating a particular message.

In a nutshell, designing Web pages that are both accessible and attractive requires only an understanding of the available technologies. With CSS technology and standard HTML, you can accomplish almost anything you want in your site design without locking out visitors, which enhances your site and helps it to serve the purpose it was created for.

21 MOVIE THEATER CAPTIONING

Movie theaters were the site of the first experiments in captioning technology when Emerson Romero began splicing text-only frames into films in 1947. "Captioning," in the form of foreign-language subtitles, has been around almost as long as talkies have.

In a home environment, a small audience typically shares a television, and there are few people to argue over whether the captions are turned on or not. In a movie theater, hundreds or even thousands of strangers gather in a room and have to agree on how to view the movie. This makes captioning in a theater a significantly different issue than TV captioning, with its own set of solutions.

Open Captions

In larger cities, movies with open captions can be enough of a draw that theaters will show special engagements of open captioned movies. InSight Cinema, for example, is a nonprofit organization that open-captions movies using a laser process to burn the text into the film (by removing the emulsion). These open captioned prints are then distributed to over 150 theaters that are participating in their program.

InSight (and its predecessor, Tripod Captioned Films) has captioned over 300 films as a part of this program. According to Insight, there are about 35,000 movie screens in the U.S., which means that this program has achieved significantly less than 1% penetration. They still have a long way to go.

Open captioning or subtitling has the advantage of being crisp and clear, and visible from everywhere in the theater. It does not require any sort of special equipment or training on the part of theater management or staff. Working through a group like InSight, theaters can get first-run films without having to wait for captions to be added in later releases.

There are disadvantages as well, though. A theater can't order a single print (set of films) of a movie and show it with captions one night and without the next. Showing the same film with and without captions requires shipping in two copies, which can be expensive (movie films are heavy). Even when a theater is showing the same movie on two screens—one with open captions and one without—groups of movie-goers must agree on which version to watch, which can be difficult. Many hearing people complain that captions are distracting, and they don't want to see a captioned movie.

Dedicated Caption Signs

The scrolling LED signs that you see in post offices, train stations, and stores have a counterpart in captioning. These signs, typically about eight feet wide and showing two to four lines of text, can be placed below a screen or even in front of the stage during a live performance.

They are used in theater settings with a live captioner or CART reporter generating the captions. Once generated, the captions can be stored and played back during future performances.

These signs have never gained wide acceptance for movie captioning, as they are expensive to install and there are few good tools for synchronizing the caption text to the movie. Like open captions, many hearing patrons consider them distracting. They can be positioned off to one side, so that they are only visible from a portion of the theater, which requires all of the deaf and hard-of-hearing people to sit in that area. In large theaters, viewers wishing to see captions on the sign won't be able to sit in the back, as the text isn't big enough.

Rear Window Captioning

In 1997, the National Center for Accessible Media (NCAM) at WGBH in Boston launched a system for closed captioning in theaters, where each individual moviegoer can choose whether to use captions. The Rear Window Captioning system works by showing the caption text reversed on a bright LED display located high on the rear wall of the theater. When deaf or hard-of-hearing patrons request captioning, they are given a transparent acrylic reflector panel on a "gooseneck" that can mount on the back of the seat in front of them or in the cup holder on the arm of their chair, as seen in figure 21-1.

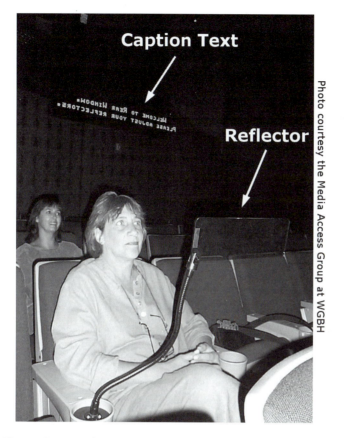

Caption Text

Reflector

Photo courtesy the Media Access Group at WGBH

Figure 21-1: Using Rear Window Captioning in a Theater

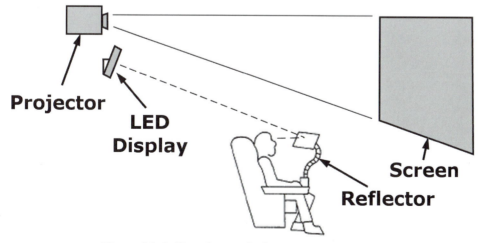

Projector

LED
Display

Screen

Reflector

Figure 21-2: How Rear Window Captioning Works

They can then adjust the panel so that it reflects the captions from the back wall, making the captioning visible only to them. The panel can be positioned so that the captions show up under the screen, or (since it's transparent) viewers can look right through the panel and see captions superimposed on the picture like line 21 closed captioning on a TV set.

Figure 21-2 shows how the system is set up. The LED display is set high on the back wall, so that reflectors at any seat in the theater can get an unobstructed line of sight. It isn't placed too close to the projector, as that would also reflect in the acrylic panel. Placement must be chosen carefully so that the reflection of the projector in the panel isn't visible to surrounding patrons, either.

When I tried out the system, I set my reflector so the captions appeared to float right at the bottom of the screen, and it worked well. People seated on either side of me couldn't see them at all.

Rear Window captioning offers many advantages over open captioning:

- The captions are out of the line of sight of everyone except the designated viewer, reducing distractions for people who don't like captions.

- Only one print of the movie is required, and some audiences can watch with captions and some without.

- Viewers can sit almost anywhere in the theater (adjusting the reflector may be difficult around the edges of the theater).

- Each viewer can position the caption text differently. Some may want it superimposed on the picture, some above it, and some below it.

Despite these advantages, Rear Window still has its detractors, who point out some of the disadvantages:

- Unlike open captioning, there is a significant start-up cost to the theater, as they must purchase and install the system and train their staff in how to use it. At the time of this writing, the cost of installing their full MoPix system (Rear Window Captioning along with the DVS Theatrical system for audio description) runs about $12,000 to $15,000. This price, of course, is subject to change.

- Only a limited number of reflectors is available in any given theater, which may prevent large groups of deaf people from seeing a movie together.

- People with bifocals or trifocals report trouble with adjusting the system so that the captions are readable when the screen is in focus.

- I have heard reports of very tall or very short people having trouble adjusting the reflectors; however, I am 6'4" tall, and my wife is 5'2", and neither of us had a problem.

The captions for Rear Window are stored electronically, separate from the movie, and automatically time synchronized, so the system can be started and then left alone as the movie runs. The cost of captioning a film is somewhat higher than captioning a videotape or DVD, but the captions can be easily loaded into a captioning system to caption the DVD or video release of the movie.

Dozens of theaters have installed the Rear Window system at this point, and first-run movies are coming out with Rear Window captioning.

Bounce-Back System

Another system similar to Rear Window is available from Cinematic Captioning Systems. The CCS Bounce-Back Mirror Image Captioning System (MICS) uses a reflector that clips onto the chair railing, and a sign at the back of the room similar to what Rear Window uses. The sign can also be moved to the front of the theater, and the supplied software can be switched to display open captioning on the sign.

CCS will either caption a film for a fee or provide a limited license to use the captions in return for a percentage of ticket sales to people using the reflectors.

Personal Captioning Systems

Personal Captioning Systems, Inc., is using an approach similar to Rear Window Captioning, but with a twist. Instead of a single caption display and inexpensive reflectors, PCS uses a transmitter and wireless receiver/display units.

One of their units, the Palm Captioning Display (shown in figure 21-3), is on a gooseneck much like the Rear Window reflector, but it's a battery-powered video display. It receives the caption text from the transmitting station, and displays it. Because it doesn't require reflection, it can be positioned at just about any angle. Unlike the Rear Window reflectors, though, it is clearly visible to the people sitting around you. This can be an advantage (it lets two people share a display) or a disadvantage (it can be distracting).

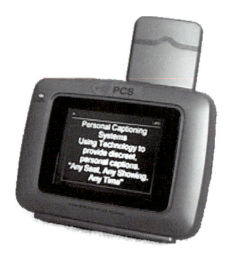

Figure 21-3: Palm Captioning Display

PCS's other display system is quite a bit different. It's a wearable unit called the Clip-On Captioning Display (see figure 21-4).

Figure 21-4: Clip-On Captioning Display

Like the Palm Captioning Display, the Clip-On Captioning Display receives a wireless transmission of the caption text. Unlike Rear Window or the Palm Captioning Display, the text is sent through a prism suspended in front of the viewer's eye—clipped to a pair of glasses.

Figure 21-5: Viewer Using a Clip-On Captioning Display

The prism's position is adjusted so that the text appears in a comfortable reading position (see figure 21-5), and the captions move as the viewer's head moves. If the captions cover a portion of the picture, simply move your head slightly or focus through the other eye, since the text is only visible in one eye.

The PCS display systems were developed for use in live theater productions, as opposed to movies, although they can be used in either venue. Because timing in a live production varies from presentation to presentation, the PCS central system does not automatically time the display of the captions. Synchronization is manual, using a theater employee or volunteer to feed out the text as the lines are spoken.

When a script has not been prepared in advance, the PCS system can take its input from a stenocaptioner, CART reporter, or voice writer.

22 CART AND LIVE EVENT CAPTIONING

Realtime closed captioning is an immense boon to deaf people who are watching educational materials. Wouldn't it be just as useful onsite at a live event?

Certainly it would, but live onsite captioning can be expensive. It requires setting up video cameras, projection systems or large-screen televisions, and a stenocaptioner with steno keyboard, a computer loaded with captioning software, and a caption encoder/decoder or character generator.

There is a less-expensive alternative, and it is called Communication Access Realtime Translation, or CART. Unlike captioning, which consists of words on a video picture, CART is just words on a screen.

CART Display Options

CART usually consists of a stenocaptioner or voice writer with their Computer-Aided Transcription (CAT) software, and a display device suitable to the audience. In cases where there is a single deaf or hard-of-hearing person at the event, the CART reporter can just bring along a notebook computer and position the screen so that they can both see it. Typically, the text is displayed in a larger-than-usual font so that it can be read at a distance.

As the size of the realtime-viewing audience increases, the viewing options change. For a small audience, an external monitor hooked to the VGA output of a notebook computer will often do. CART reporters generally select computers that allow the internal screen to be used at the same time as an external screen. This way, there's a small screen for the CART reporter and a larger one for the audience. A standard 14" or 15" monitor will work fine for a few people. A 19" monitor can accommodate as many people as you can comfortably seat within about 15 feet—typically around a dozen.

Monitors become prohibitively expensive as you move into larger sizes, so once you've outgrown a single 19" monitor, you have two choices: move to a television screen, or use multiple monitors. Several companies, such as Black Box, sell VGA video splitters that allow you to send your computer video to more than one monitor. Prices range from a couple of hundred dollars for a two-way splitter up to well over $1,000 for a high-end 10- or 12-way. An array of ten 19" monitors arranged around a room can accommodate a sizeable group.

If you wish to use television screens, you'll need a scan converter to turn that VGA output into NTSC or S-Video. Several computer manufacturers build NTSC output into their notebook computers, including Hewlett-Packard. For others, you can use anything from a hundred-dollar VGA→NTSC converter to an expensive broadcast-quality scan converter. Typically, if you are using large text with a 640×480 screen resolution, the inexpensive units are adequate.

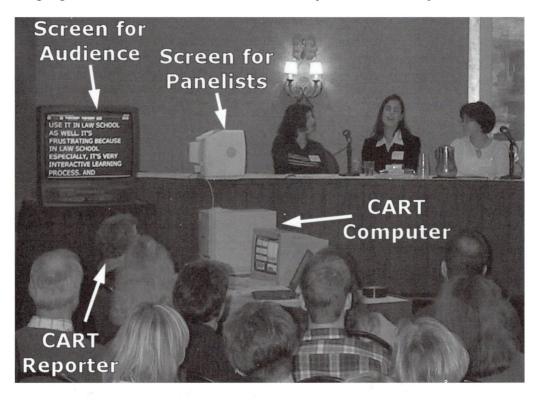

Figure 22-1: Panel Discussion with CART Reporter

Doubling the size of the screen doubles the effective reading distance. Figure 22-1 shows a panel discussion with a CART reporter (my wife, Kathy Robson). A 27" television was positioned at each side of the stage. With the settings she used (seven lines of roughly 20 to 25 characters each), they were easily readable from 45 feet. People that needed the realtime simply sat close to the sides of the room rather than the middle, and they were able to see one or the other of the two screens.

In the particular event shown in figure 22-1 (a regional meeting of the Alexander Graham Bell Association for the Deaf and Hard-of-Hearing), there were deaf panelists in addition to deaf audience members, so smaller televisions were placed near the lectern and on the panelists' table, providing realtime for everyone present.

Figure 22-2: SHHH Meeting with CART on Projection Screen

The disadvantage to locating screens away from the action like this is that people's eyes are drawn away from the people on the podium. A video projector with a screen next to or behind the lectern solves this problem by displaying large text readable by everyone in the room. This type of setup sometimes requires placing the screen significantly higher than normal or placing text only on the top half of the screen if the bottom is blocked.

Figure 22-2 shows an example of CART with a bigger screen like this. In this case, Deanna Boenau (seen at lower-left with her steno keyboard) is writing at a meeting of a Florida chapter of

Self Help for Hard-of-Hearing People (SHHH). She's using the rear-projection video system at their local library and is displaying exactly what she's seeing on her computer screen. The speaker's lectern is at the left side of the picture.

Yet another option doesn't involve video at all, but a large LED sign. An eight-foot long sign with two rows of text is clearly readable from 100 feet away or farther, and can be placed on a table in front of the people speaking or suspended above them. Another advantage to LED signs is that they don't require the lights in the room to be dimmed. They are readable from a distance even in a brightly lit environment.

CART Interaction

A significant difference between CART and captioning is that CART reporters often have the opportunity to interact with their audience, acting more as an interpreter than a part of the presentation crew.

CART is used quite often in educational settings—mostly in higher education, but increasingly in K-12 schools as well. In this case, the CART reporter works one-on-one (or one-on-few) with deaf and hard-of-hearing students, acting as their ears and sometimes their mouths as well if they don't feel comfortable speaking.

An unrealistic expectation I've encountered before is for CART reporters to write what someone else signs. American Sign Language (ASL) is not just a manual representation of English. It is a language of its own, with a unique syntax and grammar that is originally based on French rather than English. Stenocaptioning is a translation process. Captioners hear words and translate those into finger motions that produce steno strokes that aren't quite phonetic. This is a difficult process that requires years of training. Directly reporting ASL would require the captioner to see the sign, mentally convert it to English, and mentally convert *that* into steno shorthand. Only a few people are capable of this feat.

This may be one area where voice writers have an advantage. Since they are echoing English rather than translating it to an intermediate representation like steno shorthand, the task of seeing ASL and reporting English is less daunting. As I write this, I do not know of any voice writers that can report ASL directly, but I expect they will be out there soon.

CART vs. Sign Language

CART and sign language are *not* interchangeable. Despite frequent references in the popular media to the "deaf community," there is no single viewpoint or demographic representing the 26 million+ deaf and hard-of-hearing people in the United States, nor does any one group represent them all.

Different people with varying degrees and circumstances of hearing loss require different accessibility aids. The descriptions here are generalizations and will not apply to many individuals.

Prelingually Deaf

Prelingually deaf people were born deaf or lost their hearing before developing spoken language skills. There are two large subgroups of prelingually deaf. The first, referred to as the "culturally deaf" or "big-D Deaf," typically develop American Sign Language (ASL) as their primary language. The other subgroup is the oralists, who prefer lip reading and mainstream schooling over ASL and special education.

People who develop ASL skills before learning English often read at significantly slower rates, because English is effectively their second language. Since they have not actually heard spoken English, they miss the nuances of phonetics and the linguistic connections between words that sound similar while having significantly different spellings. As an example, a culturally deaf reader encountering the word "thru" for the first time would not necessarily connect it to the word "through," even though their meaning and pronunciation are identical.

On the other hand, since ASL is their native language, they are typically fully fluent with it, so that they can follow a sign language interpreter at a significantly faster pace than captioning or CART.

The oralists, on the other hand, often have English skills equivalent to those found in the postlingually deaf population, and the entire oralist culture pushes English over ASL. For them, then, captioning or CART is a far better alternative than sign interpreting.

Postlingually Deaf

This group includes late-deafened adults, as well as many younger people. The term "postlingual" refers to someone who lost their hearing after developing spoken language skills. Postlingually deaf people have English—or some other spoken language—as their native tongue. Since they have a concept of phonetics, their spelling is generally better and they can generally read faster than the prelingually deaf.

Some postlingually deaf, including late-deafened adults, begin learning sign language soon after discovering their hearing loss. Many more, on the other hand, make no attempt to learn sign, or give up in frustration. Languages such as ASL are, after all, complex languages that take just as much effort to learn as another spoken or written tongue. Even for those who do learn ASL, they are often not as fast as native ASL speakers, nor is their comprehension level as high.

For the postlingually deaf group, therefore, captioning and CART are likely to provide significantly better comprehension than a sign language interpreter would.

Hard-of-Hearing

The vast majority of the hearing-impaired population still retains a portion of their hearing. Some, through the use of hearing aids, cochlear implants, and similar technologies, can function almost as if they had no hearing loss at all. Others have varying amounts of comprehension loss along with their hearing loss.

The single largest demographic among the hard-of-hearing (HoH) is the elderly. Age-related deterioration of hearing is a common complaint. It is this group that is least likely to take on the daunting task of learning another language, such as ASL. In fact, many HoH people refuse to acknowledge their hearing loss, viewing it as a sign of age or of weakness, and will not accept any assistive technology. When presented with captioning or CART, however, they can take advantage of what's offered with no difficulty whatsoever.

For the overwhelming majority of the HoH population, ASL interpreters are simply not an option. CART or captioning, on the other hand, can provide significant assistance. Many, however, can benefit from other technologies, such as closed-loop audio, amplifiers, and hearing aids to the point where no other assistive technology is needed.

What to Offer

In setting up a live event, then, which method should you offer: CART or ASL interpreting? The best solution is to ask the people affected. They'll let you know what they need and what they prefer. In many cases, it makes sense to offer both, if the budget allows for it. I worked with one group that was putting on an awards ceremony for those who had made significant contributions to accessibility, which came up with the ideal accessibility solution.

They placed a sign interpreter on the podium where the main speakers stood—a bit to the side of the lectern. Two cameras were set up. One was zoomed in fairly tightly on the face of the person speaking, and the other showed the entire upper body of the sign interpreter. A video effects box combined the two pictures and fed it through a character generator decoder and into a projector. The projector showed the combined image with overlaid captions on a large screen behind the podium.

People who relied on ASL could focus on the interpreter on the left side of the screen. People who preferred speech reading (a term that includes lip reading along with other visual cues such as facial expressions) could focus on the speaker on the right side of the screen. For everyone's benefit, roll-up realtime captioning was placed at the top of the screen above both images.

This kind of setup, while marvelously accessible, is also quite expensive. It required a technician to set it up, and a staff of three (ASL interpreter, CART reporter, and videographers) during the event. Obviously, this would be beyond the means of a small group. In that case, fall back on a compromise between what the audience wants and what you can afford to provide.

Relative Costs

Costs for both ASL interpreters and CART reporters vary dramatically around the country, and it can sometimes be difficult to get an apples-to-apples comparison. CART reporters usually have a higher per-hour fee than ASL interpreters, but in events longer than an hour or two, you usually have to hire two ASL interpreters so that they can switch off with each other. A CART reporter, on the other hand, can take significantly longer shifts.

When hiring a CART reporter, it is very important to work out right from the beginning what equipment you need to provide and what the CART reporter is providing. Typically, they will bring their computer, software, and steno keyboard, and be ready to hook up to any video equipment you provide. Make sure they know in advance whether you'll just be using their screen, or using their VGA or NTSC output for your own displays.

ASL interpreters can generally walk into a room and start interpreting. CART reporters need to set up equipment and will often ask for a copy of agendas and notes from prior meetings to make sure that the spellings are correct on all proper names. Make sure to allow time for this.

CART vs. Electronic Note Taking [1]

In the 1980s, the National Technical Institute for the Deaf (NTID) at the Rochester Institute of Technology in New York invented a computerized note taking system they call C-Print. Since the technology really got started in 1996, hundreds of C-Print operators have been trained.

Using C-Print, a typist of modest abilities (60 wpm or better, according to NTID literature) can produce realtime text from a live lecture or meeting, just as a CART reporter can.

The difference is that C-Print produces notes rather than transcripts and makes no claim to being verbatim. C-Print operators, who unfortunately refer to themselves as "captionists" even though C-Print isn't used for captioning, use a series of abbreviations to increase their effective typing speed using a traditional QWERTY keyboard.

Just as court reporters are trained to use briefs to write long words and phrases in a few strokes, C-Print operators are taught short abbreviations of common words and phrases. For example, a

---

[1]   The majority of this discussion of C-Print is taken from my January 2001 "The Caption CART" column for the *Journal of Court Reporting*.

C-Print operator would write the sentence "This technology uses an abbreviation system" as "ts tech uses an abrevx sstm." In this particular sentence, eliminating 37% of the keystrokes allows a 60 wpm typist to write at over 95 wpm.

C-Print operates on much the same principle as the AutoCorrect feature in Microsoft Word. It uses a customized version of a commercial product called Instant Text, from Textware Solutions. The C-Print version of the software is available from NTID.

According to Pam Francis, the national training coordinator for C-Print, it typically takes four weeks of self-study and an intensive week-long training seminar to become a C-Print operator. There is no certification at this point, so anyone who has purchased the software and been trained can go to work providing C-Print services.

Of the 200 operators trained as of my discussion with Francis in late 2000, she estimated that about 150 of them were offering C-Print services at that time, and that over 90% of them were working in classrooms.

Although C-Print is often touted as a replacement for CART, the two technologies have advantages and disadvantages in different situations.

Since C-Print is not a verbatim technology, it's not appropriate in situations where a full transcript is required, or where legal matters are being discussed.

Since C-Print is less expensive, it is appropriate in educational settings where they can't afford CART. Also, many students find it easier to cope with an average of 7-10 pages per hour of C-Print notes than the full transcript generated by a CART reporter.

"It's easy for me to say I don't see C-Print as a threat to CART," said Francis, "but that's how I really feel."

She explained that there have been situations where C-Print replaced CART, but they are relatively rare. Each technology has its own application, just as neither CART nor C-Print is a replacement for sign language interpreting.

Live Event Captioning

Live captioning has been displayed on a variety of screens, all the way up to Jumbotrons in sports stadiums and amphitheaters. When the American troops returned from Operation Desert Storm, four mobile Jumbotron trucks with 40-foot displays were arrayed in the Mall in Washington, D.C., with a stenocaptioner pumping out realtime captions to the video shown on all four.

In some events, a mix of CART and captioning is used in the same event. The realtime text feed may be displayed locally as captioning, while being transmitted as CART text to a remote location.

Figure 22-3: Captioning at a Live Event

In figure 22-3, Deanna Boenau is writing realtime captions at an ADA event. In all of the illustrations in this chapter, you'll note that the captioner or CART reporter is located where she can see both the people speaking and the display screen.

The line between captioning and CART can grow fuzzy, indeed, when realtime is provided onsite for live events. The definition has become even fuzzier due to some CART reporters promoting their service as captioning even though they have neither the equipment, the software, nor the training to provide captioning.

When hiring captioners and CART reporters, have a description of what you're looking for ready, and make sure they understand precisely what they're bidding on, and get all bids in writing to avoid potential misunderstandings.

23   Audio Description for the Blind

Just as captioning provides a visual depiction of a program's audio track, audio description provides an aural description of the video images. From that definition, audio description sounds like the opposite of captioning, but it is more of a companion technology, providing the same service for blind and visually impaired people that closed captioning provides for deaf and hard-of-hearing people.

The term "audio description" is a generic one, referring to the process of describing the video on a separate audio track. The terms "descriptive video service" and DVS are registered servicemarks of the WGBH Educational Foundation (parent company to the National Center for Accessible Media), and refer to their implementations of the audio description. Just to further the confusion, the Federal Communications Commission (FCC) and the Canadian Radio-television and Telecommunications Commission (CRTC) often call it "video description" and the World Wide Web Consortium (W3C) calls it "auditory description."

Have you ever turned off the sound on your television while watching a sporting event and turned on the radio instead? Many people do this because radio broadcasters offer more complete and vivid descriptions, knowing that their listeners can't see the game. Audio description follows much the same principle.

Description is usually[1] inserted during gaps in the dialog, and explains what's happening on the screen. The concept was tested in the U.S. in 1986 and went into regular production at the WGBH Educational Foundation in 1990.

---

[1] While describers work to keep from talking over the soundtrack, sometimes it is necessary. When dialog is especially dense and there's a lot going on, a describer may need to interject short descriptions right over top of pieces of the dialog.

The first step in producing audio description for a video production is to have a describer go through the program, writing out a script that describes key visual elements. The script must be timed and trimmed to fit into the program. The describer has to make multiple passes to accomplish this. If a character drops something alongside the trail, and a different character finds it half an hour later, the describer has to go back and make sure the initial action was described, or the listener will be saying, "*what* scarf?"

Once the script is prepared, edited, and timed, a narrator dictates it. The narrator must have a clear, understandable voice, but shouldn't inject enough personality into the description that it shows. Good audio description is invisible.

The finished product is dubbed onto the program, and eventually finds its way onto the second audio program (SAP) channel in the final broadcast. Home viewers/listeners must have a SAP-enabled TV or VCR, or purchase a receiver adapter that extracts the SAP and stereo audio from the signal before passing it on to the TV.

Like captioning, audio description can be done live. The presidential inaugurations in 1993, 1997, and 2001 (Bill Clinton and George W. Bush) were described live on PBS. During live description, the narrator and the describer are the same person, and that person must make split-second decisions about what's important enough to describe and when it's important enough to talk over someone else.

At this point, audio description is more expensive than captioning. In an offline environment, an experienced captioner can be expected to caption a one-hour broadcast in about 8-12 hours. Obviously, this varies. Captioning a documentary about a classical composer that has five-minute stretches with no words will go a lot faster than captioning an hour of Abbott and Costello.

A describer/narrator team, between the two of them, can be expected to put in 20-30 hours to describe a one-hour broadcast.

Guidelines for Producing Audio Description

As of yet, there are no official guidelines or certifications for audio description in the U.S., although Audio Description International (ADI) is working on it and has a draft available. Audetel in the U.K. has a set of published guidelines, and Canadian accessibility consultant/advocate Joe Clark has his own comments to offer. Web addresses for all three of these are in Appendix 3 (Captioning Resources Online) in the Audio Description section.

Most of the goals and practices of audio description are common sense, and the three sets of recommended practices I reviewed were in general agreement on most. If you're going to be doing audio description work, I highly recommend reading all three.

Here are some of the general principles that everyone seems to agree upon:

- **Describe (only) what you see**. You are there to fill in what the viewer can't see. This includes reading subtitles and credits, filling in visual information that's required for character and plot development, and explaining what can't be deduced from the sound track alone.

- **If you can't say it all, say what's most critical**. Sometimes the action is too intense or the dialog has no pauses. There simply isn't time to describe everything. In this case, describe what matters most to the plot.

- **Don't interpret**. A statement like "the knife, a potential murder weapon, lies on the table," clearly gives away something in the plot. Obviously, most interpretation is far more subtle, from adding the describer's own interpretation of the emotion being expressed in someone's face to guessing the amount of elapsed time between scenes. State only what you see, not what you think of it.

- **Be consistent**. Don't alternate between calling the main character Henry and Mr. Higgins. Pick the one most often used and stick to it. Similarly, if you refer to the lead character's car as a light-blue sedan in one scene, don't call it a teal Ford in the next.

- **Fit in**. You're not there to be noticed. The narrator should follow the tone and vocabulary of the presentation and be an integral part of the show.

- **You don't have to fill every pause**. If there's no important information to convey at the moment, allow the listener to hear the background sounds every now and then.

These guidelines should make it clear that audio description is much more subjective than closed captioning. Two reasonably talented captioners will produce near-identical products, varying only in subtleties of timing, row division, and positioning. Two reasonably talented describers, on the other hand, could produce completely different products which both accomplish the same goal.

Audio Description Icons

There is no single icon representing audio description that has the instant recognition of the CC icon shown in figure 1-1. There are two, however, that are fairly widely used, and they are shown in figure 23-1. The one on the left is an icon that's offered copyright-free and royalty-free by the Media Access Group at WGBH. The one on the right is used by Audio Description International, and also shows up on the "generic shapes" menu of the Paint Shop Pro program from Jasc Software.

Figure 23-1: Audio Description Icons

Artwork for both of these icons is available for downloading in a variety of formats and resolutions from the Caption Central Web site at:

`www.captioncentral.com/resources/artwork/`

You can also find artwork for the generic CC icon and ratings (content advisories) icons for some of the rating systems in that same section of the Caption Central Web site.

Legal Mandates

On July 1, 2000, the Federal Communications Commission (FCC) ruled that audio description was going to be required on a limited amount of programming. The ruling took effect in April 2002, despite challenges still pending in the courts. On November 8, 2002, a Federal court vacated the ruling, removing the legal mandate to provide audio description.

There are still some stations providing audio description on portions of their programming, and a separate ruling from the FCC still requires auditory presentation of all emergency coverage.

The U.K. enacted legislation in 1996 mandating audio description of 10% of all programming within ten years of the issuance of a broadcast license.

Key Companies and Organizations

In the United States, as mentioned above, much of the work on audio description has come from the WGBH Educational Foundation. Since the FCC mandate took place, other groups have been formed and companies have jumped in to provide the service.

Audio Description International has set out to create guidelines for audio description, which are in draft form as of this writing in late 2003.

In Canada, the National Broadcasting Reading Service (NBRS) is a registered charity dedicated to improving access to print and visual media. NBRS offers free audio newspaper reading on cable TV and has a division called Audio Vision Canada, which is Canada's only audio description production center.

In the U.K., a coalition has been formed called Audio Described Television (Audetel), which is working on technologies for audio description. Since European TVs lack the second audio program (SAP) channel used for audio description in the U.S., they had to find a different means of transmitting the description, and trials are progressing using encoded audio in the Teletext signal.

24 LANGUAGE ISSUES IN LINE 21

Character Sets

Since Line 21 captioning was designed in the U.S., specifically for North American use, the needs of English-speaking Americans were quite well covered in the basic character set (see table 7-1). In addition, the £ symbol (pounds sterling) is available as a standard two-byte character (see table 7-2) for British work. Some specific concessions were made for French and Spanish although some letters are missing, and other languages certainly can be captioned using the basic line 21 technology.

An optional extended character set is also available for line 21 use. The letters shown in table 24-1 are all transmitted using two bytes (a full frame). Since they are optional, not all decoders will be able to display them. In this chapter, we'll refer to decoders that do not understand the extended character set as "basic decoders" and those that do as "extended decoders."

Any character in this table should always be transmitted with a roughly equivalent standard character in front of it. Basic decoders will show only the standard character. Extended decoders will back up one position to erase the standard character before displaying the extended character.

For example, if the caption stream contains NOEËL (4E 4F 45 12 35 4C in CC1), a basic decoder would display NOEL and an extended decoder would display NOËL. This method of handling extended characters is *required*. If the captioning system just transmits NOËL (4E 4F 12 35 4C in CC1), basic decoders will just show NOL and extended decoders will show NËL, making the word wrong in both cases.

Since the extended characters have only a single alternate character before them, the CEA committee couldn't come up with a reasonable way of handling ligatures like Æ and Œ. The readability of the word isn't affected significantly if you substitute the individual letters (using ae instead of æ, for example), so no ligature handling at all is built into the extended line 21 character set.

This system precludes transmitting an extended character in the 32nd column, which usually isn't a problem because most of them appear in the middle of words.

For decoder manufacturers that wish to support a language other than English without supporting the entire extended character set, CEA-608-B contains specific recommendations on which characters to add.

In addition to supporting languages other than English, the extended character set shown in table 24-1 also fills in some of the missing ASCII characters, such as asterisk (*) and backslash (\). It also provides a set of drawing characters to allow captions like the one in figure 24-1.

Figure 24-1: Using Drawing Characters

These same drawing characters are available in DTVCC, in the miscellaneous (G2) character set.

The drawing characters in the line 21 character set follow the same rules as the other extended characters: they must be preceded by an alternate character for basic decoders. In producing a caption like the one in figure 24-1, you need to decide what it should look like on an older decoder. If each of the extended characters were preceded by a space, then basic decoders would show the same caption, but with no box around it, as shown in the upper example in figure 24-2.

Figure 24-2: Appearance of Drawing Characters on Basic Decoders

If, on the other hand, you preceded the em dashes with hyphens (character 2D), the vertical bars with exclamation marks (character 21), and the corners with plus signs (character 2B), basic decoders would show something like the lower example in figure 24-2.

Table 24-1: Optional Extended Line 21 Character Set

Channel 1 Code	Channel 2 Code	Symbol	Description	Language(s)
12,20	1A,20	Á	Uppercase A, acute accent	Spanish, Portuguese
12,21	1A,21	É	Uppercase E, acute accent	Spanish, French, Portuguese, Italian
12,22	1A,22	Ó	Uppercase O, acute accent	Spanish, Portuguese
12,23	1A,23	Ú	Uppercase U, acute accent	Spanish, Portuguese
12,24	1A,24	Ü	Uppercase U, umlaut	Spanish, French, German, Portuguese
12,25	1A,25	ü	Lowercase u, umlaut	Spanish, French, German, Portuguese
12,26	1A,26	`	Open single quote[1]	
12,27	1A,27	¡	Inverted exclamation	Spanish
12,28	1A,28	*	Asterisk	
12,29	1A,29	'	Plain single quote	
12,2A	1A,2A	–	Em dash[2]	
12,2B	1A,2B	©	Copyright symbol	
12,2C	1A,2C	SM	Servicemark symbol	
12,2D	1A,2D	•	Round bullet	
12,2E	1A,2E	"	Open quote	
12,2F	1A,2F	″	Closing quote	
12,30	1A,30	À	Uppercase A, grave accent	French, Italian, Portuguese
12,31	1A,31	Â	Uppercase A, circumflex	French, Portuguese
12,32	1A,32	Ç	Uppercase C, cedilla	French, Portuguese
12,33	1A,33	È	Uppercase E, grave accent	French, Italian, Portuguese
12,34	1A,34	Ê	Uppercase E, circumflex	French
12,35	1A,35	Ë	Uppercase E, umlaut	French
12,36	1A,36	ë	Lowercase E, umlaut	French
12,37	1A,37	Î	Uppercase I, circumflex	French
12,38	1A,38	Ï	Uppercase I, umlaut	French, Portuguese
12,39	1A,39	ï	Lowercase I, umlaut	French, Portuguese
12,3A	1A,3A	Ô	Uppercase O, circumflex	French, Portuguese
12,3B	1A,3B	Ù	Uppercase U, grave	French, Italian, Portuguese
12,3C	1A,3C	ù	Lowercase U, grave	French, Italian, Portuguese
12,3D	1A,3D	Û	Uppercase U, circumflex	French
12,3E	1A,3E	«	Open guillemets (quotes)[3]	French
12,3F	1A,3F	»	Closing guillemets	French

---

[1] If a decoder supports the open single quote, then the apostrophe (character 27) should be curled the other way, so that it can be used as a closing single quote.

[2] The em dash extends the full width of the character cell, so two em dashes side-by-side appear connected. It can be used with the vertical bar and corner characters for drawing boxes.

[3] In French, the guillemets are used as described, «like this». In German, the opening and closing symbols are swapped, »like this«, except for German speakers in Switzerland, who use guillemets like the French.

Table 24-1: Optional Extended Line 21 Character Set (continued)

Channel 1 Code	Channel 2 Code	Symbol	Description	Language(s)
13,20	1B,20	Ã	Uppercase A, tilde	Portuguese
13,21	1B,21	ã	Lowercase a, tilde	Portuguese
13,22	1B,22	Í	Uppercase I, acute accent	Portuguese
13,23	1B,23	Ì	Uppercase I, grave accent	Portuguese, Italian
13,24	1B,24	ì	Lowercase i, grave accent	Portuguese, Italian
13,25	1B,25	Ò	Uppercase O, grave accent	Portuguese, Italian
13,26	1B,26	ò	Lowercase o, grave accent	Portuguese, Italian
13,27	1B,27	Õ	Uppercase O, tilde	Portuguese
13,28	1B,28	õ	Lowercase o, tilde	Portuguese
13,29	1B,29	{	Open curly brace	
13,2A	1B,2A	}	Closing curly brace	
13,2B	1B,2B	\	Backslash	
13,2C	1B,2C	^	Caret	
13,2D	1B,2D	_	Underscore	
13,2E	1B,2E	¦	Pipe (broken bar)	
13,2F	1B,2F	~	Tilde	
13,30	1B,30	Ä	Uppercase A, umlaut	German, Finnish, Swedish
13,31	1B,31	ä	Lowercase a, umlaut	German, Finnish, Swedish
13,32	1B,32	Ö	Uppercase O, umlaut	German, Finnish, Swedish
13,33	1B,33	ö	Lowercase o, umlaut	German, Finnish, Swedish
13,34	1B,34	ß	Esszett (sharp S)	German
13,35	1B,35	¥	Yen symbol	
13,36	1B,36	¤	Currency symbol	
13,37	1B,37	|	Vertical bar[4]	
13,38	1B,38	Å	Uppercase A, ring	Danish, Swedish
13,39	1B,39	å	Lowercase a, ring	Danish, Swedish
13,3A	1B,3A	Ø	Uppercase O, slash	Danish
13,3B	1B,3B	ø	Lowercase o, slash	Danish
13,3C	1B,3C	⌐	Upper left corner[5]	
13,3D	1B,3D	¬	Upper right corner	
13,3E	1B,3E	∟	Lower left corner	
13,3F	1B,3F	⌐	Lower right corner	

---

[4]   The vertical bar extends the full height of the character cell, so one vertical bar above another appears connected. It can be used with the em dash and corner characters for drawing boxes.

[5]   These four corner characters all extend to the edges of their character cells so that they can be used with the em dash and vertical bar to draw boxes.

Afrikaans

Afrikaans requires a large selection of vowels with accent marks in both uppercase and lowercase. Many are missing from the basic set, but by adding the extended character set, the full complement is available (áé è âêîôû ëïö ÁÉ È ÂÊÎÔÛ ËÏÖ).

Danish

The addition of A-ring (å and Å) and O-slash (ø and Ø) in the extended character set covers basic Danish, except for the ae ligature (æ). The only letters used in Danish that are not provided in the extended line 21 character set are ý and Ý.

Finnish

Few accented letters are required for Finnish. The key requirements are A and O with umlauts (diereses), which are provided in the extended character set.

French

The majority of Parisian French can be written without using the extended character set at all, as can mixed-case Quebecois. The major difference between them is that Parisians typically drop accent marks from uppercase vowels, while Quebecois keep them.

When providing the alternate letters before extended characters, Quebecois might use accented lowercase letters, turning MUSÉE and FRANÇAIS into MUSéE and FRANçAIS, while Parisians might use unaccented capitals, producing MUSEE and FRANCAIS.

The recommended alternate for both opening and closing guillemets would be the double quote mark (character 22), so that «J'apprécie le bifteck» becomes "J'apprécie le bifteck."

When the extended characters are taken into consideration, ligatures are the only thing missing from French.

Gaelic

Gaelic requires a full complement of vowels with acute and grave accents. The basic character set includes most of the lowercase letters, and the extended character set includes the rest of the lowercase and all of the uppercase.

German

The basic line 21 character set was simply not designed for German, but the extended character set fills in the gaps well. The biggest challenge with German is the letter ß (esszett, or sharp S). Unlike all of the accented letters, there is no single-character alternative to ß. When a word containing ß is rendered in a basic Latin alphabet, the ß is usually replaced with a double s (rendering, for example, "schloß" as "schloss"). Using a single s as an alternate can alter the pronunciation of the word, and impair readability. It is probably better to avoid using ß except in environments where you know the decoders can support it.

As in French, use double quote marks (character 22) as alternates for guillemets.

Irish

The only accented letters used in Irish (as distinct from Gaelic) are the vowels with acute accents. The basic character set provides lowercase, and the extended character set provides uppercase.

Italian

The extended character set provides the missing lowercase letters with grave accents, all of the required uppercase letters with grave and acute accents, and the i-umlaut (ï and Ï) required by Italian. Although there are quite a few missing pieces in the primary character set, the extended set suits Italian well.

Portuguese

The basic line 21 character set covers Portuguese fairly well in mixed-case, except for the letters ã, õ, and ü (there are others, but not as frequently used). In uppercase, however, there are quite a few holes. The extended character set plugs the holes well, filling in everything that should be needed for Portuguese captioning.

Spanish

Spanish is well covered by the main line 21 captioning character set. Not only does the primary character set include accented letters and both upper- and lowercase ñ, but the inverse (open) question mark is there as well, so that captioners can write things like: ¿Qué pasa?

With the addition of the extended characters, the only things missing for Spanish captioning are the ° and ª (masculine and feminine ordinal indicators) and inverse (open) exclamation mark (¡). The ¡ is far less important to the language than the question mark, and you can always improvise by using a lower-case "i."

Quite a bit of captioning has been done in Spanish. The majority of it has been offline (post-production) captioning, but there is realtime Spanish captioning happening as well. Professor Fernando Altamirano, in Puerto Rico, has developed a theory for writing realtime Spanish using a standard American stenotype machine. This required some modification to the basic structure and meaning of the keys, so that he could, for example, represent the ñ sound.

Swedish

Aside from the A and E with acute accents, which aren't used frequently in Swedish, the big gaps in the basic character set are the A-ring (å & Å) and vowels with umlauts (diereses), all of which are fixed in the extended character set.

Non-Latin Alphabets

Since the character set resides in the television set or decoder rather than in the encoder, there's no way to replace the alphabet. Rendering a language like Russian (which uses the Cyrillic alphabet), Arabic, Greek, or Japanese (kanji or katakana) requires that the language be rendered using the Latin alphabet.

The Consumer Electronics Association (CEA) has allowed for a method of selecting alternate character sets as an extension to CEA-608-B, and Norpak has registered command codes for selecting both Korean (Hangul) and Chinese alphabets. Several different methods for captioning in non-Latin character sets have been developed, as you can see by perusing patents filed on captioning systems.

APPENDIX 1: CAPTIONING EQUIPMENT VENDORS

Hardware Vendors

Hardware manufacturers are listed alphabetically, with the following key words to describe the products they make:

- **608 Encoders**: CEA-608-compatible caption/XDS encoding equipment for line 21 use. This category includes both analog and digital format encoders.

- **708 Encoders**: CEA-708-compatible caption encoding equipment for DTV use.

- **Bridges**: Devices that extract and reinsert captions to bridge around equipment that destroys or regenerates line 21. They may include caption relocation capabilities.

- **Character Generators**: Equipment used for open captioning or subtitling.

- **Decoders**: Devices that decode CEA-608 or CEA-708 captions and display them on a video output.

- **Grabbers**: Devices that allow a computer to extract line 21 data. Also known as data recovery decoders.

- **Monitors**: Devices that show line 21 status information to verify that captions and related data are present.

- **Theater Captioning Systems**: Closed or open captioning for movie theaters.

- **Transcoders**: Equipment to convert CEA-608 caption data to CEA-708 data.

Most of these companies are producing new products on a regular basis, so check their Web sites for updates on available products and technologies.

Adrienne Electronics
7225 Bermuda Road, Unit G
Las Vegas, NV 89119
Phone: 702/896-1858
Toll-free: 800/782-2321
Fax: 702/896-3034
Email: info@adrielec.com
Web site: www.adrielec.com

- Grabbers (PCI cards)
- Other (timecode readers & generators)

ATI Technologies
1 Commerce Valley Drive East
Markham, Ontario, Canada L3T 7X6
Phone: 905/882-2600
Fax: 905/882-2620
Email: sales@atitech.ca
Web site: www.atitech.com

- Grabbers (All-In-Wonder)

Broadcast Video Systems Corp.
40 West Wilmot St.
Richmond Hill, Ontario L4B 1H8
Phone: 905/764-1584
Fax: 905/764-7438
Email: bvs@bvs.ca
Website: www.bvs.ca

- 608 Encoders
- Bridges
- Decoders
- Transcoders

Compusult Limited
40 Bannister Street
Mount Pearl, Newfoundland, Canada
Phone: 709/745-7914
Toll-free: 888/388-8180
Fax: 709/745-7927
Email: info@captiondisplay.com
Web site: www.captiondisplay.com

- Decoders (Caption Display—large format signs that display captions outside of the TV viewing area)

Cinematic Captioning Systems, Inc.
8111 Bel Moore Blvd.
Indianapolis, IN 46259
Phone: 317/862-3418
Email: sales@moviecaptions.com
Web site: www.moviecaptions.com

- Theater Captioning Systems (MICS)

EEG Enterprises
586 Main Street
Farmingdale, NY 11735
Phone: 516/293-7472
Fax: 516/293-7417
Email: sales@eegent.com
Web site: www.eegent.com

- 608 Encoders (Smart Encoder)
- 708 Encoders (Smart Server)
- Bridges
- Character Generators
- Decoders
- Grabbers
- Monitors
- Transcoders

Evertz Microsystems
5288 John Lucas Dr.
Burlington, Ontario, Canada L7L 5Z9
Phone: 905/335-3700
Toll-free: 877/995-3700
Fax: 905/335-3573
Email: sales@evertz.com
Web site: www.evertz.com

- 608 Encoders
- 708 Encoders
- Decoders
- Grabbers
- Monitors
- Transcoders

International Computers
7245 South 76th Street
Franklin, WI 53132
Phone: 414/764-9000
Email: mail@intlc.com
Web site: www.intlc.com

- 608 Encoders (CCE)
- Grabbers (CCD)

IPCO, Inc.
3247 Waterfront Drive
Chattanooga, TN 37416
Phone: 423-894-1234
Fax: 423-894-1224

- Decoders with filtering (ProtecTV and CC+)

Link Electronics, Inc.
2137 Rust Ave.
Cape Girardeau, MO 63703
Phone: 573/334-4433
Toll-free: 800/776-4411
Fax: 573/334-9255
Email: sales@linkelectronics.com
Web site: www.linkelectronics.com

- 608 Encoders
- Character Generators
- Decoders
- Grabbers
- Monitors

National Center for Accessible Media
125 Western Avenue
Boston, MA 02134
Phone: 617/300-3400
TTY: 617/300-2489
Fax: 617/300-1035
Email: ncam@wgbh.org
Web site: ncam.wgbh.org

- Theater captioning systems (Rear Window Captioning, MoPix)

Norpak Corporation
10 Hearst Way
Kanata, Ontario, Canada K2L 2P4
Phone: 613/592-4164
Fax: 613/592-6560
Email: info@norpak.ca
Web site: www.norpak.ca

- 608 Encoders
- 708 Encoders
- Grabbers
- Monitors
- Transcoders

Personal Captioning Systems, Inc.
9401 N. Nashville
Morton Grove, IL 60053
Phone: 847/965-6544
Fax: 503/210-8789
Email: Info@PersonalCaptioning.com
Web site: www.PersonalCaptioning.com

- Theater captioning systems (Palm Captioning Display and Clip-On Captioning Display)

Principle Solutions
PO Box 670
Rogers, AR 72757
Phone: 479/986-0022
Toll-free: 800/967-7884
Fax: 479/986-0033
Email: sales@TVGuardian.com
Web site: www.tvguardian.com

- Decoders with filtering (TVGuardian)

SoftTouch, Inc.
306 Stevenson Lane
Landover, MD 20785
Phone: 301/333-6555
Fax: 301/333-6556
Email: Info@SoftTouch-Inc.com
Web site: www.softtouch-inc.com

- 608 Encoders (CCEPlus)
- Character Generators
- Decoders
- Grabbers (MagHubcap)
- Monitors

SunBelt Industries Technologies Group, Inc.
83 S. 30th Avenue
Jacksonville Beach, FL 32250
Phone: 904/249-5577
Fax: 904/241-1853
Email: sunbelt@sunbeltindustries.com
Web site: www.sunbeltindustries.com

- Grabbers (TextGrabber)

Tri-Vision International, Ltd.
41 Pullman Court
Toronto Ontario Canada M1X 1E4
Toll-free: 888/298-8551
Email: info@tri-vision.ca
Web site: www.tri-vision.ca

- Decoders (V.gis)

Ultech, LLC
125 North Benson Road
Middlebury, CT 06762
Phone: 203/758-8667
Toll-free: 888/360-0010
Fax: 203/758-8693
Email: info@ultech.com
Web site: www.ultech.com

Ultech is a wholly owned subsidiary of the National Captioning Institute.

- 608 Encoders (Insertacap)
- 708 Encoders (DTV708)
- Character Generators (Displayacap)
- Decoders
- Transcoders

ViewCast
600 Airport Blvd, Suite 900
Morrisville, NC 27560
Phone: 972/488-7200
Toll-free: 800/540-4119
Fax: 919/319-9814
Email: info@dfw.viewcast.com
Web site: www.viewcast.com

- Grabbers (Osprey)

Software Vendors

Software manufacturers are listed alphabetically, with the following key words to describe the products they make:

Offline: Includes both tape-based and nonlinear captioning systems that work off of timecodes for anything that isn't produced live.

Online: Software for live captioning, including steno-based and voice-based realtime as well as live-display (scripted or typed) realtime.

Encoding: Programs that place captions generated by an offline captioning system into the video, typically using caption encoder hardware.

Multimedia: Software for captioning video and/or audio streams for Internet broadcasts and CD-ROM presentations.

Other: Includes interactive television, XDS, realtime network messaging, and other related products and services.

Newsroom systems and prompting systems are almost all capable of producing line 21 captioning output now, and so they are not included in this listing.

Most of these companies are producing new products on a regular basis, so check their Web sites for updates on available products and technologies.

Advantage Software

925 Central Pkwy
Stuart, FL 34994
Phone: 772/288-3266
Toll-free: 800/800-1759
Fax: 772/288-1737
Email: sales@eclipsecat.com
Web site: www.eclipsecat.com

- Online & Offline (AccuCap)

AudioScribe

P.O. Box 321
Breaux Bridge, LA 70517
Phone: 337/332-0680
Toll-free: 800/869-0569
Fax: 337/332-0705
Email: info@audioscribe.com
Web site: www.audioscribe.com

- Online (SpeechCAP)

Cheetah International, Inc.

8120 Sheridan Blvd., #C206
Westminster, CO 80003
Phone: 877/333-2287
Email: sales@caption.com
Web site: www.caption.com

- Encoding (PostCAP)
- Offline (CAPtivator Offline & CAPtivator NL)
- Online (CAPtivator Online)

Computer Prompting and Captioning

1010 Rockville Pike, Suite 306
Rockville, MD 20852
Phone: 301/738-8487
Fax: 301/738-8488
TTY: 301/738-8489
Toll-free: 800/977-6678
Email: info@cpcweb.com
Web site: www.cpcweb.com

- Encoding
- Offline (CaptionMaker)
- Offline for Mac (MacCaption)
- Online (CaptionMaker)
- Multimedia

CSpeech

303 Potrero Street, Suite 42-203
Santa Cruz, CA 95060
Phone: 831/438-1498
Email: info@CSpeech.com
Web site: www.cspeech.com

- Multimedia

EEG Enterprises
586 Main Street
Farmingdale, NY 11735
Phone: 516/293-7472
Fax: 516/293-7417
Email: sales@eegent.com
Web site: www.eegent.com

- Other (iTV XPress, XDS XPress)

Evertz Microsystems
5288 John Lucas Dr.
Burlington, Ontario, Canada L7L 5Z9
Phone: 905/335-3700
Toll-free: 877/995-3700
Fax: 905/335-3573
Email: sales@evertz.com
Web site: www.evertz.com

- Offline (ProCAP)
- Other (MetaCast)

HiSoftware Company
6 Chenell Drive
Concord, NH 03301
Phone: 603/229-3055
Toll-free: 888/272-2474 (US and Canada)
Fax: 603/223-9741
Email: info@hisoftware.com
Web site: www.hisoftware.com/hmcc

- Multimedia (Hi-Caption)

ImageLogic Corporation
6807 Brennon Lane
Chevy Chase, MD 20815-3255
Phone: 301/907-8891
E-mail: info@imageLogic.com
Web site: www.imagelogic.com

- Encoding
- Offline (AutoCaption)

International Computers
7245 South 76th Street
Franklin, WI 53132
Phone: 414/764-9000
Email: mail@intlc.com
Web site: www.intlc.com

- Offline (CCE)
- Online (CCE Voice)
- Other (TVWebLinks)

NCAM
(National Center for Accessible Media)
125 Western Avenue
Boston, MA 02134
Phone: 617/300-3400
TTY: 617/300-2489
Fax: 617/300-1035
Email: ncam@wgbh.org
Web site: ncam.wgbh.org

- Multimedia (MAGpie)
- Theater (Mopix)

Norpak Corporation
10 Hearst Way
Kanata, Ontario, Canada K2L 2P4
Phone: 613/592-4164
Fax: 613/592-6560
Email: info@norpak.ca
Web site: www.norpak.ca

- Other (WHAZ-it, WHAK-it)

ProCAT Corporation
5126 Clareton Drive, Suite 260
Agoura Hills, CA 91301
Toll-free: 800/966-1221
Fax: 818/879-5620
Email: sales@procat.com
Web site: www.procat.com

- Online (CaptiVision)

RapidText
1801 Dove Street, Suite 101
Newport Beach, CA 92660
Phone: 949/399-9200
Email: info@rapidtext.com
Web site: www.rapidtext.com

- Online (RapidCaption)

Softel-USA, Inc.
1601 Cloverfield Blvd.
2nd Floor, South Tower
Santa Monica, CA 90404
Phone: 310/309-5281
Toll-free: 866/SOFTEL-4
Fax: 310/309-5288
Email: sales@softel-usa.com
Web site: www.softel-usa.com

- Encoding
- Offline (Swift)
- Online

SoftNI Corporation
11400 West Olympic Blvd., Suite 200
Los Angeles, CA 90064
Phone: 310/312-9558
Fax: 310/312-9557
Email: jmsalgado@softni.com
Web site: www.softni.com

- Encoding
- Offline (Subtitler Suite)
- Other (Open, DVD, NLE, Projection, DVB)

Speche Communications
1500 Bishop Court
Mt. Prospect, IL 60056
Toll-free: 800/323-4247
Fax: 847/803-4950
Email: Info@speche.com
Web site: www.speche.com

Speche Communications is a wholly owned
subsidiary of Stenograph, LLC.

- Multimedia

TM Systems
419A Española Way
Miami Beach, FL 33139
Phone: 305/535-6373
Fax: 305/535-6353
Email: info@tm-systems.com
Web site: www.tm-systems.com

- Offline (TranStation CC)

Ultech, LLC
125 North Benson Road
Middlebury, CT 06762
Phone: 203/758-8667
Toll-free: 888/360-0010
Fax: 203/758-8693
Email: info@ultech.com
Web site: www.ultech.com

- Encoding (CCX)
- Online (Caption Mic)

Ultech is a wholly owned subsidiary of the
National Captioning Institute.

Voice to Text, LLC
1133 Bal Harbor Blvd., Suite 1139
Punta Gorda, FL, 33950-6574
Phone: 941/639-1522
Toll-free: 888/877-3334
Fax: 941/833-0638
Email: sales@voicewrite.com
Web site: www.voicewrite.com

- Online (ISIS)

XOrbit Software Associates, Inc.
8545 Willow Wisp Court
Laurel, MD 20723
Phone: 301/362.9500
Toll-free: 877/XOrbit1
Fax: 301/362.9502
Email: sales@xorbit.com
Web site: www.xorbit.com

- Encoding/Monitoring (UltraCast)
- Offline (OmniEdit)
- Other (Sweeper, Translator, SponsorServer, TaskFlow)

Appendix 2: Captioning Service Providers

United States

Aberdeen Captioning
30211 Avenida de las Banderas, #248
Rancho Santa Margarita, CA 92688
Phone: 800-688-6621
Fax: 949-888-6623
Email: info@abercap.com
Web site: www.abercap.com

Access-USA
PO Drawer 160
242 James Street
Clayton, NY 13624
Phone: 800-263-2750
Fax: 800-563-1687
Email: info@access-usa.com
Web site: www.access-usa.com

AdTech Productions Co.
2324 Broadmeade Road
Louisville, KY 40205
Phone: 502-451-5616
Fax: 502-599-3356
Email: adtech@insightbb.com
Web site: www.adtechproductions.com

American RealTime/Captioning Services
900 NE Loop 410, Ste. 429-D
San Antonio, TX 78209
Toll-free: 888-306-ARTS
Phone: 210-805-7094
Fax: 830-626-8946
Email: monette@ARTCS.com
Web site: www.artcs.com

AmeriCaption, Inc.
Phone: 941-359-8100
Email: AmeriCaption@comcast.net
Web site: www.americaption.com

Applied Graphics Technologies
21725 Melrose Ave
Southfield, MI 48075
Phone: 248-386-0400
Fax: 248-353-6026
Email: b_faria@yahoo.com

Archive Reporting Service
2336 North Second Street
Harrisburg, PA 17110
Phone: 1-800-870-1795
Fax: 717-234-6190
Email: archivereporting@worldnet.att.net

Armour Captioning
920 Stryker Avenue
W. St. Paul, MN 55118
Phone: 651-457-6845
Email: Info@ArmourCaptioning.com.
Web site: www.armourcaptioning.com

Arthur International
3206 Fern Ave
Palmdale, CA 93550
Phone: 805-274-0822
Fax: 805-274-0822
Email: USA@Arthurint.com
Web site: www.arthurint.com

Bay Area Video Coalition
2727 Mariposa Street, 2nd Floor
San Francisco, CA 94110
Phone: 415-861-3282
Fax: 415-861-4316
Email: bavc@bavc.org
Web site: www.bavc.org

Buyers & Kaczor Reporting Services, Inc.
14 Lafayette Square
Buffalo, NY 14203
Phone: 716-852-2223
Fax: 716-852-8271

Calabro Reporting Services
549 N. 6th Ave.
Tucson, AZ 85705
Phone: 520-798-1808
Fax: 520-620-0660
Email: admin@calabroreporting.com
Web site: www.calabroreporting.com

Capitol Caption
6515 Spelling Bee
Columbia, MD 21045-4636
Phone: 410-312-7289
Email: capcap95@aol.com

Caption 2000+
5910 N. Central Expressway
Suite 100
Dallas, TX 75206
Phone: 214-987-5550
Fax: 214-361-5126
Email: dbrown@caption2000.com

Caption Advantage
4440 Ashfield Terrace
Syracuse, NY 13215-2463
Phone: 877-227-2382
Fax: 315-492-1426
Email: CaptionAdv@aol.com
Web site: www.captionadvantage.com

Caption Colorado
7935 East Prentice Avenue
Suite 310
Greenwood Village, CO 80111
Toll-free: 800-775-7838
Main: 720-489-5662
Fax: 720-489-5664
Web site: www.CaptionColorado.com

Caption Communication Services
201 N. Franklin Street
Tampa, FL 33602
Phone: 813-223-3344
Fax: 813-229-1774

Caption Connection
P.O. Box 11
Hampstead, NH 03841
Phone: 603-329-7321
Fax: 603-329-7321
Email: captconn@aol.com

Caption Graphics
201 Bonhill Drive
Fort Washington, MD 20744
Phone: 301-203-0680
Fax: 301-203-0680

Caption House
779 N 1180 E
Orem, UT 84097
Phone: 801-224-7684
Fax: 801-224-7223
Email: jaborn@aol.com

Caption Minnesota
14286 Dulcimer Way
Apple Valley, MN 55124-5954
Phone: 612-322-2113

Caption Perfect
P.O. Box 12454
Research Triangle Park, NC 27709-2454
Phone: 919-942-0693
TTY: 919-942-0436
Fax: 919-942-0435
Web site: members.aol.com/captioning/

Caption Reporters, Inc.
5801 Allentown Road, Suite 209
Camp Springs, MD 20746
Phone: 301-316-3131
TTY: 301-316-3138
Fax: 301-316-3139
Email: info@captionreporters.com
Web site: www.captionreporters.com

Caption Services of Hawaii
PO Box 755
Honolulu, HI 96808
Phone: 808-534-0191
Fax: 808-538-6458

Caption Services of Kansas
1118 E. 1600 Rd., P.O. Box 3593
Lawrence, KS 66046
Toll-free: 888-745-5380
TTY: 785-842-9994
Fax: 785-842-8997
Email: AnneCSK@cs.com
Web site: www.captionservices.com

Caption Technologies, Inc.
16273 FM 1778
Farmersville, TX 75442
Phone: 972-843-4400
Fax: 972-843-4700
Email: lisa@captiontechnologies.com
Web site: www.captiontechnologies.com

Caption Technology Inc.
42 Harthorn Avenue
Bangor, ME 04401-5904
Phone: 207-945-6209
Email: jvardamis@aol.com

Caption Unlimited
2424 Magog Rd.
Palmyra, NY 14522
Phone: 315-597-6097

CaptioNation
12401 Schoolhouse Street
Raleigh, NC 27614
Phone: 919-570-6210

Captioned Communication
445 George Street
New Haven, CT 06511
Phone: 203-785-8795
Fax: 203-785-9132

Captioning Company
4100 Burbank, Suite 300
Burbank, CA 91505
Phone: 818-848-6500
Web site: www.captioningcompany.com

Captioning Company
P.O. Box 1534
Clear Lake Shores, TX 77565
Email: TxActCap@aol.com
Web site:
www.angelfire.com/tx/closedcaption

Captioning Group, Inc. (USA)
11149 Acama Street
Studio City, CA 91602
Toll-free: 800-717-9707
Fax: 877-822-3394
Web site: www.captioning.com

Captioning Resources of Western New York
P.O. Box 708
Honeoye, NY 14471
Phone: 716-367-3190

CaptionLit
1700 Harris Road
Glenside, PA 19038
Phone: 215-485-0094
Fax: 215-836-9348
Email: sales@captionlit.com
Web site: www.captionlit.com

CaptionMax
530 North Third Street, Suite 210
Minneapolis, MN 55401
Phone: 612-341-3566
Fax: 612-341-2345
Email: derek@captionmax.com
Web site: www.captionmax.com

CaptionPlus
1800 Ignacio Blvd.
Novato, CA 94949-4900
Phone: 415-382-7735
Email: kruss768@concentric.net

Captions Direct
6401 East Rogers Circle
Suite 11
Boca Raton, FL 33487
Phone: 561-997-8006
Fax: 561-997-6653
Email: rose@captionsdirect.com

Captions Now, Inc.
1111 West Holly
Suite F
Bellingham, WA 98225
Phone: 360-738-2880
Fax: 360-671-6298
Email: cni4robin@aol.com

Captions West
1656 Sunset Drive
Kaysville, UT 84037
Phone: 801-544-2059
Fax: 801-544-2217
Email: utsten@xmission.com

Captions, Inc.
901 W. Alameda Ave
Burbank, CA 91506
Phone: 818-729-9501
Fax: 818-729-9519
Email: rob_troy@captionsinc.com
Web site: www.captionsinc.com

Cardinal Captioning Center
53 Orange St.
P.O. Box 7294
Asheville, NC 28802
Phone: 704-252-4738
Fax: 704-253-3897
Email: RealtimeCC@aol.com

CCaption
132 Buckhorn Drive
Springfield, IL 62707
Phone: 217-522-0842
Email: CCaption@aol.com

ClosedCaption Maker
1500A Lafayette Road, #226
Portsmouth, NH 03801
Phone: 800-527-0551
Email: wGallant@CCmaker.com
Web site: www.CCmaker.com

Chicago Captioning
205 Regency Drive, Suite 512
Bloomingdale, IL 60108
Phone: 630-893-0996
Email: info@chicagocaptioning.com
Web site: www.chicagocaptioning.com

Christian Captions and Subtitle Services
Cherry Creek Commons
2631 E. Cass Street, 2nd floor
Joliet, IL 60432
Phone: 815-740-1009
Toll-free: 866-230-1009
Fax: 815-740-6270
Email: info@christiancaptions.com
Web site: www.christiancaptions.com

Classic Worldwide Productions
5001 East Royalton Road
Cleveland, OH 44147
Phone: 440-838-5377
Fax: 440-838-1240
Web site: www.classicworldwide.com

Closed Caption Productions
6622 W Maya Way
Phoenix, AZ 85085
Phone: 623-566-1333
Email: info@ccproductions.com
Web site: www.ccproductions.com

Closed Captioning Services, Inc.
6159 28th Street SE, Suite 16
Grand Rapids, MI 49546
Phone: 616-940-9444 ext 16
Fax: 616-940-0440
Email: rleet@ccscaption.com
Web site: www.ccscaption.com

Communication Connections
410 N Third Street
Malta, IL 60150
Phone: 815-825-2781

Communication Works of the Deaf, Inc.
24780 Hathaway, Suite 201
Farmington Hills, MI 48335
Phone: 248-615-5070
Fax: 248-615-5088
Email: captworks@aol.com
Web site: www.captworks.com

Complete Captions
5183 Maison Avenue
Los Angeles, CA 90041
Phone: 213-257-7704

CompuScripts Captioning
1825 Gadsden Street
Columbia, SC 29201
Phone: 803-988-8438
Fax: 803-988-0094
Email: staceywilson@compuscriptsinc.com
Web site: www.compuscriptsinc.com

Computer Engineering Associates
8227 Cloverleaf Drive, #308
Millersville, MD 21108
Phone: 410-987-7003

**CPC Computer Prompting and
Captioning Co.**
1010 Rockville Pike, Suite 306
Rockville, MD 20852
Phone: 301-738-8487
Fax: 301-738-8488
TTY: 301-738-8489
Toll-free: 800-977-6678
Email: info@cpcweb.com
Web site: www.cpcweb.com

CTV Captioning
400 Pacific Ave Fl 2W
San Francisco, CA 94133-4607
Phone: 415-677-9924

Custom Captions
458 South 2470 West
Provo, UT 84601
Phone: 801-370-9878
Email: adurrant@mstar2.net

Dallas Prompter & Captions
Po Box 280413
Dallas, TX 75228
Phone: 214-328-4700
Email: Dprompter@aol.com

Davideo Productions
3060 Sutherland Springs
Seguin, TX 78155
Email: DAVIDEO@satx.rr.com

Deaf Video Communications of America, Inc.
PO Box 4307
Lisle, IL 60532-9307
Phone: 630-964-0909
Email: dvcdeaf@ix.netcom.com

DeBee Communications
3900 Monet Court South
Pittsburgh, PA 15101-3221
TTY: 412-492-8214
Fax: 412-492-8215
Email: sales@debee.com
Web site: www.debee.com

Dubscape
3614 Overland Avenue
Los Angeles, CA 90034
Phone: 310-202-2974
Fax: 310-202-6088
Email: info@dubscape.com
Web site: www.dubscape.com

eCaptions
1106 Second St., #282
Encinitas, CA 92024
Phone: 858-794-6811
Fax: 858-794-6812
Email: Info@ecaptions.com
Web site: www.ecaptions.com

Florida Captioning Services
P.O. Box 150898
Altamonte Springs, FL 32715
Phone: 407-331-7950
Fax: 407-831-5570
Email: PBelflower@aol.com

Garman Productions, LLC
825 N.W. 58th Street
Oklahoma City, OK 73118
Voice: 405-254-2500
Fax: 405-254-2507
Toll-free: 800-747-5699
Email: steve@garman.com
Web site: www.garman.com

Green Mountain Reporters & Captioners
P.O. Box 1311
Montpelier, VT 05601
Phone: 802-229-9873
Fax: 802-223-4716
Email: gmrptrs@together.net

Gwenn Bever Captioning Services
N4246 Sunset Road
Medford, WI 54451
Phone: 715-748-6282
Fax: 715-748-6406
Email: gbever@midway.tds.net

Hear Ink
11118 Lindbergh Business Ct.
St. Louis, MO 63123
Toll-free: 888-314-2811
Phone: 314-638-1113
Fax: 314-638-4513
TTY: 314-638-4514
Email: info@hearink.com
Web site: www.hearink.com

In Touch Services
1904 Hillcrest Drive
Coshocton, OH 43812
Phone: 740-295-0511
Email: intouch2@core.com
Web site: www.intouchservices.com

Line of Sight Captions
2829 N Glenoaks Blvd
Burbank, CA 91504-2660
Phone: 818-843-8506
Email: rbag@ix.netcom.com

LNS Captioning
9498 SW Barbur Blvd.
Portland, OR 97219
Phone: 503-299-6200
Toll-free: 800-366-6201
Fax: 503-299-6839
Email: officemgr@LNScourtreporting.com
Web site: www.lnscourtreporting.com

Media Access Group at WGBH
125 Western Avenue
Boston, MA 02134
Phone: 617-300-3600 (voice/TTY)
Fax: 617-300-1020
Email: access@wgbh.org
Web site: access.wgbh.org

Media Captioning Services
2141 Palomar Airport Road, #330
Carlsbad, CA 92009
Phone: 760-431-2882
Fax: 760-431-8735
TTY: 760-431-8795
Email: mediacap3@earthlink.net
Web site: www.mediacaptioning.com

Mundomedia Digital Studios, LLC
1935 Lochmore Dr.
Longmont, CO 80501
Phone: 720-260-8462
Fax: 303-651-7605
Email: mds@mundomedia.tv
Web site: www.mundomedia.tv

Mujtabaa Captioning
95-780 Paikauhale St
Mililani, HI 96789-2839
Phone: 808-623-7475

National Capitol Captioning
820 S. Lincoln St.
Arlington, VA 22204
Phone: 703-920-2400
Email: info@capitolcaptioning.com
Web site: www.capitolcaptioning.com

National Captioning Services
6119 28th Street S.E., Suite 2A
Grand Rapids, MI 49546
Phone: 616-974-0811
Fax: 616-974-9054
Email: info@netcapinc.com
Web site: www.netcapinc.com

New Day Media
8282 S. Memorial Suite, #102
Tulsa, OK 74133
Toll-free: 800-834-6606
Fax: 918-294-1186
Email: mail@newdaymedia.com
Web site: www.newdaymedia.com

NJCaptions
418 Rowan Avenue
Hamilton Twp, NJ 08610
Phone: 609-392-7329
Fax: 609-392-4315

Pacific Caption Company
6200 East Thomas Road
Suite 103
Scottsdale, AZ 85251
Phone: 480-429-5070
Fax: 480-429-5071
Email: PACAP@aol.com

Paradigm Reporting & Captioning
1400 Rand Tower
527 Marquette Avenue South
Minneapolis, MN 55402-1331
Phone: 612-339-0545
TTY: 612-339-5941
Toll-free: 800-545-9668
Fax: 612-337-5575
Email: caption@paradigmreporting.com
Web site: www.paradigmreporting.com

Philadelphia Captioning Services, Inc.
400 Market Street
11th Floor
Philadelphia, PA 19106
Fax: 215-627-0555
Email: Highrobert@aol.com

Puzzle International
8365 Nestle Ave.
Northridge, CA 91325-3741
Toll-free: 888-522-8903
Phone: 818-886-7915
Fax: 818-886-5523
Email: sales@puzzlecorp.com
Web site: www.puzzlecorp.com

Rapid Text
1801 Dove Street, Suite 101
Newport Beach, CA 92660
Phone: 949-399-9200
Email: info@rapidtext.com
Web site: www.rapidtext.com

Realtime Reporters
303 Potrero Street, Suite 42-203
Santa Cruz, CA 95060
Phone: 831-335-7792
Email: info@rtreporters.com
Web site: www.rtreporters.com

Regis Realtime Captioning
P.O. Box 1832
Olympia, WA 98507-1832
Phone: 360-754-0902
Email: Regisrealtime@hotmail.com

Riverside Captioning Company
621 Second Street
Hudson, WI 54016
Phone: 715-386-0799
Email: info@closed-captioning.com
Web site: www.closed-captioning.com

Softitler
9255 W. Sunset Boulevard
Mezzanine
West Hollywood, CA 90069
Phone: 310-288-9200
Fax: 310-288-9255
Email: info@softitler.com
Web site: www.softitler.com

Soundwriters
5-30 50th Avenue LIC
New York, NY 11101
Phone: 718-786-0010
Fax: 718-482-0990
Email: info@soundwriters.com
Web site: www.soundwriters.com

Tele-Print Digital Media Center
3361 Boyington Dr., Suite 160
Carrollton, TX 75006
Phone: 972-702-8388
Toll-free: 800-628-1124
Web site: www.tele-print.com

Tempo Media Network
4585 E. Speedway #110
Tucson, AZ 85712
Phone: 520-760-9896
Fax: 520-760-9897
Email: captioning@tempomedia.net
Web site: www.tempomedia.net

Texas Closed Captioning
310 East 34th Street
Austin, TX 78705
Phone: 512-480-0210
Fax: 512-480-0225
Email: txcaption@austin.rr.com
Web site: www.texascaption.com

U.S. Captioning Company L.L.C.
2079B Lawrence Drive
De Pere, WI 54115
Phone: 920-338-9201
Fax: 920-338-9202
Email: director@uscaptioning.com
Web site: www.uscaptioning.com

UnitedCaption, Inc.
19785 W 12 Mile Road, #404
Southfield, MI 48076
Toll-free: 1-866-225-6766
Fax: 1-248-357-9704
Email: info@unitedcaption.com
Web site: www.unitedcaption.com

VIA Communications
12550 Biscayne Blvd, Suite 306
N. Miami, FL 33181
Phone: 305-893-2202
Fax: 305-893-6554
Email: mail@viacommunications.com
Web site: www.viacommunications.com

Visual Data Media Services
145 West Magnolia Boulevard
Burbank, CA 91502-1722
Phone: 818-558-3363
Toll-free: 888-418-4782
Fax: 818-558-3368
Web site: www.closedcaptions.com

Video Services International
27 Kreiger Lane
Glastonbury, CT, 06033
Phone: 860-652-8972
Toll-free: 800-827-3382
Fax: 860-652-9276
Email: vsi@tapedub.com
Web site: www.tapedub.com

Video Solutions
512 North Washington Street
Alexandria, VA 22314
Phone: 703-683-5305
Web site: www.thevideosolution.com

VITAC
101 Hillpointe Drive
Canonsburg, PA 15317-9503
Toll-free: 800-278-4822
Phone: 724-514-4000
Fax: 724-514-4111
TTY: 724-514-4100
Web site: www.vitac.com

Western Video Services
1331 120th Ave. NE
Bellevue, WA 98005
Phone: 425-454-5253
Email: wvs@westernvideo.com
Web site: www.westernvideo.com

Australia

Australian Caption Centre
Level 4
187 Thomas Street, Haymarket
Sydney, NSW 2000
Phone: 800 777 801
Fax: +61 (0) 2 9281 2198
Email: acc@auscap.com.au
Web site: www.auscap.com.au

Comcopy
235 Normanby Road
South Melbourne, VIC 3205
Phone: +61 3 9646 7466
Fax: +61 3 9646 9411
Email: maryg@broadcast-rentals.com.au

Canada

Broadcast Captioning & Consulting Services
150 Laird Drive, Suite 302
Toronto, Ontario M4G 3V7
Phone: 416-696-1534
Fax: 416-421-7603
Email: hallahan@closedcaptioning.com
Web site: www.closedcaptioning.com

Captioning Group, Inc. (Canada)
Suite 500, 1550 - 8th Street S.W. T2R 1K1
Calgary, Alberta T2R 0A4
Toll-free: 800-717-9707
Fax: 877-822-3394
Web site: www.captioning.com

cc Caption, Inc.
215 Spadina ave #360
Toronto, Ontario M5T 2C7
Phone: 416-367-8464
Fax: 416-367-8466
Email: info@cccaption.com
Web site: www.cccaption.com

Centre National du Sous-Titrage Inc.
1975, rue Falardeau
Bureau 220
Montreal, Quebec H2K 2L9

CFA Communications
786 King Street West
Toronto, Ontario M5V 1N6
Phone: 416-504-5071
Fax: 416-504-7390
Email: info@cfacommunications.com
Web site: www.cfacommunications.com

Closed Caption Services
41 Brodeur Crest
Ottawa, Ontario K2L 1Z2
Phone: 613-592-9800
Fax: 613-599-5598
Email: lgavin@ibm.com

Comprehensive Distributors
635 Queen St. East
Toronto, Ontario M4M 1G4
Phone: 416-778-9800
Fax: 416-778-9799

Intercaption Canada (ICC)
172 Gainsborough Road
Toronto, Ontario M4I 3C4
Phone: 416-532-8212
Fax: 416-462-9609
Email: info@intercaption.com
Web site: www.intercaption.com

Line 21 Media Services
122 - 1058 Mainland Street,
Vancouver, British Columbia V6B 2T4
Phone: 604-662-4600
Fax: 604-662-4606
Email: line21@line21cc.com
Web site: www.line21cc.com

Media House Productions
430 McDonald Street
Regina, Saskatchewan S4N 6E1
Phone: 306-359-0977
Fax: 306-569-2240
Email: media.house@dlcwest.com

Nathanail Captioning
147 Signal Ridge Link SW
Calgary, Alberta T3A 4R4
Phone: 403-286-9696
Fax: 403-286-0987
Email: natcap@home.com

National Alternate Media
1154 Adirondack Drive
Ottawa, Ontario K2C 2V1
Phone: 613-224-2829
Fax: 613-224-5957
Email: davegill@magma.ca

National Captioning Centre
388 King St
Toronto, Ontario M1B 1A1
Phone: 416-599-0223

New World Media Artists
18 Port Of Newcastle Drive
Newcastle, Ontario L1B 1M8
Phone: 905-987-1771
Email: info@nwmartists.com
Web site: www.nwmartists.com

Softitler Canada, Inc.
1255 Philips Square
Suite 901
Montreal, Quebec H3B 3G1
Email: info@softitler.com
Web site: www.softitler.com

Sous-Titrage Plus Inc.
1453 Amherst #101
Montreal, Quebec H2L 3L2
Phone: 514-521-4460
Fax: 514-521-3985

Vertical Sync
#402 - 2206 Dewdney Avenue
Regina, Saskatchewan S4R 1H3
Email: tbennett@sasktel.net
Web site: www.verticalsync.com

Germany

Titelbild Subtitling and Translation GmbH
Joachim-Friedrich-Straße 37
D- 10711 Berlin
Phone: +49.30.890 923 39
Fax: +49.30.892 96 51
Email: info@titelbild.de
Web site: www.titelbild.de

Vicomedia
Wareka & Frühauf GbR
Burgstraße 6
34233 Fuldatal
Phone: (0 56 07) 93 42 – 0
Fax: (0 56 07) 93 42 – 30
Email: info@vicomedia.de
Web site: www.vicomedia.de

New Zealand

Captioning NZ
PO Box 3819
Auckland
Phone: 09 916 7787
Fax: 09 916 7902
Email: captioning@tvnz.co.nz
Web site: www.captioningnz.co.nz

Spain

Cinematxt
Benavente, 5 Bajo Izq.
Madrid
Phone: +34 91 6380026
Fax: +34 91 6345471
Email: albenito@teleline.es

United Kingdom

European Captioning Institute
First Floor, The Media Centre
3 - 8 Carburton Street
London, W1W 5AJ
Phone: +44 (0)20 7323 4657
Fax: +44 (0)20 7886 0819
Email: Info@ecisubtitling.com
Web site: www.ecisubtitling.com

IMS
21 Soho Square
London W1V 5FD
Phone: +44 (0)20 7440 5400
Fax: +44 (0)20 7440 5410
Email: ims@dial.pipex.com
Web site: www.imsmediasupport.com

Intelfax Ltd
Lincoln House
75 Westminster Bridge Road
London SE1 7HS
Phone: (020) 7928 2727
Fax: (020) 7928 1836
Web site: www.intelfax.co.uk

Independent Television Facilities Centre Ltd.
28 Concord Road
Acton, London W3 0TH
Phone: +44 (0) 20 8752 0352
Fax: +44 (0) 20 8993 6393
Email: webmaster@itfc.com
Web site: www.itfc.com

Visiontext Ltd
48 Charlotte Street
London W1T 2NS
Phone: +44 (0) 20 7016 2200
Fax: +44 (0) 20 7016 2222
Web site: www.visiontext.com

Venezuela

HispanoCaptions
Calle El Recreo, Torre Farallón
Bello Monte
Caracas 1051
Phone: +582 2379898
Fax: +582 7614337
Email: hispanocaptions@cantv.net

APPENDIX 3: CAPTIONING RESOURCES ONLINE

General Closed Captioning Information

- Caption Central – A general closed captioning resource site
  www.captioncentral.com

- CMP – Captioned Media Program
  www.cfv.org

- Insight Cinema – Open captioned first-run movies in the theaters
  www.insightcinema.org

- Joe Clark's media access pages – Caption-related articles and research
  www.joeclark.org/access/

- MoPix – Closed captioned and described movies
  www.mopix.org

- NCAM – National Center for Accessible Media
  ncam.wgbh.org

Captioning Products and Services

See Appendix 1 and Appendix 2 for a list of companies providing products and services for closed captioning, including complete contact information and product names.

Broadcasting Associations and Standards Bodies

- ANSI – American National Standards Institute
  www.ansi.org

- ATSC – Advanced Television Systems Committee
  www.atsc.org

- CEA – Consumer Electronics Association
  Publishers of the EIA and CEA standards—a sector of the EIA.
  www.ce.org

- EBU – European Broadcasting Union
  www.ebu.ch

- IEEE – Institute of Electrical and Electronics Engineers
  www.ieee.org

- IEC – International Electrotechnical Commission
  www.iec.ch

- ISO – International Organization of Standardization
  www.iso.ch

- NAB – National Association of Broadcasters
  www.nab.org

- NABA – North American Broadcasters Association
  www.nabanet.com

- RTNDA – Radio and Television News Directors Association
  www.rtnda.org

- SBE – Society of Broadcast Engineers
  www.sbe.org

- SMPTE – Society of Motion Picture & Television Engineers
  www.smpte.org

- STLD – Society of Television Lighting Directors
  www.stld.org.uk

- W3C (World Wide Web Consortium) Web Content Accessibility Guidelines
  www.w3.org/TR/WCAG10/

Deafness

- ALDA – Association of Late-Deafened Adults
  www.alda.org

- Alexander Graham Bell Association for the Deaf and Hard of Hearing
  www.agbell.org

- ASTLA – American Sign Language Teachers Association
  www.aslta.org

- Hearing Exchange – For people with hearing loss, parents, and professionals
  www.hearingexchange.com

- Hearing Loss Web – For people with hearing loss that aren't part of the Deaf community
  www.hearinglossweb.com

- IDRT – Institute for Disabilities Research and Training
  www.idrt.com

- NAD – National Association of the Deaf
  www.nad.org

- NTID – National Technical Institute for the Deaf (at Rochester Institute of Technology)
  ntidweb.rit.edu

- SayWhatClub – A worldwide forum for people with hearing loss
  www.saywhatclub.com

- SHHH – Self Help for Hard-of-Hearing People
  www.shhh.org

- TDI – Telecommunications for the Deaf, Inc.
  www.tdi-online.org

Disabilities Rights and ADA

- DREDF – Disability Rights Education and Defense Fund, Inc.
  www.dredf.org

- CCC Live Caption – Reimbursement for live captioning of courses offered within the California Community Colleges
  `www.ccclivecaption.com`

Stenocaptioning and CART

- CARTWheel – Communication Access Realtime Translation
  `www.cartwheel.cc`

- Communication Access Information Center
  `www.cartinfo.org`

- NCRA (National Court Reporters Association) CART Special Interest Group
  `cart.ncraonline.org`

- NCRA (National Court Reporters Association) Closed Captioning SIG
  `www.ncraonline.org/captioning`

Voice Writing and Speech Recognition

- Dragon NaturallySpeaking
  `http://www.dragontalk.com/`

- IBM ViaVoice
  `www.ibm.com/software/voice/viavoice/`

- NVRA (National Verbatim Reporters Association)
  `www.nvra.org`

Related Government Sites

- CBC – Canadian Broadcasting Corporation
  `www.cbc.ca`

- CRTC – Canadian Radio-television and Telecommunications Commission
  `www.crtc.gc.ca`

- Disability-related government resources
  `www.disabilityinfo.gov`

- FCC – Federal Communications Commission
  `www.fcc.gov`

- FCC Disability Issues (including the main FCC closed captioning section)
  `www.fcc.gov/cgb/dro/`

- Section 508 (Rehabilitation Act) compliance
  `www.section508.gov`

- U.S. Access Board
  `www.access-board.gov`

Audio Description

- Audio Description International
  `www.adinternational.org`

- Independent Television Commission Audio Description Guidelines and Standards
  `www.itc.org.uk/itc_publications/codes_guidance/audio_description`

- Joe Clark's audio description site
  `www.joeclark.org/access/description`

APPENDIX 4: STANDARDS DOCUMENTS

Standards Organizations

ANSI Standards

ANSI sells its standards through the online ANSI store in electronic form and through Global Engineering Documents in hardcopy.

> **American National Standards Institute**
> 25 West 43rdStreet
> 4th Floor
> New York, NY 10036
> Phone: 212/642-4900
> Web site: www.ansi.org

ATSC Standards

Standards from the Advanced Television Systems Committee (ATSC) may be downloaded directly from their Web site.

> **Advanced Television Systems Committee**
> 1750 K Street N.W., Suite 1200
> Washington, DC 20006
> Phone: 202/872-9160
> Fax: 202/872-9161
> Downloads: www.atsc.org/standards.html

CEA/EIA Standards

CEA/EIA standards are available through Global Engineering Documents.

Consumer Electronics Association
2500 Wilson Blvd.
Arlington, VA 22201-3834
Phone: 703/907-7625
Fax: 703/907-7693
Email :   standards@ce.org
Web site: www.ce.org

IEC Standards

IEC standards are available through Global Engineering Documents (hardcopy) and the ANSI online store (electronic).

International Electrotechnical Commission
3, rue de Varembé
P.O. Box 131
CH-1211 Geneva 20
Switzerland
Phone: +41 22 749 01 11
Fax: +41 22 749 01 55
Email: mbinfo@iso.ch
Web site: www.iso.ch

ISO Standards

The ISO Web site has an online store, or their standards are available through Global Engineering Documents (hardcopy) and the ANSI online store (electronic).

International Organization for Standardization
1, rue de Varembé
P.O. Box 56
CH-1211 Geneva 20
Switzerland
Phone: +41 22 749 01 11
Fax: +41 22 749 01 55
Email: mbinfo@iso.ch
Web site: www.iso.ch

SMPTE Standards

Purchase directly from the SMPTE store on their Web site.

Society of Motion Picture and Television Engineers
595 West Hartsdale Avenue
White Plains, New York 10607
Phone: 914/761-1100
Fax: 914/761-3115
Email: smpte@smpte.org
Web site: www.smpte.org/

Global Engineering Documents

Most of the standards referenced in this book are available from Global Engineering Documents, a "one-stop shop" for hundreds of thousands of documents from hundreds of organizations. To purchase standards from Global Engineering Documents, contact them at:

Global Engineering Documents
World Headquarters
15 Inverness Way East
Englewood, CO USA 80112-5776
Phone: 303/397-7956
Toll-free: 800/854-7179
Fax: 303/397-2740
Email: global@ihs.com
Web site: global.ihs.com

GLOSSARY

—A—

AARP – American Association of Retired Persons. A fast-growing demographic of caption users.

ACC – Australian Caption Centre, headquartered in Sydney, New South Wales.

acute accent – An accent mark that slopes upward over a letter (e.g., á). Known in French as an "aigu" accent.

ADA – Americans with Disabilities Act.

AEA – American Electronics Association.

ALDA – Association of Late-Deafened Adults. An organization created by and for postlingually deaf people, most of whom lost their hearing later in life. It addresses issues not faced by those deaf since birth.

ANSI – American National Standards Institute.

ASCII – American Standard Code for Information Interchange. A simple 7-bit character set for computers.

ASL – American Sign Language.

aspect ratio – The ratio of the width of an image to its height. Standard NTSC video has a 4:3 aspect ratio, and wide-screen DTV uses 16:9. There are other aspect ratios in use as well, but 4:3 and 16:9 are the most common.

asynchronous data – Data in line 21 that does not have to be synchronized with the audio.

ATSC – Advanced Television Systems Committee. The group that defined the standards for DTV (both HDTV and SDTV).

ATV – Advanced Television. Systems with better audio and video than the standard NTSC analog system used in North America today. ATV is often used interchangeably with DTV or HDTV.

audio description – Narration on an alternate audio track (such as SAP) that describes the video for blind people.

—B—

bandwidth – The amount of information that can be carried in a signal.

Baudot – A character set that predates ASCII and is still used in TTYs. Named for French inventor J.M.E. Baudot.

bit – A contraction for "binary digit." A bit is the smallest unit of information that a computer can hold. A bit has only two possible values: on and off (usually represented as 0 and 1).

BITC – Burned-In Time Code. Timecode that's visible on the video signal. Also referred to as a "window burn."

BNC – Bayonet connector for coaxial cables. Typically, BNC connectors are used in professional video equipment, as opposed to the RCA connectors or F connectors used in home video equipment. BNC connectors slide onto a post, and then twist to lock in place, using one pin on each side of the post.

bps – Bits per second. A measurement of transmission rate that is *not* the same as baud rate, although the terms are often used interchangeably.

Bps – Bytes per second. Note that the letter "B" is capitalized to differentiate Bps from bps.

bridge – A device that extracts and reinserts captions to bridge around DVE (digital video effects) units and other equipment that destroys or regenerates line 21. Bridges may or may not include caption relocation capabilities.

BS – Backspace command.

bug – An icon or logo in the corner of a TV picture, identifying the broadcaster. Also used to refer to a design or implementation error in a piece of hardware or software.

–C–

CAB – Canadian Association of Broadcasters.

CART – Communication Access Realtime Translation. Realtime text used to provide accessibility for deaf and hard-of-hearing people at live events.

CAT – Computer-Aided Transcription. Computer systems providing translation and editing capability for steno-based court reporters.

CATV – Cable television. The acronym comes from the original name for cable TV: Community Antenna Television.

CC1 through **CC4** – The four "channels" of captioning information in line 21 captioning. CC1&2 are in field 1, and CC3&4 are in field 2.

CCDA – Canadian Captioning Development Agency.

CCITT – Comité Consultatif International de Telecommunications et Telegraphy (in English, the International Telegraph and Telephone Consultative Committee). It is a standards committee that makes technical recommendations about communications equipment, both voice and data. CCITT is now a part of ITU (the International Tele-communication Union), a United Nations agency.

CEA – Consumer Electronics Association. A sector of the EIA with over 1,000 member companies in the consumer technology business.

CEA-608 – The standard for broadcasting captions, extended data services, and other data in line 21 of an NTSC television signal. Formerly known as EIA-608.

CEA-708 – The standard for broadcasting captions in a DTV signal. Originally known as EIA-708.

CES – Consumer Electronics Show. A conference put on by CEA in Las Vegas every year.

cedilla – The "hook" under the letter ç in French and Portuguese to specify that it is pronounced as an "s" rather than as a "k," as in "façade" or "français."

CFD – Captioned Films for the Deaf. An organization that provides open-captioned movies for deaf and hard-of-hearing people.

CGMS – Copy Generation Management System.

checksum – An error-detection scheme that involves adding up all of the bytes of data in a packet and discarding remainders. The receiving device calculates a checksum and compares it with the transmitted checksum. If they match, there were no errors. ITV links and XDS packets both use checksums, although the algorithms are different.

chording – Pressing more than one key at a time on a keyboard.

circumflex – A caret-shaped accent placed over a letter, as in ô.

clock run-in – A waveform that is generated just prior to a data signal that gives the receiving device a chance to "lock on" to the frequency of the transmission.

closed captioning – Captions that can be turned on or off by the viewer.

codec – Coder/decoder. The piece of software or hardware that encodes or decodes a signal in a given format.

computerized note taking – The use of a fast typist to simulate realtime by typing a summary of events as they happen. These notes can be displayed as standard captions, just more slowly.

conflict – Two or more words that are written the same in stenotype, but are spelled differently. Typically these are homonyms, but there are other types of conflicts as well.

C-Print – A method of computerized note taking that doesn't use captioning equipment or stenocaptioners. Similar to CART, C-Print uses typists with a collection of macros and abbreviations to increase their effective typing speed. It provides a summary of important (in the mind of the C-Print operator) points rather than a verbatim or near-verbatim transcript.

CR – Carriage Return. An ASCII character that signifies the end of a line of text.

crawl – Text that scrolls horizontally across the TV screen, usually at the bottom. Crawls are often used for emergency notification, breaking news stories, or financial data.

CRR – Certified Realtime Reporter. A certification given by NCRA, designed to test writing and technical skills relating to realtime court reporting and captioning. The test consists of setting up realtime computer equipment and writing literary dictation at speeds ranging from 180 to 200 wpm. The examinee is graded on the accuracy of the test as written in realtime. The final portion of the test involves copying the unedited file to a 3½" floppy diskette in ASCII format.

CRTC – Canadian Radio-television and Telecommunications Commission (*Conseil de la Radiodiffusion et des Télécommunications Canadiennes*). The group that oversees television broadcasters in Canada – the approximate equivalent of the FCC in the United States.

CSS – Cascading Style Sheets. A standard for embedding formatting in Web sites completely separate from the content. This approach is highly recommended for accessibility.

–D–

data recovery decoder – A caption decoder designed to be connected to a computer. For example, an offline captioning system can be connected to a data-recovery decoder to allow it to capture existing captions from a videotape and modify them rather than starting from scratch.

data channel – The destination or intended purpose of line 21 data. CEA-608 defines four caption and four text data channels.

decoder – A device that extracts closed caption data from the video signal and makes it visible as text.

DER – Delete to End of Row.

diacritical – An accent mark placed over a letter, such as an acute, grave, circumflex, or dieresis.

dieresis – A double dot placed over a letter, as in ü. Also called an umlaut.

DirectShow – A standard Microsoft Windows interface for playing digital video and audio.

downconverting – Translation of caption data from digital CEA-708 format to analog CEA-608 format.

dropframe timecoding – Omitting frame numbers in SMPTE timecodes every so often to compensate for the fact that there are 29.97 frames in a second rather than 30. This is rather like the way leap years are handled on the calendar.

DTV – Digital Television. Includes HDTV, EDTV, and SDTV.

DVD – A 5¼-inch disc format similar to CD, but with significantly greater capacity. Used for storing video.

DVE – Digital Video Effects. DVE generators often regenerate the VBI, thus destroying the captions and necessitating the use of a caption bridge to preserve them.

DVR – Digital Video Recorder. A device like the TiVo or ReplayTV that records television programs onto a built-in hard disk or other digital media rather than using videotape.

DVS – Descriptive Video Service. A voice-over on an auxiliary channel such as SAP, containing a description for blind people of what's going on in a video program. DVS is a registered servicemark of the WGBH Educational Foundation.

–E–

EBU – European Broadcasting Union. EBU is an organization, but the term is mostly encountered when talking about the 25-frame-per-second PAL timecoding standard.

ECI – European Captioning Institute. The European subsidiary of NCI, located in Peterborough, U.K.

EDM – Erase Displayed Memory. The command character that blanks line 21 captions.

EDTV – Enhanced Definition Television. Digital TV with at least 480 progressive active scan lines.

EIA – Electronic Industries Alliance. The parent organization of CEA, whose R4.3 subcommittee produces standards for captioning and other data transmission on TV signals.

EIA-608 – Now called CEA-608.

EIA-708 – Now called CEA-708.

EIA-744 – Standard for V-Chip data in XDS. EIA-744 has been incorporated into the latest version of CEA-608.

encoder – A device that "hides" captions on a video picture, to be later extracted and viewed by a decoder.

ENM – Erase Nondisplayed Memory.

EOC – End Of Caption.

–F–

FAQ – Frequently Asked Question. FAQs are available on the Internet on many subjects. The Closed Captioning FAQ is on www.CaptionCentral.com.

FCC – Federal Communications Commission. The organization in the United States that oversees and regulates broadcast television and radio.

field – Half of an interlaced television frame. A full frame of video is built by transmitting every other line, and then making a second pass to fill in the blanks.

field 1 – The first half of the line 21 data, containing CC1, CC2, TEXT1, and TEXT2.

field 2 – The second half of the line 21 data (actually video line 284), containing CC3, CC4, TEXT3, TEXT4, and XDS data.

fps – Frames per second. The unit of measure for frame rates.

frame – One of the many still pictures that, when shown in rapid succession, make up a moving video picture. In interlaced video like NTSC, each frame has two fields.

frame rate – The number of frames presented in one second of video. In North America, using NTSC video, the frame rate is about 30 fps. In other parts of the world, using PAL or SECAM, it is 25 fps. Frame rates on streaming and computer media can vary widely.

–G–

Gallaudet – Four-year university for deaf and hard-of-hearing people, located in the Washington, D.C., area.

grave accent – A down-sloping accent mark placed over a letter, as in è.

–H–

HBI – Horizontal Blanking Interval. The space in the video signal between the end of one line of video and the beginning of the next.

HDTV – High Definition Television. Digital TV with at least 720 progressive or 1,080 interlaced active scan lines.

hertz (Hz) – The standard unit of measurement for frequency, named for physicist Heinrich Hertz. One Hz is equivalent to one cycle per second.

HoH – Hard-of-hearing. The preferred term for someone with some level of hearing loss less than that required to be considered completely deaf.

HTML – HyperText Markup Language. The native language of the World Wide Web, standardized by the W3C and used for coding Web pages. HTML tags are also used in caption file formats such as SAMI and RealText. See also XHTML.

–I–

IEC – International Electrotechnical Commission.

interlacing – A video display system that splits each frame into two fields, each containing every other scan line. With NTSC, the first field contains all of the odd numbered scan lines and the second field contains the even numbered ones.

IRC – Internet Relay Chat. A system that's been used for transmitting realtime streaming text.

IRE – An arbitrary unit for the amplitude of the video signal. Black is 0 IRE and pure white is 100 IRE.

ISO – International Organization for Standardization. A consortium that defines many of our transmission and storage formats.

ITV links – An Internet address (URL) embedded in line 21 to connect the TV program to a Web site, email address, or Usenet newsgroup.

–J–

Java – An object-oriented programming language designed for platform independence, commonly used on the Web.

JavaScript – A scripting language designed to be embedded in Web pages. Despite the similarity in names, JavaScript is quite different from Java.

JPEG – Joint Photographic Experts Group. This is a standards group, working under ISO, to define standards for compression and storage of still pictures. Most of the photo-quality pictures you'll find on the Web are stored in JPEG format, as it provides very good quality in a fairly small amount of space.

–K–

kanji – The Japanese "alphabet" of symbols, derived from Chinese characters.

Katakana – Another Japanese writing system (see "kanji"), often used for writing words borrowed from other languages.

–L–

ligature – Two letters written together, like the "æ" in "encyclopædia." Ligatures are a typesetting phenomenon in English, but are actual letters in some other languages.

line 21 – The VBI line containing North American standard closed captioning for analog TV broadcasts.

line 284 – The VBI line containing field 2 of line 21, which is used for additional captioning and related data.

live display – Hand-timing captions from a script during live programming. Used when somebody is reading from a script or a prompter.

LTC – Longitudinal Time Code. One of the SMTPE timecode standards, where the timecodes are on an audio track.

–M–

mask reporter – A generic term for a Stenomask reporter, now generally referred to as a voice writer.

mid-row text attribute code – A code that changes appearance of text in the middle of a line. Contrast with PAC.

misstroke – A misfingering on a stenotype keyboard.

MPAA – Motion Picture Association of America. The organization that created the movie rating system (G, PG, PG-13, R, NC-17, and X) used in the U.S.

MPEG – Motion Picture Experts Group. MPEG is used to refer to both the ISO committee which came up with the standard for digital storage and compression of video and audio signals, and to refer to the standard itself. MPEG compression is used in DTV and DVD.

–N–

NAB – National Association of Broadcasters.

NABTS – North American Broadcast Teletext Specification.

NAD – National Association of the Deaf.

NCAM – National Center for Accessible Media. An nonprofit R&D organization formed by the Corporation for Public Broadcasting and the WGBH Educational Foundation. NCAM researches and develops technologies that create access to public mass media.

NCI – National Captioning Institute. A not-for-profit captioning company in Virginia that performs captioning services. NCI also designed the TeleCaption line of caption decoders.

NCRA – National Court Reporters Association. The group that developed certification standards for stenocaptioners.

NCTA – National Cable Television Association.

newsroom captioning – Creation of captions for live programming using prompter scripts and stories from a newsroom computer system.

NLE – Nonlinear Editing. A video editing system that works from digital video on a disk instead of analog video on tapes.

nonsynchronous caption service – Captions that may be moved earlier or later in time and do not have to be timed to coincide with specific events in the audio or video of the program. CC2 and CC4 are nonsynchronous caption services.

NRB – National Religious Broadcasters association.

NRZ – Non-Return to Zero.

NTSC – National Television Systems Committee. The term "NTSC" is used to refer to the EIA committee that came up with the television format used in North America and Japan, and to refer to the format itself. The NTSC format was developed to provide a way to place color information on a television signal while remaining compatible with black-and-white televisions. The format was adopted by the FCC in 1953. NTSC has difficulty with color consistency, and video engineers often claim it stands for Never The Same Color.

NUL – A zero byte (character).

NVRA – National Verbatim Reporters Association. The main association for voice writers in the United States. NVRA developed the RVR certification.

NWPC – National Working Party on Captioning. An Australian group established to facilitate communication between the consumers of captioning and the providers of the service. The NWPC also acts as a consumer lobbying group for captioning.

–O–

offline captioning – Captioning done on a videotape or digital video in a studio. This does not require a realtime stenocaptioner or voice writer.

online captioning – Captioning produced live in realtime. Can use prompter scripts or realtime generated by stenocaptioners and voice writers.

open captioning – Captions that cannot be turned off by the viewer. No decoder is required, as they are "burned" onto the video.

OSD – On-Screen Display.

–P–

PAC – Preamble address code. A code that precedes a row of caption data and specifies the style and position of the caption. PACs can also be used to specify some text attributes.

paint-on captions – Line 21 captions that are visible as they are being drawn, anywhere on the screen, without the scrolling behavior associated with roll-up captions.

PAL – Phase alteration line. PAL is the color television standard format throughout most of Europe (pretty much everyone except France, which uses SECAM). It is higher resolution than the NTSC used in North America, using 625 lines of video instead of 525, but it has a lower frequency (50 Hz interlaced, yielding 25 frames per second).

PAL-M – A 525-line version of PAL used in Brazil.

pixel – Short for "picture element," which refers to a single image-forming dot on a video screen. Also called a "pel."

pop-on captions – Line 21 captions that are rendered in a nondisplayed memory and then displayed "instantly." You can't see them being drawn, as you can with paint-on and roll-up captions.

PSA – Public Service Announcement.

–Q–

Quicktext – A caption format used in QuickTime video.

QuickTime – A digital video standard from Apple Computer. Also used to refer to Apple's media player.

QWERTY keyboard – The standard keyboard used on computers and typewriters for typing languages that use Latin Alphabets, such as English. It was named for the sequence of letters in the top row.

–R–

RCA – Connector used for home video and audio equipment.

RCL – Resume Caption Loading. The command that sets a line 21 caption decoder in pop-on caption mode.

RDC – Resume Direct Captioning The command that sets a line 21 caption decoder in paint-on caption mode.

realtime captioning – Verbatim or near-verbatim captions generated during a live event. This requires a stenocaptioner or voice writer.

RealText – File format for caption text in the RealOne media player. Used with SMIL control files.

RFC – Request for comment. Despite the name, an RFC is an Internet standards document. RFC 1071, for example, describes the checksum system used for ITV links.

RGB – Red, Green, Blue. Colors on a video system are often expressed by listing their relative levels of red, green, and blue. This system is also used for component video signals on three wires.

RLE – Run-Length Encoding. A system for compressing pictures that's used for the subpicture (subtitle) information on DVDs.

roll-up captions – Captions that are visible as they are rendered (like paint-on captions), where the new text is added to the bottom row, which scrolls up when it's full.

RS-232 – The transmission standard used for most serial communications from computers. Serial (or "COM") ports on most personal computers are RS-232 compatible, and are typically DB-9 or DB-25 connectors.

RS-422 – A transmission standard designed for longer distances than RS-232. For that reason, it is often used in broadcast equipment like tape decks that may be quite a distance from the control system. RS-232 and RS-422 are not compatible, although adapters are available.

RTD – Resume Text Display. The command that sets a line 21 caption decoder in text mode.

RVR – Realtime Verbatim Reporter. The certification given by NVRA to voice writers. Requirements are similar to NCRA's CRR exam.

–S–

safe image area – TV manufacturers make the case around the television set cover part of the edge of the picture tube. This is done for aesthetic reasons, to compensate for differences in manufacturing process from time to time, or factory to factory, and so that when the tube gets old and the picture starts to shrink, you don't see a black border around it. The safe image area is defined as the portion of the picture that is guaranteed to be visible on all televisions.

safe title area – The area of the TV screen in which captions may be placed.

SAMI – Synchronized Accessible Multimedia Interchange. The format used for captioning data for Microsoft's Media Player.

SAP – Second Audio Program. An additional audio track that can be used for audio description, or for a second language.

SDTV – Standard Definition Television. TV with lower resolution than EDTV. Sometimes used to refer only to low-resolution DTV, and sometimes includes analog NTSC TV as well. In this book, it means digital.

SECAM – *Sequential Couleur Avec Memoire* (sequential color with memory). Other sources list it as "*Système Electronique Couleur Avec Memoire*," or "electronic system for color with memory." SECAM is the French color TV standard, also adopted in the old USSR. It uses 625 lines of video at 50 Hz interlaced (25 frames per second), like PAL does.

SHHH – Self Help for Hard-of-Hearing People.

SMIL – Synchronized Multimedia Integration Language (pronounced "smile"). File format adopted by W3C for captioning and other information coordinated with video. Used for all captioned material viewed with the RealOne media player.

SMPTE – Society of Motion Picture & Television Engineers. SMPTE developed, among other things, the standard for

timecoding that is used by most broadcast and captioning equipment.

speech recognition – A computer system that can automatically convert speech to text. See also "voice writers," and contrast with "voice recognition."

start bits – One or more bits transmitted at the beginning of a character to ensure that the receiver is correctly locked on.

stenocaptioner – A person who performs realtime captioning using a stenotype keyboard.

Stenomask reporter – A court reporter that records proceedings by repeating everything into a special microphone with a surrounding mask to reduce ambient noise. These people, now known as voice writers, are starting to work in the realtime closed captioning field.

stenotype keyboard – A keyboard that uses "chording" (a system of pressing more than one key at a time) to allow much faster writing than a traditional QWERTY or Dvorak keyboard.

streaming audio or video – Audio or video that is transmitted over the Internet to a media player that begins playing before receiving the entire file.

stroke – A combination of one or more keys pressed all at one time on a stenotype keyboard. One stroke usually represents one syllable or word.

subpicture – A static image that can be displayed over top of MPEG-encoded video. Subpictures are used for subtitling on DVDs.

subtitling – In the U.S., subtitling refers to open captions created with a character generator or to captions on a DVD. In the U.K., "subtitling" is a synonym for "closed captioning."

Supertext – Captions produced by the ACC. "Supertext" is a registered trademark of the Australian Caption Center.

synchronous caption service – Captions that are timed to coincide with specific events in the audio or video part of the program, and should not be moved earlier or later when adding new line 21 information. CC1 and CC3 are synchronous caption services.

–T–

TCL – Television Crossover Link. An obsolete term for an Interactive TV link, or ITV link.

TDCA – Television Decoder Circuitry Act of 1990. Legislation which mandates that every television set 13" or larger manufactured for sale in the United States must have a caption decoder chip in it.

TDD – Telecommunication Device for the Deaf. This term has fallen out of favor, and TDDs are more commonly known now as TTYs.

TDI – Telecommunications for the Deaf, Inc. Although TDI functions principally as an advocacy group for equal access via telephone (using TTYs), they have also been involved in captioning issues.

TeleCaption I – Original home set-top caption decoder from NCI, distributed by Sears.

Teletext – A system used in the U.K. and other parts of Europe for transmitting textual data in a TV signal.

TER – Total error rate. This is how captioners measure their accuracy. It involves counting words in a selection of caption text, and marking errors to find a ratio.

TEXT1 through **TEXT4** – The four data channels reserved in line 21 for caption-like scrolling text which covers anywhere from half the screen to the entire screen when displayed.

TIFF – Tagged Image File Format. A rasterized format for pictures. Often used as the format for sending rendered subtitles to a DVD authoring system.

tilde – A wavy line ($\sim$) placed over a letter, as in ñ.

timecode – Unique time identifier stamped on each frame of video. SMPTE defines two ways of storing timecodes: LTC goes on a linear (audio) track, and VITC goes in the VBI.

TO1, TO2, TO3 – Tab Offset 1, 2, or 3 columns.

transcoding – The conversion of caption data from analog CEA-608 format to digital CEA-708 format.

transparent space – A space character for captioning which does not generate a background behind it.

TSID – Transmission Signal Identifier. A unique 16-bit number assigned to each broadcast licensee.

TTY – The "text telephone" used by deaf and hard-of-hearing people. This basically consists of a keyboard connected to an old-style Baudot modem, so that two people can connect TTYs to their telephones and type messages to each other.

–U–

UI – User interface. The part of a computer program or electronic device that interacts with human beings.

UIMSBF – Unsigned integer most significant bit first.

umlaut – The double dot over vowels in German, as in "München," and French, as in "Noël." Also called a dieresis.

upconverting – Translation of caption data from analog CEA-608 format to digital CEA-708 format.

upstream captions – Captions placed on the video before it is processed by the encoder. This may be done in a studio or by another encoder in the video loop.

–V–

VBI – Vertical Blanking Interval. The "blank" lines of video picture between the bottom of one frame and the top of the next. Line 21 of the VBI is where closed captions are stored.

video description – See audio description.

VFS – Virtual Frame Store. A sequence of frames shown on a nonlinear captioning system's screen to allow captioners to more easily find shot changes.

VITC – Vertical Interval Time Code. One of the SMTPE timecode standards, where the timecodes are embedded in the VBI.

VITS – Vertical Interval Test Signal.

voice recognition – A computer trained to recognize the identity of a person by his or her speech patterns. This is usually used in security systems and is very different from speech recognition.

voice writer – Someone who creates realtime text by speaking into a trained speech recognition system.

VTR – Video tape recorder. This acronym is more common with professional, broadcast, and studio equipment than "VCR," which is usually reserved for consumer (home) electronics.

–W–

widescreen – A picture wider than the standard 4:3 aspect ratio. In DTV and DVD, widescreen usually means 16:9.

WMP – Microsoft's Windows Media Player.

wpm – Words per minute. The unit of measure for caption delivery speed (reading rate).

WST – World System Teletext.

W3C – World Wide Web Consortium. The organization responsible for standards like HTML and SMIL.

–X–

XDS – Extended Data Services. Data packets carried in Field 2 of Line 21, containing information like time of day, network name, program name, National Weather Service alerts, parental guidelines ("V-Chip") information, and so forth.

XHTML – Extensible HyperText Markup Language. The standardized language planned as the replacement for HTML.

XML – Extensible Markup Language. Similar to HTML, except that tags are user-definable and that XML is designed to focus on describing data rather than specifying how it will be displayed.

INDEX

CRB0246